The Globalization and Corporatization of Education

The forces associated with globalization, whether economic or social, have conditioned the ways educators operate, and have profoundly altered people's experiences of both formal and informal education. Globalization, as a multidimensional, multilevel process, is unequivocally, but not exclusively, based on the economics of neoliberalism. This book chronicles new sites of tension in education that are a result of an ever-globalizing economy and its accompanying neoliberal practices in the United States, Costa Rica, and the US territories in the Caribbean. The contributions are grouped into two areas: institutionalized schooling practices and non-formal educational practices that focus on identities and language.

Each chapter questions the neoliberal market mantra that education must be rebranded into a marketable product and consumed by individuals, making a complex and compelling ethnographic argument that the market mantra is bankrupt. The authors argue that globalization produces liminal subjects and leads to the destruction of social institutions like education that are essential to democratic governance. The aim of each article is to uniquely disentangle the dynamics of the process, so as to resolve the mystery of how globally inspired paradigms and policies mix with locally defined structures and cultures. In assessing globalization's relationship to educational change, we need to know how globalization and its ideological packaging affect schooling, from transnational paradigms, to national policies and to local practices.

This book was originally published as a special issue of the *International Journal of Qualitative Studies in Education*.

Denise Blum is an Associate Professor of Social Foundations in the School of Educational Studies at Oklahoma State University, USA. Her research focuses on political economy in Mexico, Cuba and the United States, looking at neoliberalism and equity issues and how young people are negotiating their identities in contexts of educational reform. She is author of *Cuban youth and revolutionary values: Educating the new socialist citizen* (2012).

Char Ullman is an Associate Professor of Literacy/Biliteracy and Educational Anthropology in the Department of Teacher Education at the University of Texas at El Paso, USA. Her research focuses on globalization and language use among Mexican (Im)migrants to the United States. She explores the ways in which people construct and are constructed by identities and ideologies, with an emphasis on nationalism. Her current project is about translanguaging on the Mexico-US border.

The Globalization and Corporatization of Education
Limits and Liminality of the Market Mantra

Edited by
Denise Blum and Char Ullman

LONDON AND NEW YORK

First published 2014
by Routledge
2 Park Square, Milton Park, Abingdon, Oxfordshire OX14 4RN

and by Routledge
711 Third Avenue, New York, NY 10017

First issued in paperback 2015

Routledge is an imprint of the Taylor & Francis Group, an informa business

© 2014 Taylor & Francis

All rights reserved. No part of this book may be reprinted or reproduced or utilised in any form or by any electronic, mechanical, or other means, now known or hereafter invented, including photocopying and recording, or in any information storage or retrieval system, without permission in writing from the publishers.

Trademark notice: Product or corporate names may be trademarks or registered trademarks, and are used only for identification and explanation without intent to infringe.

British Library Cataloguing in Publication Data
A catalogue record for this book is available from the British Library

ISBN 13: 978-1-138-95350-5 (pbk)
ISBN 13: 978-0-415-72472-2 (hbk)

Typeset in Times New Roman
by Taylor & Francis Books

Publisher's Note
The publisher accepts responsibility for any inconsistencies that may have arisen during the conversion of this book from journal articles to book chapters, namely the possible inclusion of journal terminology.

Disclaimer
Every effort has been made to contact copyright holders for their permission to reprint material in this book. The publishers would be grateful to hear from any copyright holder who is not here acknowledged and will undertake to rectify any errors or omissions in future editions of this book.

Contents

Citation Information vii
Notes on Contributors ix

Introduction: The globalization and corporatization of education: the limits and liminality of the market mantra
Denise Blum and Char Ullman 1

1. A good investment? Race, philanthrocapitalism and professionalism in a New York City small school of choice
   Amy Brown 9

2. Hip hop as empowerment: voices in El Alto, Bolivia
   Ariana Tarifa 31

3. The play of risk, affect, and the enterprising self in a fourth-grade classroom
   Steven Bialostok and George Kamberelis 51

4. "English for the global": discourses in/of English-language voluntourism
   Cora Jakubiak Neisser 69

5. "My grain of sand for society": neoliberal freedom, language learning, and the circulation of ideologies of national belonging
   Char Ullman 87

6. Floating migration, education, and globalization in the US Caribbean
   Mirerza González and Nadjah Ríos-Villarini 105

7. Neoliberalism and the demise of public education: the corporatization of schools of education
   Marta Baltodano 121

Index 143

Citation Information

The chapters in this book were originally published in the *International Journal of Qualitative Studies in Education*, volume 25, issue 4 (June 2012). When citing this material, please use the original page numbering for each article, as follows:

Introduction
   The globalization and corporatization of education: the limits and liminality of the market mantra
   Denise Blum and Char Ullman
   International Journal of Qualitative Studies in Education, volume 25, issue 4 (June 2012) pp. 367-374

Chapter 1
   A good investment? Race, philanthrocapitalism and professionalism in a New York City small school of choice
   Amy Brown
   International Journal of Qualitative Studies in Education, volume 25, issue 4 (June 2012) pp. 375-396

Chapter 2
   Hip hop as empowerment: voices in El Alto, Bolivia
   Ariana Tarifa
   International Journal of Qualitative Studies in Education, volume 25, issue 4 (June 2012) pp. 397-416

Chapter 3
   The play of risk, affect, and the enterprising self in a fourth-grade classroom
   Steven Bialostok and George Kamberelis
   International Journal of Qualitative Studies in Education, volume 25, issue 4 (June 2012) pp. 417-434

Chapter 4
   "English for the global": discourses in/of English-language voluntourism
   Cora Jakubiak Neisser
   International Journal of Qualitative Studies in Education, volume 25, issue 4 (June 2012) pp. 435-452

CITATION INFORMATION

Chapter 5
"My grain of sand for society": neoliberal freedom, language learning, and the circulation of ideologies of national belonging
Char Ullman
International Journal of Qualitative Studies in Education, volume 25, issue 4 (June 2012) pp. 453-470

Chapter 6
Floating migration, education, and globalization in the US Caribbean
Mirerza González and Nadjah Ríos-Villarini
International Journal of Qualitative Studies in Education, volume 25, issue 4 (June 2012) pp. 471-486

Chapter 7
Neoliberalism and the demise of public education: the corporatization of schools of education
Marta Baltodano
International Journal of Qualitative Studies in Education, volume 25, issue 4 (June 2012) pp. 487-508

Please direct any queries you may have about the citations to clsuk.permissions@cengage.com

Notes on Contributors

Marta Baltodano, Urban Education, Loyola Marymount University, USA

Steven Bialostok, Literacy Education, University of Wyoming, USA

Denise Blum, School of Educational Studies, Oklahoma State University, USA

Amy Brown, Critical Writing Project, University of Pennsylvania, USA

Mirerza González, English Department, College of Humanities, University of Puerto Rico, PR, USA

Cora Jakubiak Neisser, Education Department, Grinnell College, USA

George Kamberelis, Literacy Education, University of Wyoming, USA

Nadjah Ríos-Villarini, Graduate Program of Linguistics, University of Puerto Rico, PR, USA

Ariana Tarifa, School of International Studies, Oklahoma State University, USA

Char Ullman, Department of Teacher Education, University of Texas at El Paso, USA

INTRODUCTION

The globalization and corporatization of education: the limits and liminality of the market mantra

Denise Blum and Char Ullman

What are some of the ways in which neoliberalism is impacting the practice and experience of education? People worldwide are being forced to negotiate their identities for survival in a globalized world. How are ideologies of national identity and belonging negotiated in educational contexts across the globe? In what ways are teachers and their curricula perpetuating, as well as resisting, the corporatization of education and its resulting inequities? Academic capitalism has entered classrooms at all levels, redefining everything from the interaction between teachers and students to the existence of academic disciplines. This special issue is grounded in the ethnographic analysis of specific educational formations that are simultaneously social, cultural, political, economic, historical, and transnational. In this introduction, the authors offer ways to think about how the market mantra has been internalized in communities worldwide, along with the ways in which it is questioned, resisted, and ultimately, transformed.

Introduction

The forces associated with globalization, whether economic or social, have conditioned the context in which educators operate, and have profoundly altered people's experiences of both formal and informal education. Globalization, as a multidimensional, multilevel process, is unequivocally but not exclusively based on the economics of neoliberalism. This special issue continues the conversation on neoliberalism and education that guest editors Bronwyn Davies and Peter Bansel started in the 2007 special issue of the *International Journal of Qualitative Studies in Education*. Davies and Bansel called into question the notion that neoliberal regimes are specific to the northern hemisphere, by presenting cases both compelling and disturbing, of neoliberal practices and policies in education taking place in Australia and New Zealand. We continue the chronicling of new sites of tension in education as a result of the global economy and accompanying neoliberal practices in the US, Costa Rica, and the US territories in the Caribbean.

The market mantra and its consequences

The Keynesian approach to the problem of class conflict inherent in the structure of liberal democracies has been for there to be governmental support in the form of educational and healthcare benefits that benefit working-class people. This system has been in place, to varying degrees, in many advanced capitalist nations (with the US lagging behind much of the Global North) for much of the twentieth century, and its goal was to push the possibility of violent revolution into a permanently blurry future time frame. These social programs allowed for a minimally more equitable social order, in which some people (certainly not everyone), with government support, achieved their status based on talent and hard work. While the liberal state only slightly lessened the role of ascribed status (the idea that people succeed both as individuals and as groups, through the status ascribed to them through their race, gender, or class status), the reality is that the twentieth century has been characterized in the Global North by a combination of achievement and ascription, making success about both "who you know and where you are from" as well as "pulling yourself up by the bootstraps".

The late-twentieth-century shift to a neoliberal regime has meant the steady destruction of collective bargaining rights (unions), combined with the corporatization of hospitals, schools, and many other parts of modern life. Healthcare and education were once considered to be part of the social good, factors that combined to produce a stable social and economic order. In the neoliberal state, healthcare and education have been transformed through the market mantra, into products that individuals can buy and sell. Education, or "lifelong learning" became essential to the creation of the neoliberal subject, leading to the notion that "the most worthy citizen is a flexible homo economicus" (Ong 2003, 9).

For decades now, neoliberal economics has been reshaping democratic agendas by invoking market discourses (e.g. choice) to describe both the problem and utility of public schools (McLaren and Farahmandpur 2001). Neoliberal discourses commodify public education by depicting it as an economic drain linked to an unsustainable welfare state (Burchell 1996). In fact, in neoliberal societies, "there is nothing distinctive or special about education or health; they are services and products like any other, to be traded in the marketplace" (Peters 1999, 2). The result has been a drive toward the achievement of specified outcomes and the adoption of standardized teaching models. The emphasis is less on community and equity, and rather more on individual advancement and the need to satisfy investors and influential consumers. Education has come to resemble a private, rather than public good.

While private and public interests will likely always intertwine in a neoliberal democracy, the encroachment on the public good by private and special interests takes us further away from a participatory democracy. The surrendering of public schools to market pressures, and to the privileged within those markets, benefits those who have access to power within both sectors. The revolving door between governmental agencies and the private educational sector is ripe for personal gain and corruption at the public's expense.

Schools and colleges have, for example, become sites for branding and the targets of corporate expansion. Many policymakers automatically look to the market for alleged solutions. The impact and pervasiveness of these forces of globalization make them a necessary focus for scholarship on education and learning, but there are powerful currents running against thoughtful, honest work in this area. In this special issue, we explore some of what we believe to be the more significant impacts of globalization with regard to the practice and experience of education.

The papers we have assembled for this special issue question the effects of the neoliberal market mantra that education must be rebranded into a marketable product to be consumed by individuals. Together, they make a complex ethnographic argument that the market mantra is bankrupt, and that it produces liminal subjects, and leads to the destruction of social institutions, like education, that are essential to democratic processes. Wrestling with the process of globalization in terms of education, each of the contributors has sought to uniquely disentangle the dynamics of the process, so as to resolve the mystery of how globally inspired paradigms and policies mix with locally defined structures and cultures. We have divided the contributions into two categories: institutionalized schooling practices and non-formal educational practices that focus on identities and language.

Institutionalized schooling practices

Globalization is having a significant impact on educational systems worldwide. International institutions have generated powerful ideologies of how educational delivery needs to be changed and they have played a prominent role in the economic restructuring of the world economy. We need to ask how this larger ideological package – which includes, but is not limited to, decentralization and privatization, choice and accountability, testing and assessment – affects education. The way knowledge is delivered in the classroom is an important aspect of knowledge production, and the classroom has seemed largely untouched. But the classroom is only one part of the knowledge production process, and the forces of globalization are subtly, but ultimately, transforming it as well. In assessing globalization's true relationship to educational change, we need to know how globalization and its ideological packaging affect the overall delivery of schooling, from transnational paradigms, to national policies, to local practices.

We have three such articles that shed light on the delivery of schooling in elementary, secondary, and post-secondary institutions.

Within the institution of formal schooling, Steven Bialostok and George Kamberelis' study of a fourth grade classroom reveals new capitalist discourses that circulate and encourage children to become "enterprising selves." The teacher does not so much consciously determine the children's capitalist subjectivities, but rather elicits, fosters, and fundamentally, promotes them. School children learn to enter into high levels of risk-taking behavior and how to manage risk and affect.

At a small New York school of choice, Amy Brown chronicles high school students' negotiation and resistance to contesting corporate ideals of professionalism and "college readiness." Students recognize the system of "performative professionalism" that earns them points. Brown critiques the ways that the increasing privatization and corporatization of schools in the US reinforces racism and inequality. She outlines instances where students redefine achievement by performing professionalism in classrooms without coercion, and discusses possibilities for intellectual, rather than performed, classroom professionalism.

The globalizing political economy affects the way universities are governed, and Marta Baltodano offers a powerful critique of the privatization of public schooling and how this affects colleges of education. She discusses practices such as managerialism, accountability, and privatization, which represent a shift toward business values and a market agenda. She looks at the exclusive use of standardized testing to gauge academic achievement and teacher quality, along with the weakening of teacher unions (Weiner 2007), as neoliberal techniques that have wrought fundamental changes to the way schools of education prepare professional educators. She considers the ways in which the market mantra has led to new products: charter school administrators and teachers, and fast-track EdDs whose job is to train school administrators to raise test scores. Colleges of education are now competing with online and for-profit colleges to "train" people to work in education.

Academic capitalism has entered into the classroom and has redefined the academic premises upon which the entire higher education system was instituted. How can schools of education promote the development of public intellectuals when their curricula are shaped by corporate agendas? What are the implications of this new educational arrangement for the very purpose of education and the development of a critically informed mass of democratic citizens? Baltodono argues that university faculty must become more conscious of neoliberalism in higher education, and she proposes that we create alliances with parents, unions, and grassroots organizations to stop the demise of public education.

Non-formal educational practices and the role of languages and identities

Educational practices are profoundly impacted by the notion of the neoliberal subject, both within and outside of formal educational settings. Because neoliberal regimes of power reposition the education and healthcare of the populace from a state responsibility to an individual responsibility, the role of the neoliberal subject is greatly expanded in neoliberal states. Issues of language variety and language choice have become central to determining who belongs to the nation and who does not, which brings questions of identity to the fore. Neoliberal subjects must be self-regulating, and must continually reevaluate their abilities and knowledge, in order to respond to the constantly changing relationship between "the state, the economy, civil society, government, the market, and the subject" (Bansel 2007, 285). That means that constructing the right kind of identity and using the right kind of language to do it are primary preoccupations for contemporary citizens. The neoliberal subject must become, as Nikolas Rose says, "an entrepreneur of the self" (Rose 1999, 142).

Neoliberal subjects are formed through what Foucault identified as governmentality, which he described as the processes by which governments work to produce citizens who help them enact their policies. But how is it that governments conduct this work? It is accomplished in large part through what Foucault termed "technologies of the self" (Martin, Gutman, and Hutton 1988), the process of internalizing social norms that produce particular kinds of citizens. It is through self-policing, and controlling thoughts and behaviors in relation to social norms, that people become neoliberal subjects. This process happens in non-formal educational settings, and can be accomplished through popular books, media, and non-governmental organizations (NGOs). It often involves monitoring which language one uses where, as well as the variety of language deemed appropriate to a particular situation.

Neoliberal discourses demand that restrictions on the movement of capital be removed, while the movement of workers (i.e. migration) continues to be highly problematic and state controlled. The development of new, flexible workers who are self-regulating, and who continually re-educate themselves to meet the demands of the marketplace is the foundation of neoliberalism. And what is the role of language in the production of this neoliberal subject? Cameron (2001) reminds us that globalization has led governments and corporations to understand language as a commodity with market value. Heller (2011) notes that globalization and neoliberal governments have lessened the role of the manual laborer, and have led to the preeminence of the language worker, transforming "the *workforce* into the *wordforce*" (20). The following set of papers explores the particularities of how neoliberal subjects are formed in relation to language in a variety of non-formal locales. One is through floating migration among teachers in the Caribbean; another is through English-language voluntourism in the Global South; and still another is through an intensely marketed English-language program called *Inglés Sin Barreras* [English without Barriers], which is advertised on Spanish-language television. The final paper in this special issue explores the role of codeswitching in hip hop among Indigenous people who have organized to protest neoliberal regimes.

Mirerza González and Nadjah Ríos-Villarini analyze transnational teacher identities in the Caribbean islands of Vieques and St. Croix, a context of circular migration produced by global markets and the need for cheap labor. They examine the role of language in globalized identity construction, and the ways in which producing Otherness serves to mediate anxieties related to students' transnational identities and cultural differences.

Cori Jakubiak discusses short-term, volunteer English language teaching, or English language voluntourism, a practice in which native speakers of prestige-variety English work as unpaid English as International Language (EIL) instructors in the Global South. She argues that voluntourism recreates a discourse of what Dicken (2003) calls hyperglobalism. Coming largely from the Western business world, it augurs a future in which all countries are equally interconnected by a single, global economy and in which the primary role of the nation-state is to aid the global economic network rather than to provide social welfare services. Refracted through this hyperglobalist lens, English language skills alone become the proposed solution to a myriad of complex, structural problems in the Global South.

Char Ullman looks at the pop-culture phenomenon, *Inglés Sin Barreras* [English without Barriers], an English-language program for Spanish-speakers that retails for up to $3000 (with most people buying it at 21% interest). More advertised than Coca-Cola or McDonald's, ads for the program appear every 15 minutes from dawn to dusk on both Univisión and Telemundo. For immigrants whose bodies, cultural practices, and languages are marginalized, migration is a "life-long process of negotiating identity, difference, and the right to fully exist in the new context" (Benmayor and Skotnes 2005, 8). Ullman discusses the ways in which ideologies of Latindad and national belonging to the US for Latinos are circulated through *Inglés Sin Barreras*, the commodity.

In the final contribution to this special issue, Ariana Tarifa examines the ways in which young people in Latin America have increasingly used hip hop music as a means of unifying and educating Indigenous people in El Alto, Bolivia. Indigenous people have been encouraged to use their native dialects in creating this music, and they also use hip hop as a means to protest neoliberal policies and assert Indigenous identities. Nina Uma, a prominent Bolivian hip hopper sees the young Alteños' musical development as a "Hip hop revolution"; hip hop that criticizes and questions the social, political, and economic structure, the differences between the haves and the have-nots, and proposes using hip hop to spread "education as cultural action of freedom" (Freire 2000, 7).

These collected papers demonstrate that neoliberalism continues to be understood and enacted in multiple ways in different parts of the globe. People simultaneously seek to become neoliberal subjects, fail at the attempt, and mobilize against neoliberal regimes. Becoming an "entrepreneur of the self," while widely encouraged throughout the world, continues to be contested. In these times, "the economic fates of citizens within a national territory are uncoupled from one another, and are now understood and governed as a function of their own particular levels of enterprise, skill, inventiveness, and flexibility" (Miller and Rose 2008, 96). The neoliberal imposition threatens the sustainability of democracy.

Neoliberal policies are transforming the delivery of public education. Schooling as a public benefit and common good has been supplanted by the ideology of privatization. Our educational institutions have become reterritorialized with business-driven imperatives that legitimize the symbolic capital of entrepreneurial and individualized selves. Schools have accepted the bulk of the blame for our economic problems despite the reality that educators have been virtually disempowered at every level. The truth is that our worldwide economic problems have little to do with the school-based preparation of human capital, but instead are deeply tied to the limits of market capitalism.

Historically, education and training developed locally and were supported at the state or national level. However, globalization continues to intensify the authority of neoliberal policies through the World Bank and the International Monetary Fund, altering this process. The concept of government as an equalizing force appropriately belongs to the Keynesian school of economics, which is in sharp decline today. As neoliberal strategies are shifting production from a nation-state function to a global one, the form of the human being is changed and challenged by new uses of education. At the same time, people continue to question these shifts, to resist the notion that the neoliberal subject is the only human subject, and to organize to return educational practices and institutions to a more democratic vision.

References

Bansel, P. 2007. Subjects of choice and lifelong learning. *International Journal of Qualitative Studies in Education* 20, no. 3: 283–300.

Benmayor, Rina, and Andor Skotnes. 2005. *Migration and identity*. New Brunswick, NJ: Transaction.

Burchell, Graham. 1996. Liberal government and the techniques of the self. In *Foucault and political reason: Liberalism, neoliberalism, and rationalities of government*, ed. A. Barry, T. Osbourne, and N. Rose, 19–37. Chicago, IL: The University of Chicago Press.

Cameron, Deborah. 2001. *Good to talk?* London: Sage.

Davies, Bronwyn, and Peter Bansel. 2007. Neoliberalism and education. *International Journal of Qualitative Studies in Education* 20, no. 3: 247–59.
Dicken, Peter. 2003. *Global shift: Reshaping the global economic map in the 21st century*. 4th ed. New York, NY: Guilford Press.
Freire, Paulo. 2000. *Cultural action for freedom*. Cambridge, MA: Harvard Education Press.
Heller, Monica. 2011. *Paths to postnationalism: A critical ethnography of language and identity*. Oxford: Oxford University Press.
Martin, Luther H., Huck Gutman, and Patrick H. Hutton. 1988. *Technologies of the self: A seminar with Michel Foucault*. Amherst, MA: University of Massachusetts Press.
McLaren, Peter., and Ramin Farahmandpur. 2001. Teaching against globalization and the new imperialism: Toward a revolutionary pedagogy. *Journal of Teacher Education* 52, no. 2: 136–50.
Miller, Peter, and Nikolas Rose. 2008. *Governing the present: Administering economic, social and personal life*. Cambridge, UK: Polity Press.
Ong, Aiwa. 2003. *Buddha is hiding: Refugees, citizenship, and the new America*. Berkeley, CA: University of California Press.
Peters, Michael. 1999. Neoliberalism. The encyclopedia of philosophy of education. http://www.vusst.hr/ENCYCLOPAEDIA/neoliberalism.html.
Rose, Nicolas. 1999. *Powers of freedom: Reframing political thought*. Cambridge: Cambridge University Press.
Weiner, L. 2007. A lethal threat to U.S. teacher education. *Journal of Teacher Education* 58, no. 4: 274–86.

A good investment? Race, philanthrocapitalism and professionalism in a New York City small school of choice

Amy Brown

Incorporating data from two years of ethnographic teacher-research, this article explores how a curriculum of "professionalism" resonates with teachers and students in a small New York City school of choice. Using the literature on Critical Whiteness Studies and philanthrocapitalism in the context of New York City Mayor Michael Bloomberg's education reforms, the paper critiques the ways that the increasing privatization and corporatization of schools in the US reinforces racism and inequality. The discussion concludes by outlining instances where students and teachers resist market-based pedagogies of professionalism, and discusses the importance of critical intellectualism and humanizing pedagogy in a climate of market-based reforms in education.

Introduction

During my two years of teacher-research at the College Preparatory Academy (hereafter "College Prep"[1]), a public high school in New York City, students lent special insight into the school's emphasis on performative professionalism,[2] the explicit demonstration of "appropriate" behaviors for college or a corporate career. When asked on a school-wide questionnaire given in the spring of 2010, "What is your opinion of professionalism/professionalism points at College Prep?" some students responded:

[Professionalism/Professionalism points are] bull, I'm already professional. (ninth grade)

College Prep instills a professional environment but us as students don't uphold it, i.e. dress code, respect for ourselves and others. (ninth grade)

I don't think professionalism points should make up a majority of our grades because it pulls down our GPA significantly. Plus, schools aren't supposed to do that. (eleventh grade)

Nobody is good in being professional. (twelfth grade)

Sometimes points are taken away because of extremely frivolous things like not directly looking at a teacher during a lesson. (twelfth grade)

It's ridiculous, we're not little kids. It's important, but repeating it every day is not necessary. (twelfth grade)

These students illustrate critiques of College Prep's pedagogy and curricula of professionalism. Some of the students who are critical of performative professionalism display their opinions through resistant behavior in hallways and classrooms. In this paper, I argue that students' resistance to school expectations of professionalism demonstrates mediation of and response to experiences of raced, classed and gendered structures of domination and constraint (Giroux 1983).

Importantly, College Prep created its own in-house nonprofit organization, which I call "the Foundation," in order to solicit funds from private donors. Although never explicitly stated in the school's contracts with its funders, the school's insistence on students' performative professionalism is grounded in a larger project of image management in the context of its dependence on the private sector for resources. Using the literature on Critical Whiteness Studies and philanthrocapitalism in the context of New York City Mayor Michael Bloomberg's education reforms, I critique the ways that the increasing privatization and corporatization of schools in the United States reinforces inequality and racism, a "fundamental characteristic of social projects which create or reproduce structures of domination based on essentialist categories of race" (Omi and Winant 1994, 162) in an already classist society, using College Prep as an example. My use of the term "racial philanthrocapitalism" is rooted in Robinson's (1983) "racial capitalism." Robinson foregrounds racism (and more specifically White supremacy[3]) as he traces the origins of world capitalism and western hegemony; in other words, he posits that European racialism was integral to the development of modern capitalism. In using "racial philanthrocapitalism," I emphasize that the maintenance of White privilege is foundational to philanthropy and privatization in US schools. First, I describe the continued production of a marketable school that appeals to funders within the context of racial philanthrocapitalism. Secondly, I describe how College Prep's environment attempts to produce individuals who display neoliberal conceptions of upward mobility. Finally, I outline ways that teachers and students attempt to humanize the classroom experience at College Prep.

Context: Bloomberg, philanthrocapitalism, and the small schools movement

In 2002, the state granted New York City Mayor Michael Bloomberg control of the city's 1400 public schools. As part of a larger small schools movement in the United States, Bloomberg focused on developing small, themed schools of choice (SSCs) as a response to the failure (by national and state standards of accountability) of the city's large, factory-style high schools (Ancess and Allen 2006). SSCs were created with the goal of preparing disadvantaged students from historically underserved communities in the city for the competitive demands of the world economy. Since the start of his administration, Bloomberg has closed more than 90 "underperforming" public high schools in the name of college or career readiness for all students (Robinson 2011).

When schools are closed, they undergo a restructuring process that involves either "transformation" or "restart." Transformation typically involves a longer school day and more professional development, and may involve replacing the principal and part of the school's staff. "Restart" involves bringing in an outside educational organization (such as a private entity) to run the school (Fertig 2011).

In the name of contributing to economic growth, Bloomberg's search for the panacea that will guarantee "success" for the city's public school students in a climate of competition, accountability and the pressure to innovate is marked by a reliance on private monies. The administration often relies on philanthropists and nonprofit intermediary organizations to implement new programs and practices (Foley 2010). For example, the Gates Foundation started investing in small school intermediaries called "school developers" in New York City in 2001. Along with the Carnegie Corporation and the Open Society Institute, the Gates Foundation made a grant totaling 30 million dollars to New Visions for Public Schools, New York City's largest school reform association, to establish 75 small schools by 2005. Additional investments by the Gates Foundation came about in 2002 when Bloomberg centralized control of the schools (Foley 2010). In total, Bloomberg and former US deputy attorney and antitrust lawyer Joel Klein – who became Bloomberg's first chancellor of city schools – created 333 new public schools, and more than 80 charters between 2002 and 2009. They used a total of 70 million dollars of outside funding from organizations, relying heavily on the nonprofit New Visions for Public Schools as a developer (Goldsmith, Georges, and Burke 2010).

Although high school graduation rates and test scores have increased, critics argue that standards were lowered in order to ensure this ostensible gain (Ravitch 2011). Bloomberg has been criticized for other decisions about the city's schools, for instance, appointing the chairwoman of Hearst magazines, Cathie Black,[4] who lacked a graduate degree and had no experience in education, to replace Joel Klein as school chancellor. Recently, Bloomberg controversially voiced his support of laying off teachers and increasing class sizes in public schools (Giordano and Phillips 2011). He has been criticized for the emphasis on high-stakes test scores and for the lack of services for special education and disabled students in many SSCs (Otterman and Kopicki 2011), as well as his continuing mission of closing "underperforming" schools with little regard for the ways that these closures affect students and communities (Giordano 2011; Tarras and Gokey 2011).

The small schools movement has not resulted in college or career readiness for all students. For example, according to a recent *New York Times* article, many of the city's public high school graduates attend college in the City University of New York (CUNY) system (Garvey 2011). Yet the six-year graduation rate for all full-time, first-time freshmen enrolled in degree programs at CUNY is only 17% for associate degrees and 11% for baccalaureate degrees; 8.2% are still enrolled (Garvey 2011), despite the city's reliance on private funding.

Bloomberg's support of private investment in public services demonstrates what Bishop and Green (2009) call philanthrocapitalism. Philanthrocapitalists argue that an entrepreneurial approach is the most effective way of solving problems. For example, Steven Goldsmith, former mayor of Indianapolis and self-professed admirer of neoliberal economist Milton Friedman, argues that rich philanthropists provide "catalytic capital," or capital that is invested with a private approach but with a partial social return (Goldsmith, Georges, and Burke 2010). Catalytic capital, according to Goldsmith, inspires "new and creative innovations for combating social problems." Goldsmith believes in philanthropic investors of capital "turning risk into reward;" in fact, in a chapter that bears this title, he focuses on investors cultivating the ability to understand and underwrite risk in a way that unlocks value for investors, and enhances participation (in free market capitalism) for "marginalized populations" (Goldsmith, Georges, and Burke 2010).

Goldsmith, Georges, and Burke (2010) cite Bloomberg's "entrepreneurial approach" to public school reform as particularly effective. Along with Joel Klein, Bloomberg joined with civic entrepreneurs in order to inspire "innovation." As Goldsmith says, by partnering with nonprofits and the private sector, Bloomberg:

> ... infused the system with catalytic talent from nontraditional areas, partnered with private sector entrepreneurs to widen choice, disrupted traditional school management by developing new routes for advancement, and granted managers the authority and autonomy to innovate. (204)

Through greatly expanding the number of privately run charter schools, and increasing the role of both nonprofit and for-profit intermediaries in the public school system, Bloomberg merged private interest with public good in an unprecedented fashion, ensuring that private entities could maintain a large degree of control over education policy and reform.

College Prep and philanthrocapitalism

College Prep, which opened in 2004, is an SSC. The school's mission states that students will graduate with an understanding of social justice, and that these students, "most of whom come from the city's historically least served communities, graduate ready to succeed in college and effect change in society." College Prep enacts its version of social justice by providing students from under-resourced communities with the opportunity to go to college and become successful professionals, and thus proactive participants in the free market.

Mirroring citywide reforms, College Prep created the Foundation, its in-house nonprofit, in 2008 in order to solicit funds from the private sector. The school is located on a busy street in a newly remodeled building in a commercial and business centered neighborhood in New York City. Thanks to the large donations that the Foundation accrues, clean and freshly painted classrooms boast of up-to-date equipment, including LCD projectors and interactive whiteboards. The large windows that look out onto the street are adorned with banners that advertise the colleges that College Prep alumni attend.

Media portrayals of progress-minded, accountability-driven College Prep demonstrate the philanthrocapitalistic model so popular in many of New York City's small schools; College Prep's website thanks five foundations, seven elected officials, and 34 companies and organizations for their charitable donations to the school, and also thanks more than 300 individuals who have each donated 5000 dollars or more to the Foundation. In addition to these donors, the website boasts of more than 25 links to articles in newspapers and magazines that praise the school for its ambitious mission, its talented teachers, and its propensity for receiving generous grants and donations.

Of the 458 students enrolled in the school, grades 9 through 12, 81% identify as "Black," 17% as "Hispanic," 1% as "Asian/or Pacific Islander," and less than 1% "White" or "American Indian." According to the New York City Department of

Education's profile of College Prep, 62% of its students are eligible for free lunches and 16% are eligible for reduced price lunch (nysed.gov. 2008–2009). Most of College Prep's students do not live in the immediate neighborhood; they commute from various boroughs of the city to attend the school. In the 2009–2010 school year, of the school's 35 teachers, 65% identify as "White," 20% identify as "African-American" or "Black," 9% as "biracial" or "mixed-race" (one African American and White, two Latino and White) and 6% as "Latino." Most teachers identify as coming from middle-class backgrounds. Media portrayals enhance the image of the school as one that provides, as philanthrocapitalist Andrew Carnegie might say, a "hand up, not a hand-out" (Bishop and Green 2009) for Black and Brown, urban poor but hardworking students to become college ready.

Importantly, Bishop and Green point to an essay that Carnegie wrote, "The gospel of wealth" (Carnegie 1889), as a favorite of philanthrocapitalist Bill Gates. Carnegie, a devotee of Herbert Spencer and Charles Darwin, argues that capitalism, competition and economic "survival of the fittest" are not only inevitable; they are essential to civilization. Millionaires aid those whom they deem worthy, assuming that the masses, if left to their own devices or if given resources to use on their own, would squander them through vice and laziness.

Bishop and Green argue that philanthrocapitalists are interested in "maximizing the leverage of their money" (2009, 6) through a market-oriented approach. Based on a strong belief that profit motive can achieve social good, the authors argue that:

> If [philanthrocapitalists] can use their donations to create a profitable solution to a social problem, it will attract far more capital, far faster, and risk provoking the public into a political backlash against the economic system that allowed them to become so wealthy. (6)

In other words, philanthrocapitalism is based on faith that free market capitalism is the antidote to social ills. The richesse oblige of these social innovators helps to maintain the "unstable equilibrium" (Gramsci 1975) of neoliberal hegemony. While predominantly White funders and teachers choose to engage the vocabulary of "need" and "risk" rather than the vocabulary of race when talking about donations or opportunities for students, racial formation theory (Omi and Winant 1994) provides a useful heuristic with which to name and trouble the raced model of need and privilege demonstrated through College Prep's model.

Philanthrocapitalistic education reform and race

Racial formation refers to: "the process by which social, economic and political forces determine the content and importance of racial categories, and by which they in turn are shaped by racial meanings" (Omi and Winant 1994, 61–2). Racial meaning is socially constructed and contested yet has concrete implications for the distribution of power, resources, opportunities and life chances. "Race," Omi and Winant write, "[is] a central axis of social relations which cannot be subsumed under or reduced to some broader category or conception" (Omi and Winant 1994, 62). One might view College Prep's model as one that is contingent upon privileged philanthropic donors providing resources for "needy" or "at-risk" students and their teachers. Although less explicit, the social, economic and political forces of philanthrocapitalism define and recreate racial meanings in the school through a hierarchical social and financial relationship.

Despite a colormute (Pollock 2004) discourse, politicized concepts of both risk and humanitarianism reinforce racism (Benton 2011; Fassin 2007; Hartigan 2009): at College Prep, White bodies are individuated as humanitarian or philanthropic "risktakers" (donors who take a risk with their money, young, idealistic teachers who make the sacrifice to teach in a high-needs school) while Black and Brown students are grouped and labeled as "at-risk" and in need of being "saved" in the context of the neoliberal market. Fassin (2007) argues that humanitarian intervention constitutes the politics of life – whose lives are to be saved and whose are to be risked. This distinction, he states, implies a radical inequality in the human condition. One could make a similar argument about College Prep's dependence on private and corporate philanthropy.

Critical Race Theorists expose the relationship between liberalism, meritocracy and the maintenance of White supremacy (Crenshaw et al. 1995; Freeman 1995); colorblindness (as opposed to race-consciousness) is a norm in post-civil rights US racial discourse. Rather than eradicating racism and racial disprarity, colorblindness maintains structures of White supremacy while at the same time perpetuating a false narrative of meritocracy and individual achievement (Bonilla-Silva 2006). Critical Race Theorists see racial domination and the struggle for civil rights as evolving through particular political, institutional conflicts and negotiations. Through race-conscious critiques, Critical Race Theory seeks to upend common sense structures of White supremacy, as well as other forms of class, gender and sexual domination, and to understand how racial power and domination are reproduced, especially within legal and liberal discourse (Crenshaw et al. 1995).

Critical White Studies, which grew out of Critical Race Theory, seeks to expose the operation and practice of normalized Whiteness as social category and creation (Frankenberg 1993; Ignatiev 1996; Leonardo 2004; Roediger 1991), and critiques Whiteness as a key element of oppressive social relations (Delgado and Stefancic 1997; Kincheloe et al. 1998). Like Critical Race Theorists, Critical Whiteness Studies theorists critique the ways that normalized liberal discourse masks and upholds White supremacy. Recently, Critical Whiteness Studies theorists in education have made critiques of the liberal trope of the "good White teacher" who "just wants to help." This is contingent upon a hierarchical relationship with people of color where Whites are the "givers" and people of color are the "recipients" (Picower 2009). This relationship maintains White dominance as well as ideologies of colorblindness, meritocracy and individual choice (Applebaum 2005).

Fine (1997) describes the operation of Whiteness as an "intricate institutional webbing that connects 'Whiteness' and 'other colors'" (58). In other words, institutions like schools and work "do not merely *manage* race; they *create* and *enforce* racial meanings" (Fine 1997, italics in original). Fine argues that Whiteness is coproduced with and against other "colors." This maintains White privilege by withholding opportunity from and denigrating that which is Black (60). At College Prep, the hierarchy of need and privilege between donors/funders, teachers, and students operationalizes Whiteness. Whites accumulate and maintain racial privilege and merit at College Prep through: (1) defining and then policing students' performed professionalism; and (2) maintaining an explicitly racial hierarchical structure of need and privilege.

Du Bois names the ideology of White supremacy that kept White and Black workers from unifying as a class during US Reconstruction the "wages of Whiteness" (Du Bois 1965; Smith 2006). This idea forms a foundation for scholars who posit that Whiteness reproduces itself as an ontological, psychological and financial investment (Fanon 1967; Harris 1993; Lipsitz 2006; Roediger 1991). College Prep staff explicitly teach professionalism as a set of performances that emphasize a punctual, dutiful and diligent worker who is also an individual achiever – as teachers attempt to make all students "college ready" (Conley 2005; Holland and Farmer-Hinton 2009). Performative professionalism furthers the view that students can meritocratically exceptionalize themselves from structural forms of oppression through the performance of marketability, yet in reality, serves to reinforce and reproduce White dominance because it does not critique structures of race and class privilege.

Lipman (2005) calls for an educational ethnography that: "engages relationships between cultural and social processes and policies in schools and the larger social situation – an educational ethnography that links micro with macro from an anti-imperialist, anti-neoliberal position" (319). I respond to this call, and seek to use the ethnographic data below to synthesize two distinct bodies of literature. One, Critical Race Theory, primarily focuses on race. The other, philanthrocapitalism, primarily focuses on class and globalization. In a move toward a more intersectional and qualitatively grounded critique of privatization of public education, I attempt to show how racial philanthrocapitalism, a manifestation of neoliberalism, reifies racist practices in schools and society.

My identity as student, teacher, and researcher

I was born and raised in a predominantly White college town in the Northeastern United States, and attended a predominantly White high school. I began in the classroom as a New York City Teaching Fellow. I have taught in New York City public schools for five years; two of those years included my dissertation fieldwork. I taught English at College Prep from 2008 to 2010. When I applied for the job, I told the principal that I was interested in conducting my dissertation research as well as teaching.

During the 2008–2009 school year, I developed close working and personal relationships with colleagues. I told them about my dissertation research in informal conversations and at staff meetings. I also told the students in my classroom about my research, although I did not interview them or their families until the following year, when I was no longer their teacher. I recorded daily fieldnotes, photocopied student work, did preliminary interviews with teachers, and collected school memos and documents. I paid a great deal of attention to how the school marketed itself to funders. I attended one of the school's annual benefits, which was a formal, private evening function that solicited donations from individual and corporate funders.

During the second year of my fieldwork, I taught at College Prep part time in order to have more time to focus on data collection. I collaborated with teachers and students on authoring and disseminating a school-wide questionnaire about students' home life, school life, personal interests, and aspirations.[5] Wanting to gain a better understanding of the physical and emotional experience of being a College Prep student, I decided to shadow various students on Mondays in the spring of

2010 (Ferguson 2001). In all grades, I sought teachers' recommendations, and told them that in exchange for having me as an extra "student" in their room for the day, I would share the field notes that I took from their classes with them if students gave me their permission. I also sought parent permission from the students whom I asked to shadow. If teachers and students gave their permission, I would compile the notes from the whole day together, and share them with the grade team so that they would have a sense of a "day in the life" of a College Prep student.

Jokingly, during one meeting, a teacher suggested to me that I wear the school uniform. I loved the idea, thinking that this would give me a better sense of the experience of moving through the building marked as a student. I turned out to be right: wearing the uniform sent the message to both teachers and students who saw me on those days that I was "student for a day;" both parties allowed me to play somewhat with the borders between student and staff at College Prep. One day in a ninth grade class, I blended in too well; a substitute teacher insisted that I sign in on the student attendance sheet, much to the delight of the students in the class, who laughed and played along.

After shadowing the students for the day, I interviewed them about the experience, asking about what it was like for them to be shadowed, and asking for their general impressions of College Prep. Professionalism came up often in the interviews, because it is such a large part of students' everyday experience and academic standing. I collaborated with teachers in choosing students to shadow and interview: three young men (one in 10th grade, one in 11th grade and one in 12th grade), and five young women (one in ninth grade, and four in 11th grade), all African-American. I was especially curious about when and why students rejected the school's implicit and explicit expectations about classroom, cafeteria and hallway conduct, and so I told students (and informed school staff beforehand) that I was officially off the clock as a teacher when I was wearing the students' uniform: black or khaki pants or a skirt with a blue collared shirt, instead of the more formal, business casual clothes I wore when I came to work as a teacher.

My physical appearance and positionality affected my data collection in instrumental ways: while I look younger than my age (28 at the time of my data collection), which at times proved to be an asset when I shadowed students, my Whiteness separated me from the racial positionalities of College Prep's students. My Whiteness seemed to facilitate White teachers sharing their politics in regard to race in our interviews.

Throughout the process of gathering data, I employed a "grounded theory" approach, constantly combining coding with analysis, and inductively developing theory in constant interaction with data (Glaser and Strauss 1967). I audio-recorded semi-structured interviews with 45 members of the school staff (including administrators, security guards, guidance/college office staff, and deans of discipline), 14 alumni of the school, 14 parent/guardians, and 10 students. My insider role as a teacher at College Prep helped me to develop rapport and trust with subjects before and during the interview process (Spradley 1979). I transcribed interviews and moved from open to focused coding as themes began to emerge (Emerson, Fretz, and Shaw 1995; LeCompte and Schensul 1999). At opportune moments, more informal interviews took place at work and in social settings, allowing me to member check my initial ideas and preliminary findings (Maxwell 1996).

Defining professionalism

I was first introduced to the concept of professionalism at College Prep in August 2008, during a 10th grade team meeting before the first day of school. During this meeting, Matt Randall, a White social studies teacher, and head of the 10th grade team, told us that we all needed to "be on the same page" in terms of how much professionalism counted for students' grades. "Professionalism is great," Mr Randall told Ms Williams, a newly hired, African-American, history teacher and me, "students really care about their professionalism points, and it's a great management tool. Like if you see them doing something bad, just start docking their professionalism points, and they'll stop." Students could be penalized by losing professionalism points as a result of inappropriate classroom behavior, or of being out of uniform, or rewarded by gaining points for their punctuality, organization, and preparedness in and for class. Typically, professionalism counted for approximately 10% of students' marking period grades.

Ninth grade teachers were more likely to be explicit with students about professionalism. They used a professionalism rubric that encompassed three categories of assessment for professional behavior: getting started in class, classwork, and exiting the room. According to the professionalism points rubric developed by ninth grade teachers, students are evaluated based on whether their conduct in class leads their teachers to believe that they are prepared, purposeful, focused, respectful, professional and prepared with questions or a summary of the lesson at the end of class. Teachers in the upper grades were more likely to grade for professionalism "intuitively" and subjectively.

College Prep professionalism, as Ms Carr, a White teacher, described:

> Is about giving students an opportunity to practice the social skills required for middle-class success, upper-middle, or upper-class success ... it's about equipping them for what's expected or required in a university setting and in a professional job setting.[6]

Ms Carr's statement shows how professionalism, central to discourse about college and career readiness at College Prep, becomes synonymous with how achievement is defined in this school (i.e. if a student is not professional, he or she is not seen as a high achiever or as one who is upwardly mobile). Along with prioritization of the performance of corporate professionalism comes the realization for students that the appearance of learning takes precedence over learning itself. The discourse of professionalism is taught without explicit social or racial critique, masking and upholding, rather than exposing or critiquing socially constructed racial hierarchies (Leonardo 2006; Pollock 2004). College Prep's pedagogy of professionalism carries with it a White supremacist logic that is dependent on classic liberal moral discourses of colorblindness, meritocracy, and individual choice. These logics masquerade as anti-racism or social justice while upholding the status quo (Applebaum 2005) by purportedly giving students from "under-resourced communities" access to the free market.

Performative professionalism at College Prep represents a neoliberal culture and politic of marketable respectability that is enforced by school administrators and Foundation staff in order to remain interesting to funders. College Prep professionalism also represents the belief that the performance of particular behaviors deemed "professional" will lead to college matriculation and upward mobility. In this privatized school model, a combination of philanthropy and careful image management is supposed to exceptionalize some College Prep students from deeply rooted racial and social inequities.

Many students reject or resist the school's top-down push for the performance of professionalism while simultaneously embracing professionalism in self-identified contexts, opting to remain connected to their support network of friends, family, and community. These points of resistance demonstrate an important counter-discourse to, and tension with and within the school discourse. The resistance represents a critique of the movement toward valorization of marketable respectability, as well as a critique of the devaluing of community control and democracy (Apple 2006), all in the name of agency and self-determination.

Marketing the institution
College matriculation as image management

The Foundation funds two staff members who are in charge of extracurricular opportunities for students and three college advisors. Beginning in the ninth grade, students follow a scope and sequence to ensure that they all matriculate into college. This includes college visits and curricula for "college readiness" (Conley 2005) in all classes, although the college office is more concerned with matriculation and with good-looking applications than with academic preparedness. For example, teachers complained about grade inflation at after-school meetings, and wondered about the difference between editing students' college application essays and writing them for students. College Prep does not keep accurate data on retention rates for students who matriculate to college, but some staff members whom I interviewed were sure that many struggled in college, or did not stay past their freshman year.

Ms Barnes, one of the college advisers, meets with students during the fall of their junior year and creates a file on each one that incorporates information about their family situation (household income and obligations to family members), their aspirations for careers and majors, and their academic standing. College Prep mandates that every student apply to at least six colleges in the CUNY system. As students complete their applications, the college office reviews them to make sure that applications are complete. College office staff also ensure that FAFSA[7] forms are filled out and that a member of College Prep's staff proofreads students' personal essays.

Urban, racially segregated schools are often aligned with a lack in opportunity or resources for students (Anyon 1997; Bowles and Gintis 1976; Kozol 2005; Massey and Denton 1993; Oakes 2005; Wacquant 1994). College Prep does not fall into this category. The school's 93% graduation rate, and 97% college acceptance rate for seniors stands out as atypical compared to New York City's average graduation rate of 62.7% (schools.nyc.gov 2010). Through college matriculation, school staff members strive to manage College Prep's external image in order to convince outsiders of the school's adeptness at its mission of social justice (see above), regardless of whether students are academically prepared for college or not.

The focus or emphasis is more on professionalism than content knowledge. For example, the nine students (eight African-Americans and one Latina) who were chosen to represent the school at an annual benefit (held at the corporate office of one of the school's primary funders) had rarely been written up for dress code or uniform violations. These students of color can perform the school's version of middle-classness or Whiteness believably, regardless of their actual class status. They are polished at engaging middle- or upper-class adults in polite conversation, and will highlight positive school experiences in conversations. These students are adept at code-switching into standard English from their primary dialect, are punctual, are involved in extracurricular activities, do their homework, do not get involved in physical or verbal altercations in or outside of school, and have relatively high grades. In other words, to be chosen to represent the school to outsiders, students are expected to blend seamlessly into corporate-class social settings; they are expected to "cover" (Yoshino 2006) those aspects of their identities that do not align with corporate-class norms. This is not to say that nonconformity is limited to students who are not middle class. Rather, those students who are hand-picked to represent the school are the ones who choose to show that they can fluidly move between the "cash language" (Little 2003) of corporate-class America and their home discourse, whatever it may be. Although it may have seemed that the students at the benefit needed the funders to attain upward mobility, in reality the funders also needed the students to reinforce their own social and economic standing. In this sense, Whiteness produces and protects itself as a merit or advantage through what Fine (1997) calls a "parasitic interdependence" on Blackness; Whiteness needs Blackness in order to become privileged. Students who represent College Prep at the benefit are expected to perform in ways which funders deem respectable in order to access their generosity. Generosity towards the "other" becomes a means to defend race and class privilege.[8]

The keynote speech given at the benefit by the guest of honor, to a mostly White, male corporate audience of about 150 people, highlighted the idea that students at College Prep come from the most desperate of circumstances and most needy backgrounds. This statement indexes larger discourses about Black and Latino students in urban public schools. At the benefit, students' color and school uniforms marked them as "underprivileged" and "needy," while their discourse led predominantly White guests to see them as successful meritocratic climbers who, with corporate help, could continue to be social climbers. At the end of the benefit, Mr Thomas, the head of the Foundation, was present, as guests dropped donations into a box, which, he recorded, added up to 34% of the Foundation's 2010–2011 budget, and was the second largest source of revenue for the school after a grant from the Robin Hood Foundation.

Professionalism and deficit discourse

As Ms Carr, the White teacher whom I mentioned earlier and I spoke with about professionalism, said:

> I think that some kids learn [professionalism] at home, I mean, I think a lot of kids learn that at home, but I think that having a place to practice that where that expectation is constant, I think that's what we provide. Because when they are hanging out with their friends, and say, for instance, when they live in the projects, and they are surrounded by people that are ... not necessarily following those values, it's easy to fall into the trap of, well I don't have to excuse myself, because nobody else does, or I don't have to expect this of myself because nobody else does.

Here, Ms Carr notes that most students practice "middle-class" or "upper-middle-class" codes of culture in the school, ascribing a deficit discourse (Valencia 2010) to some home cultures, conflating race, class and place (Gregory 1998), as she uses Black or Brown students who live in public housing as an example of students who lack the social skills required for upward mobility and personhood.[9] She demonstrates how the pedagogy of professionalism is explicitly raced and classed; these "middle-class or upper-middle-class codes of culture" are qualities that school staff members believe predominantly Black and Brown students need to be taught by predominantly White College Prep staff to be prepared for success and upward mobility in the world outside of College Prep. Professionalism points operate under the guise of staff members' self-imposed refusal to see or acknowledge the salience of race while maintaining structures of White privilege; many teachers view professionalism as a "color-blind" (Bonilla-Silva 2006; Leonardo 2004, 2007) cultural code of upward mobility and meritocracy.

At College Prep, I found that professionalism is supposed to be a way to teach students what Demerath (2009) calls "the Wilton Way," a competitive class culture of personal advancement and individual achievement. In Demerath's high school setting, 10% of the (mostly White middle and upper-middle class) senior class is named valedictorians. In this environment, these students' efforts at individual achievement and personal advancement are maximized in the name of "excellence." On the other hand, at College Prep where there is one senior valedictorian each year, as soon as students enter the building, they may be penalized by losing professionalism points, affecting their transcript grades. In other words, not only are the students in Demerath's study assumed to already be professional due to the lack of an explicit curriculum of professionalism, the structure of the school is such that their actions are likely to carry them on the path to "success." As compared to the deficit-based system of College Prep, the asset-based system in Demerath's high school setting demonstrates how the "wages of Whiteness" are protected, nurtured, and maximized (Du Bois 1965; Roediger 1991). The very existence of professionalism points at College Prep not only assumes that College Prep students are not professional, but sets up a structure in which it is expected that their behavior and cultural norms will lessen the likelihood of personal advancement or achievement.

In the following sections, I demonstrate the pedagogy of professionalism both in the context of College Prep as a "total institution" as well as its "underlife" (Goffman 1961). I discuss how despite the school's attempts at producing individuals who perform neoliberal conceptions of upward mobility, students and some teachers counter this process of dehumanization.

Teachers and professionalism

As a member of both the ninth and the 10th grade teams during 2008–2010, I was regularly copied in on e-mails that teachers sent to parents, and to each other, about students who resisted performative professionalism. These e-mails documented students who were out of uniform, who had a "negative attitude" or "muttered things under their breath," who "stuck post-its or tape all over themselves," or who mocked other students. Teachers often became quite upset when students showed that they did not buy into the logic of performative professionalism, and did not self-regulate their behavior, thus rejecting College Prep's version of Foucaultian governmentality, which holds that the "educated subject" should be self-governing

(Fendler 1998). In the context, then, of neoliberalism, the ostensibly individualized subject imagines him or herself to be free, yet a discourse of obedience strongly governs desires and agency; the responsible citizen must become the economic entrepreneur of his or her own life (Davies and Bansel 2007). This was demonstrated by teachers' frustration in a series of faculty meetings where the agenda included how to "change school culture" and "get students to buy in." When I interviewed Mr Fulton, a White ninth grade teacher, he said:

> Kids will do fine in the classroom, but ... the way kids behave in the hallways is evident of the culture you have built in the school. Like you can walk into the worst school, with a particular teacher and a group of kids, and you can see great things happening. But when you let kids just walk around, without an authority figure hovering over them, then you see how this school is. And it makes me really sad because I almost don't think there is an adult that can walk into a hallway here and kids will listen to them – principal, dean, nothing. And it's almost like they step out there, and it's just like, "fuck you" to everyone – we're cursing, we're play fighting, we're throwing garbage on the floor, we throw food, we're going late to class, the bathrooms ... I feel like you can walk into a school bathroom and you can see evidence of how happy kids are. Every day, written in the bathroom here: "College Prep sucks dick, F-this." The paper towels are in the urinal toilet by 10:00. Where is this coming from? 'Cause I know they are not doing this in their homes. And it's like wow, this is the place where they spend the majority of their teenage years and they hate it. And I don't know how to change it.

Mr Fulton takes issue here with the fact that while some students at College Prep might work well in supervised classrooms, students refuse to externalize school-sanctioned "professional" values or culture where there is no visible controlling power.

During the spring of 2010 students took their hallway unprofessionalism to the next level; many chose to ignore the late bell and instead talked and laughed with friends. To ameliorate this, teachers tried locking their doors after the bell rang, so that students would have to knock before they entered. This proved ineffective, especially because students would knock on the door after the class had started. The deans of discipline participated in hallway sweeps, where any student caught after the bell was marched to the guidance suite and issued a detention, which most students did not fulfill. As a result of missing detention, they were barred from "privileges" like school dances, basketball games or extracurricular activities. Still, this did not seem to be enough of a disincentive.

In May of 2010, there were 342 students out of a total 458 who were barred from their privileges as a result of having between three and 50 unserved detentions. During an "emergency meltdown" meeting about student discipline, Ms McGoldrick, a White ninth grade teacher, said:

> They say to themselves: why do I care if I have 27 detentions? They feel that we [adults] are fighting the fight and that they don't have to – they know that we have to make our school look good. Students know that our results are published, and that it makes the school look better if our numbers look good.

Despite the fact that students do not perform the raced and classed "culture" that teachers deem necessary for their college and career readiness, for teachers, the school's image and competitiveness for funding take precedence over finding creative ways to get all students to invest. Students, meanwhile, achieve the right to opt out of College Prep professionalism.

When Ms Meehan, a White college advisor and I spoke informally one day about professionalism, she said:

> You know, most of us come here, and we have to put on a little bit of a face to be good at our jobs, to be professional. I think that's true about people who are professionals all over the country. But at the same time, we don't mind doing that, because it's not like anyone is criticizing who we really are on the inside when we have to put on a "face" for work. I always know I can celebrate who I am. With our kids, it's totally different – there is no place to celebrate who they are. That's the problem.

Students pick up on the implicit assumption behind the ostensibly colorblind discourse of professionalism that knowledge of how to be professional (punctual, properly dressed, well-behaved) is something that predominantly Black and Brown College Prep students lack; this is something that they are supposed to learn from predominantly White and/or middle-class teachers. Ms Meehan's quote demonstrates that a different version of racial philanthrocapitalist logic or richesse oblige can masquerade underneath White teachers' good intentions about what is best for students (Ferguson 2001; Hyland 2005). For example, Ms Elliott, a White teacher, shared with me that she believes that College Prep teachers work for social change by:

> Confer[ring] as much of our privilege that we were lucky enough or coincidentally fortunate enough to grow up with on our students. We give them the opportunity to have them enter whatever social sphere they would like ... we give them the opportunities that their racial group traditionally or stereotypically doesn't have.

Casting herself as a neoliberal savior, Ms Elliott hides a deficit discourse behind a deracinated narrative of meritocracy for students. She does not give the school her money, but because she is privileged, she sees it as her duty to help "save" her less privileged students without ever having to face or critique oppressive social structures. She protects her White privilege here while at the same time casting herself as the "good White teacher" (Hytten and Warren 2003) who "just wants to help" (Picower 2009) her students by upholding White neoliberal subjecthood as the reference point for civilization, moral development, and rationality (Leonardo 2004).

Resistance as humanization

Students often resisted teachers' efforts at trying to "save" their students. For example, several teachers on the team struggled with Nakisha, a student who acted, in her words, "goofy" when she was "bored." Teachers complained not only about Nakisha's fighting, but also about other "unprofessional" behaviors: speaking out of turn in class, distracting other students, cutting class, and wandering in the halls. She played on the school's basketball team, but the coach had benched her to punish her for her poor class behavior as reported to the coach by her teachers. Her grandmother, her primary guardian, received so many behavior-related calls from the school that she came close to transferring Nakisha to another school.

I shadowed Nakisha, and her behavior was not always problematic; I observed her performing professionalism. Clearly she knew how to be professional; she just was not always willing to do so. Her choice to perform professionalism was especially evident in classrooms where teachers and students shared power, where teachers had developed personal rapport with their students, and where teachers did not coerce students into professionalism through a points system.

Nakisha told me that Ms Leon, her math teacher was one of her favorite teachers; she learned well from her. Ms Leon is African-American. Ms Leon, Nakisha said, "can laugh with [students], but she lets us know when it's time to be serious." I noticed, observing in Ms Leon's class on several occasions, that she did not fight students for power, but established herself as being organized and in full control. She used this control, though, to make sure that students had fun, while at the same time remaining consistent with her routines. In her class I never heard her explicitly mention professionalism points.

Following Ms Leon's lesson, Nakisha and I worked through a review packet; Nakisha showed me how to calculate mean, median and mode. At the end of the class, Nakisha volunteered to be one of three students to go up to review concepts aloud in front of the class. As she did this, I noticed a marked contrast between her behavior in classes during her 10th grade year, and this 11th grade class. Although, I thought, Nakisha was older, this change also seemed to be due to the rapport that she had with Ms Leon, as well as her own confidence in her knowledge of the material; she drew this confidence from both teaching me about it as well as teaching the class.

I knew that Nakisha's behavior had not changed in all of her classes based on interactions that I observed with two other teachers. I noticed that teachers were quite wary of Nakisha's movements and behaviors around the room. In her history class, for example, Nakisha got up from her desk and started walking across the room towards the teacher, Ms Gomez's desk. Ms Gomez stopped giving directions to the class at this point and said "Nakisha ..."

"What!?" said Nakisha, "I am just going to get the stapler!"

Ms Gomez nodded, and continued instruction. A similar incident occurred in Mr Gonzaga's chemistry class. Nakisha got up. "Nakisha, what are you doing?" asked Mr Gonzaga. "I am just going to the trash!" she said. Like Ms Gomez, he nodded and continued instruction. I noted that other students got up and moved around the room without any comment from teachers. Nakisha was watched so closely, I suspect, because she continued to cultivate a reputation as being disruptive or unpredictable in class, and had the potential for deviant behavior.

Based on many of my observations and research, students are more likely to perform as intellectuals and achieve in school-sanctioned ways when the authority in the room does not utilize deficit discourse, or coerce performed professionalism through a points system (Kohn 1999). Instead, establishing intellectual rather than performed professionalism as a norm seems more effective at encouraging students to perform school-sanctioned professionalism. As the agendas of the private and corporate elite make their way into urban public schools, which are pressured to gain more private support from philanthrocapitalists and corporations by making needy students marketable by national and global standards of professionalism and college or career readiness, it becomes especially important to recognize what is neglected by the neoliberal agenda.

Humanizing pedagogy through grounded agency

> Professionalism: Being dressed and well behaviored and manored [sic] for the real world here in "White America" (A 12th grade student's definition of professionalism on the school-wide questionnaire)

Humanizing pedagogy (Freire 1970) is based in the idea that student-teachers and teacher-students engage one another in becoming critical and maintaining a sense of community. This pedagogy is counter to a "banking" model, where students are seen as receptacles into which a teacher "deposits" knowledge. Rooted in deficits about students' backgrounds and communities, the pedagogy of professionalism assumes that students do not have needed qualities for acceptance as professionals in the mainstream. Because staff members assume that students are not professional, opportunities for a more dialogic or humanizing pedagogy become stifled. The pedagogy of professionalism, taught through a deficit lens, serves to reify the privilege of the predominantly White power structure in the school.

The student quoted in the introduction of this section expresses an awareness of "playing the game" as a Black agent in a White supremacist market. She clearly positions herself in the context of the racial state (Omi and Winant 1994), and demonstrates the pervasive discourses of neoliberal capitalism and marketability (Hursh 2007, 2009). Are there possibilities for professionalism at College Prep that both critique White supremacist and neoliberal discourses and set students up for success (Delpit 1998; Giroux 2004; Spears-Bunton and Powell 2008)?

Professionalism cannot be defined as something that students lack and must learn exclusively at a school such as College Prep. In order to see oneself as a professional, one must feel oneself valued as an intellectual, and a nuanced and knowledgeable human being, beyond the performance of professionalism. This is what College Prep's current pedagogy of professionalism neglects. Students like Nakisha already express a critique of performative professionalism through performing unprofessionalism when they are seen as "bundles of skill sets" instead of as people (Urciuoli 2010). When teachers see students as already professional and intellectual beings (as in Ms Leon's class) they are less likely to resist prescribed forms of professional behavior.

Public schools that are increasingly dependent on private funding from philanthrocapitalists and corporations for their survival must provide both students and teachers with a simultaneous critique of the culture of personal advancement and marketability, either explicitly or through curricula that challenge students to perform as intellectuals, and valorize (as opposed to applying a deficit to) students' families, home communities, and backgrounds. It may be unrealistic that schools like College Prep distance themselves from entrenched dependence on private funds, but teachers and students can make and enact a critique, on an everyday level, of social structures that encourage the needy to depend on the privileged, and that perpetuate essentializing tropes of need and privilege that often conflate race, class, and place (Gregory 1998).

Concluding thoughts

It is ironic that if College Prep were truly a social-justice school, its mission would be to eradicate itself; it could not exist in a socioeconomically equitable society. In other words, College Prep depends on economic inequity and racial hierarchy to exist. The school's rhetoric of meritocracy and college matriculation through the performance of professionalism is an attempt to smooth over the explicitly race- and class-based inequities of the school's hybrid public/private model, under the guise of social justice and moral responsibility (Applebaum 2005). The Bloomberg administration enacts the same politics on a larger scale as it facilitates the increase of private or corporate control – that is, structures of privilege are reified under the guise of social justice.

Leonardo (2007) and Gillborn (2005) have argued that education policy in the United States upholds White supremacy through normalizing Whiteness and rendering it invisible. The pedagogy of professionalism directly reflects state-mandated discourses of accountability in its attempt to make student behaviors numerically quantifiable. Grande (2000) uses the term "Whitestream" to refer to "the cultural capital of Whites in almost every aspect of society." Urrieta (2006) refers to Whitestream as: "the official and unofficial texts used in US society that are founded on the practices, principles, morals, values and history of White Anglo-American culture, i.e. White cultural capital." In this case, racial philanthrocapitalism and performative professionalism function as texts founded on White cultural capital. Neoliberal standards of marketability, furthered through racial philanthrocapitalism and the pedagogy of professionalism's deficit discourse, benefit Whitestream society through promoting a belief in US meritocracy, and through promoting colorblindness. This maintains, rather than critiques the status quo.

While racial philanthrocapitalism in education will not promote real social equity, it is unlikely that we will see this model change anytime soon. Private and philanthropic influences continue to expand in and beyond New York City. Critiques can start from within, and urban schools can push themselves to respond to the needs of the students they serve in order to interrupt the pervasive deficit discourses linked to those communities (Stovall 2007). Specifically, teachers can work toward an antiracist, asset-based, more democratic pedagogy, thus teaching respectful conduct in an atmosphere that upholds students' personhood.

When one student was asked on the school-wide questionnaire whether she was a confident student and why, she responded: "Yes. My pride, my respect for myself. I think it is College Prep [that] bring[s] down my confidence." This comment resonates with the pedagogy of professionalism at College Prep. In depending on racial philanthrocapitalism and in teaching professionalism through a raced and classed deficit model, College Prep encourages students to manage their public image, but simultaneously discourages them from aligning professionalism with their own backgrounds, or with critical thought and integrity. The former cannot take place without the latter.

Acknowledgements

I thank those who participated in the *Social Life of Achievement* panel at the 2010 annual meeting of the American Anthropological Association, where I presented and received valuable feedback on a first version of this paper. Additionally, I thank Denise Blum and Char Ullman for including me in this special issue. Unfortunately, I use pseudonyms for College Prep teachers, students, and families and cannot name them here, but I thank them for their patience and insight in regard to this study. I also wish to thank Denise Blum, David J. Brown, Laura S. Brown, Nadine Bryce, Clifton Colmon, Sharon Givens, Liz Knauer, Christopher Loperena, Kofi Ofori, Naomi Reed, Teresa von Fuchs, Char Ullman, and those who anonymously reviewed this article, for their insightful and critical commentary. I am grateful to Lane Stilson and Orson Robbins-Pianka for invaluable statistical assistance. This manuscript also benefited from the ongoing mentorship and support of Keffrelyn Brown, Peter Demerath, Kevin Foster, Edmund T. Gordon, Douglas Foley, and Joao Costa Vargas.

Notes

1. I refer to this school as "CPA" in a previous article (Brown 2011).
2. In this paper, when referring to College Prep's version of performed professionalism, I use "performative professionalism" and "professionalism" interchangeably.
3. I capitalize racial markers (i.e. White, Black and Brown) in order to highlight race as a central aspect of my analysis. In making this choice, I index the socio-historical construction and continued maintenance of race, racial meaning, and racial privilege in the United States. I also capitalize these terms to refer to the specific ideologies or practices related to racial concepts or identities (see Collins [2004, 17, 310] and Vargas [2006, 249] for related discussions). I also use ethnic markers in this article, such as "African-American" and "Latino." These terms often overlap with racial markers in the United States, and represent other ways that subjects are sometimes, but not always, identified.
4. According to a 7 April 2011 *New York Times* article, Mayor Bloomberg asked Ms Black to resign three months after her appointment due to her unpopularity and incompetence. He replaced her with deputy mayor Dennis M. Walcott (Barbaro et al. 2011, A1). State Commissioner David Steiner, who gave Black the waiver to be Chancellor without any background in education, resigned as well.
5. At each grade team, college office, and enrichment office meeting, I showed staff members an initial list of questions. This was developed largely from Demerath's (2009) school-wide questionnaire in *Producing Success*, which focused on the school experiences and emotional well being of students in the context of a school's competitive culture of achievement. The questionnaire was subsequently expanded with my own revisions as well as feedback from school staff members. The revised questionnaire focused on three general areas of students' lives: "Background and Home," "School" and "Outside of School." Students responded to a series of unstructured and structured questions that explored their experiences in regard to their peers, their families, their teachers, and their aspirations. After entering questionnaire data into an *Excel* spreadsheet, I conducted bivariate analyses in order to establish relationships between dependent variables (such as grade level or gender) and independent variables (such as students' opinion of school professionalism points, or students' goals or aspirations) (LeCompte and Schensul 1999).
6. In accordance with the Institutional Review Board at the University of Texas at Austin, all interviews were held in confidentiality, and the names of interviewees have been changed by mutual agreement.
7. Free Application for Federal Student Aid.
8. While it is not my intention to conflate the racial experiences of non-White communities in the United States, in this section I find it useful to theorize the experiences of both Black and Brown students at College Prep through the lens of Blackness. This serves to highlight the somewhat binary formation of race at this school; e.g. White vs. non-White, privilege vs. need, professional vs. unprofessional, teacher or funder vs. student, etc.
9. Although College Prep does not use Ruby Payne's (1996) *A Framework For Understanding Poverty*, this discourse resonates with her theories, as well as with other recycled "culture of poverty" discourses that trace back to Lewis (1959) and Moynihan's (1965) deficit-based arguments. The idea of a "culture of poverty" continues to be heavily contested in the social sciences, because it tends to "blame the victim," and lacks any structural critique. For example, see Good and Eames (1996), Foley (1997) and Valencia (2010) for critiques or the recycled "culture of poverty" in anthropology and education.

References

Ancess, Jacqueline, and David Allen. 2006. Implementing small theme high schools in New York City: Great intentions and great tensions. *Harvard Educational Review* 76, no. 3: 401–37.
Anyon, Jean. 1997. *Ghetto schooling: A political economy of urban educational reform.* New York, NY: Teachers College Press.
Apple, Michael. 2006. *Educating the "right" way: Markets, standards, God, and inequality.* 2nd ed. New York, NY: Routledge.
Applebaum, Barbara. 2005. In the name of morality: Moral responsibility, whiteness and social justice education. *Journal of Moral Education* 34, no. 3: 277–90.
Barbaro, M., S. Otterman, and J.C. Hernandez. 2011. After 3 months, mayor replaces school leader. *New York Times*, April 7. http://www.nytimes.com/2011/04/08/education/08black.html?pagewanted=all.
Benton, Adia 2011. Race, risk and the humanitarian politics of life. Paper presented at the American Anthropological Association annual meeting, November 16–20, in Montreal, Quebec, Canada.
Bishop, Matthew, and Michael Green. 2009. *Philanthrocapitalism: How the rich can save the world.* New York, NY: Bloomsbury Press.
Bonilla-Silva, Eduardo. 2006. *Racism without racists: Color-blind racism and the persistence of inequality in the United States.* 2nd ed. Oxford: Rowman and Littlefield.
Bowles, Samuel, and Herbert Gintis. 1976. *Schooling in capitalist America: Educational reform and the contradictions of economic life.* New York, NY: Basic Books.
Brown, Amy. 2011. Consciousness-raising or eyebrow-raising? Reading urban fiction with high school students in Freirean cultural circles. *Penn GSE Perspectives on Urban Education* 9, no. 1. http://www.urbanedjournal.org/archive/volume-9-issue-1-fall-2011/consciousness-raising-or-eyebrow-raising-reading-urban-fiction-hi.
Carnegie, Andrew. 1889/2006. The gospel of wealth. In *Andrew Carnegie: The "gospel of wealth" essays and other writings*, ed. D. Nasaw, 1–12. New York, NY: Penguin Books.
Collins, Patricia Hill. 2004. *Black sexual politics: African Americans, gender, and the new racism.* London: Routledge.
Conley, David T. 2005. *College knowledge: What it really takes for students to succeed and what we can do to get them ready.* San Francisco, CA: Jossey-Bass.
Crenshaw, Kimberlé, Neil Gotanda, Gary Peller, and Kendall Thomas, eds. 1995. *Critical race theory: The key writings that formed the movement.* New York, NY: The New Press.
Davies, Bronwyn, and Peter Bansel. 2007. Neoliberalism and education. *International Journal of Qualitative Studies in Education* 20, no. 3: 247–59.
Delgado, Richard, and Jean Stefancic. 1997. *Critical white studies: Looking behind the mirror.* Philadelphia, PA: Temple University Press.
Delpit, Lisa. 1998. The silenced dialogue. *Harvard Educational Review* 58, no. 3: 280–98.
Demerath, Peter. 2009. *Producing success: The culture of personal advancement in an American high school.* Chicago, IL: University of Chicago Press.
Du Bois, W.E.B. 1965. *Black reconstruction in America: An essay toward the history of the part which folk played in the attempt to reconstruct democracy in America.* New York, NY: The Free Press.
Emerson, Robert M., Rachel I. Fretz, and Linda L. Shaw. 1995. *Writing ethnographic fieldnotes.* Chicago, IL: University of Chicago Press.
Fanon, Frantz. 1967. *Black skin, white masks.* Trans. C.L. Markmann. New York: Grove Press. (Original edition, 1952).

Fassin, Didier. 2007. Humanitarianism as a politics of life. *Public Culture* 19, no. 3: 499–520.
Fendler, Lynn. 1998. What is it impossible to think? A genealogy of the educated subject. In *Foucault's challenge: Discourse, knowledge and power in education*, ed. T.S. Popkewitz and M. Brennan, 39–63. New York, NY: Teachers College.
Ferguson, Ann Arnett. 2001. *Bad boys: Public schools in the making of black masculinity*. Ann Arbor, MI: The University of Michigan Press.
Fertig, Beth. 2011. Between state-city tensions lie plans to improve schools. *New York Times*. http://www.nytimes.com/schoolbook/2011/12/07/between-state-city-tensions-lie-plans-to-improve-schools/?scp=2&sq=bloomberg%20school%20closure&st=cse.
Fine, Michelle. 1997. Witnessing whiteness. In *Off white: Readings on race, power and society*, ed. M. Fine, L. Powell, L. Weis, and L. Mun Wong, 57–65. New York, NY: Routledge.
Foley, Douglas. 1997. Deficit thinking models based on culture: The anthropological protest. In *The evolution of deficit thinking: Educational thought and practice*, ed. R. Valencia, 113–31. London: Falmer.
Foley, Eileen. 2010. *Approaches of Bill & Melinda Gates foundation-funded intermediary organizations to structuring and supporting small high schools in New York City*. Washington, DC: Policy Studies.
Frankenberg, Ruth. 1993. *White women, race matters: The social construction of Whiteness*. Minneapolis, MN: University of Minnesota Press.
Freeman, Alan David. 1995. Legitimizing racial discrimination through antidiscrimination law: A citical review of Supreme Court doctrine. In *Critical race theory: The key writings that formed the movement*, ed. K. Crenshaw, N. Gotanda, G. Peller, and K. Thomas, 29–46. New York, NY: The New Press.
Freire, Paulo. 1970. *Pedagogy of the oppressed*. New York, NY: Continuum International.
Garvey, John. 2011. *Are New York City's public schools preparing students for success in college?* Providence, RI: Annenberg Institute at Brown University.
Gillborn, David. 2005. Education policy as an act of White supremacy: Whiteness, Critical Race Theory and education reform. *Journal of Education Policy* 20, no. 4: 484–505.
Giordano, Mary Ann. 2011. Sadness and anger over school closings. *New York Times*. http://www.nytimes.com/schoolbook/2011/12/09/sadness-and-anger-over-school-closings/?scp=1&sq=bloomberg%20school%20closure&st=cse.
Giordano, Mary Ann, and Anna Phillips. 2011. Mayor hits nerve in remarks on class sizes and teachers. *New York Times*, December 2, A19.
Giroux, Henry A. 1983. Theories of reproduction and resistance in the new sociology of education: A critical analysis. *Harvard Educational Review* 53, no. 3: 257–93.
Giroux, Henry A. 2004. *The terror of neoliberalism: Authoritarianism and the eclipse of democracy*. Boulder, CO: Paradigm.
Glaser, Barney, and Anselm Strauss. 1967. *The discovery of grounded theory: Strategies for qualitative research*. Chicago, IL: Aldine.
Goffman, Erving. 1961. *Asylums: Essays on the social situation of mental patients and other inmates*. New York, NY: Anchor Books.
Goldsmith, Stephen, Gigi Georges, and Tim Glynn Burke. 2010. *The power of social innovation: How civic entrepreneurs ignite community networks for good*. San Francisco, CA: Jossey Bass.
Good, Judith G., and Edwin Eames. 1996. An anthropological critique of the culture of poverty. In *Urban life: Readings in urban anthropology*, ed. G. Gmelch and W. Zenner, 405–17. Prospect Heights, IL: Waveland.
Gramsci, Antonio. 1975. *The prison notebooks*. Trans. G. Einaudi. Vol. 2. New York, NY: Columbia University Press.
Grande, Sandy. 2000. American Indian geographies of identity and power: At the crossroads of indígena and mestizaje. *Harvard Educational Review* 70, no. 4: 467–98.
Gregory, Steven. 1998. *Black corona: Race and the politics of place in an urban community*. Princeton, NJ: Princeton University Press.
Harris, Cheryl. 1993. Whiteness as property. *Harvard Law Review* 106, no. 8: 1709–91.

Hartigan, John 2009. Individuating Obama: Maneuvers through American racial discourse. Paper presented at the annual meeting of the American Anthropological Association, December 2–6, in Philadelphia, PA, USA.

Holland, N.E., and Raquel Farmer-Hinton. 2009. Leave no schools behind: The importance of a college culture in urban public high schools. *The High School Journal* 92, no. 3: 24–43.

Hursh, David. 2007. Marketing education: The rise of standardized testing, accountability, competition, and markets in public education. In *Neoliberalism and education reform*, ed. E.W. Ross and R. Gibson, 15–34. Cresskill, NJ: Hampton Press.

Hursh, David. 2009. Beyond the justice of the market: Combating neoliberal educational discourse and promoting deliberative democracy and economic equality. In *Handbook of social justice in education*, ed. W. Ayers, T. Quinn, and D. Stovall, 152–64. New York, NY: Routledge.

Hyland, Nora E. 2005. Being a good teacher of Black students? White teachers and unintentional racism. *Curriculum Inquiry* 35, no. 4: 429–59.

Hytten, Kathy, and John Warren. 2003. Tiffany, friend of people of color: White investments in antiracism. *International Journal of Qualitative Studies in Education* 16, no. 1: 17–29.

Ignatiev, Noel. 1996. *How the Irish became White*. New York, NY: Routledge.

Kincheloe, Joe, Shirley Steinberg, Nelson Rodriguez, and Ronald Chennault, eds. 1998. *White reign: Deploying whiteness in America*. New York, NY: St. Martin's Press.

Kohn, Alfie. 1999. *Punished by rewards: The trouble with gold stars, incentive plans, A's, praise, and other bribes*. Boston, MA: Houghton Mifflin.

Kozol, Jonathan. 2005. *The shame of the nation: The restoration of apartheid schooling in America*. New York, NY: Three Rivers Press.

LeCompte, Margaret, and Jean Schensul. 1999. *Analyzing and interpreting ethnographic data. Ethnographer's toolkit*, Vol. 5. Walnut Creek, CA: AltaMira Press.

Leonardo, Zeus. 2004. The color of supremacy: Anti-racist education and white domination. *Journal of Educational Philosophy and Theory* 36, no. 2: 137–52.

Leonardo, Zeus. 2006. Through the multicultural glass: Althusser, ideology, and race relations in post-Civil Rights America. *Policy Futures in Education* 3, no. 4: 400–12.

Leonardo, Zeus. 2007. The war on schools: NCLB, nation creation and the educational construction of whiteness. *Race, Ethnicity and Education* 10, no. 3: 261–78.

Lewis, Oscar. 1959. *Five families: Mexican case studies in the culture of poverty*. New York, NY: Basic Books.

Lipman, Pauline. 2005. Reflections on the field: Educational ethnography and the politics of globalization, war and resistance. *Anthropology and Education Quarterly* 36, no. 4: 315–28.

Lipsitz, George. 2006. *The possessive investment in Whiteness: How White people profit from identity politics*. Philadelphia, PA: Temple University Press.

Little, Sandy. 2003. The "cash" language: Whose standard? *Field Notes* 13, no. 1. http://sabes.org/resources/publications/fieldnotes/vol13/fl31little.htm.

Massey, Douglas, and Nancy Denton. 1993. *American apartheid: Segregation and the making of the underclass*. Cambridge, MA: Harvard University Press.

Maxwell, Joseph. 1996. *Qualitative research design: An interactive approach*. Thousand Oaks, CA: Sage.

Moynihan, Daniel Patrick. 1965. *The Negro family: The case for national action*. Washington, DC: Department of Labor.

nysed.gov. 2008–2009. *The New York state school report card*. Albany, NY: NY State Education Department, Office of Assessment Policy, Development and Administration. https://www.nystart.gov/publicweb.

Oakes, Jeannie. 2005. *Keeping track: How schools structure inequality*. 2nd ed. New Haven, CT: Yale University Press.

Omi, Michael, and Howard Winant. 1994. *Racial formation in the United States: From the 1960s to the 1990s*. New York, NY: Routledge.

Otterman, Sharon, and Allison Kopicki. 2011. New Yorkers say mayor has not improved schools. *New York Times*. http://www.nytimes.com/2011/09/07/education/07poll.html?pagewanted=all.

Payne, Ruby. 1996. *Understanding the framework of poverty.* Highlands, TX: Ruby K. Payne.

Picower, Bree. 2009. The unexamined whiteness of teaching: How white teachers maintain and enact dominant racial ideologies. *Race Ethnicity and Education* 12, no. 2: 197–215.

Pollock, Mica. 2004. *Colormute.* Princeton, NJ: Princeton University Press.

Ravitch, Diane. 2011. *The death and life of the great American school system.* New York, NY: Teachers College Press.

Robinson, Cedric. 1983. *Black Marxism: The making of the black radical tradition.* Chapel Hill, NC: The University of North Carolina Press.

Robinson, Gail. 2011. With more school closings, debate about policy continues. *Gotham Gazette.* http://www.gothamgazette.com/article/education/20110131/6/3460.

Roediger, David. 1991. *The wages of whiteness.* New York, NY: Verso.

schools.nyc.gov. 2011. Cohorts of 2001 through 2005 (classes of 2005 through 2009) graduation outcomes. New York City Board of Education 2010. http://schools.nyc.gov/Accountability/data/GraduationDropoutReports/default.htm.

Smith, Sharon. 2006. Race, class and "Whiteness theory". *International Socialist Review* 46. http://www.isreview.org/issues/46/whiteness.shtml.

Spears-Bunton, Linda, and Rebecca Powell, eds. 2008. *Toward a literacy of promise: Joining the African-American struggle.* New York, NY: Routledge.

Spradley, James. 1979. *The ethnographic interview.* New York, NY: Holt, Rinehart and Winston.

Stovall, David. 2007. Towards a politics of interruption: High school design as politically relevant pedagogy. *International Journal of Qualitative Studies in Education* 20, no. 6: 681–91.

Tarras, Elizabeth Stieglitz, and Denise Gokey. 2011. City policies undermined Jane Addams High. *New York Times.* http://www.nytimes.com/schoolbook/2011/12/06/city-policies-undermined-jane-addams-h-s/.

Urciuoli, Bonnie. 2010. Neoliberal education: Preparing the student for the new workplace. In *Ethnographies of neoliberalism*, ed. C.J. Greenhouse, 162–76. Philadelphia, PA: University of Pennsylvania Press.

Urrieta, Luis. 2006. Community identity discourse and the heritage academy: Colorblind educational policy and white supremacy. *International Journal of Qualitative Studies in Education* 19, no. 4: 455–76.

Valencia, Richard. 2010. *Dismantling contemporary deficit thinking: Educational thought and practice.* New York, NY: Routledge.

Vargas, Joao Costa. 2006. *Catching hell in the city of angels: Life and meanings of Blackness in South Central Los Angeles.* Minneapolis, MN: University of Minnesota Press.

Wacquant, Loic. 1994. The new urban color line: The state and the fate of the ghetto in post-Fordist America. In *Social theory and the politics of identity*, ed. C. Calhoun, 231–76. Malden, MA: Blackwell.

Yoshino, Kenji. 2006. *Covering: The hidden assault on our civil rights.* New York, NY: Random House.

Hip hop as empowerment: voices in El Alto, Bolivia

Ariana Tarifa

> In response to neoliberal policies that have been in place since 1985, Bolivian young people have increasingly used hip hop music as a means of protest and to reclaim social and political participation. Hip hop in Latin America tells the story of the struggles that marginalized people have suffered, and speaks to the effects of international policies fueled by globalization. This paper focuses on what the Bolivian hip hopper Nina Uma calls "Hip hop revolution": a hip hop that critiques and interrogates the social, political, and economic structure, the differences between the haves and the have nots, and proposes using hip hop to spread "education as cultural action of freedom". This article examines the ways young people of El Alto, Bolivia are making sense of their social, political, and economic context.

> We've already warned you, the Aymara men are better than the system. (On a banner at the entry of El Alto, Bolivia)[1]

Abraham Bojórquez, an Aymaran hip hopper and member of the hip hop group Ukamau y Ke, was 26 when he died on 20 May 2009 in El Alto, Bolivia. Bojórquez was nationally and internationally known for his revolutionary lyrics, and his criticism of politicians, of the political and economic system, and of the media. The sudden death of Bojórquez meant a great loss not only for the hip hop movement but also for Indigenous youth in El Alto who used hip hop as a form of creative expression to promote social, economic, and political equity in Bolivian society amidst the neoliberal policies in place since 1985. These policies included the privatization of national oil and gas companies, railroads, and mines and left thousands of Bolivians, mainly Indigenous, unemployed and displaced. The policies pushed many to migrate to cities such as El Alto, which were unprepared to accommodate the new residents. As poverty increased, the informal economy in the cities grew, and cultural ruptures occurred among migrants and people of Indigenous descent.

The imposition of western cultural, social, and economic trends over nonwestern countries that comes with globalization has shaped Bolivian society. Globalization marginalizes Indigenous people from mainstream political and economic practices. Ironically, it is within this context of globalization that Alteños[2] found hip hop as a critical tool for expression and protest. Bojórquez and the hip hop movement in El

Alto was a response to the oppressive conditions of neoliberal policies and the capitalistic system.

This article shows the ways Alteño Indigenous youth use hip hop for empowerment. They respond to neoliberal practices which were put in place almost three decades ago, yet still affect them today. First, I provide a historical overview of neoliberal policies in Bolivia and El Alto in particular. Second, I explain the ways Paulo Freire's critical pedagogy articulates with these policies. I detail the methods of this study, and share findings from interviews and analysis of hip hop lyrics. Lastly, I discuss the meanings and implications of the hip hop movement for the Indigenous in this neoliberal context.

From indios to citizens: "El Alto siempre de pie, nunca de rodillas"[3]

El Alto, once a part of the neighboring city of La Paz, is situated in the *Altiplano*,[4] on the southwest side of the urban center of La Paz (Arbona and Kohl 2004). El Alto is home to close to one million people, 90% of whom are Indigenous, with a majority identifying as Aymara (74.2%) and to a lesser extent Quechua (6.4%) (Albó 2006). Poverty and the quickly growing population of El Alto greatly aggravate the living conditions in this city. El Alto's population increases by 10% annually, which has strained the city's economy (Crowder 2003). Initially El Alto was a transitory settlement for poor, Indigenous people who were looking to migrate to La Paz. Nowadays, El Alto has outgrown La Paz in population and has developed its own identity, which according to Lazar (2008, 31) is one of an "Indigenous city." With the fastest growing population in Latin America, El Alto has become a center of rebellious social movements, and home of the "hip hop revolution."

Since the sixteenth century, Bolivian Indigenous people have suffered displacement and exploitation; however, they have always asserted and defended themselves. Indigenous insurrections protesting taxes, lack of land ownership, exploitive mine work, and forced settlements were common. One of the most famous insurrections occurred in 1781: Tupac Katari positioned his army toward La Paz from what is now the city of El Alto; the siege lasted for approximately eight months (Albó 2006). Two centuries later, another milestone in Bolivian history occurred: the 1952 revolution brought changes in the economic and social structure in the country (De Mesa, Gisbert, and Mesa Gisbert 2001). The triumph of the revolution not only meant the implementation of universal suffrage, allowing women and Indigenous the right to vote, but also a huge agrarian reform. According to De Mesa, Gisbert, and Mesa Gisbert (2001), the Agrarian reform of 1952 meant the end of the *latifundio*[5] and the elimination of a system of exploitation of peasants by land owners. Huge pieces of land were returned to the Indigenous population, and the basic principle of "la tierra es de quién la trabaja"[6] was put into practice. Small pieces of land were given to the peasants, creating a *microfundio*[7]. This broke the Aymara-Quechua tradition of communitarian work of the land. This division of the land allowed Indigenous people to incorporate themselves into the economic market, but with a limited amount of agricultural production. The peasant status changed from servant to landowner. This situation forced many peasants to leave their land and migrate to the city of El Alto.

In the 1980s, two events provoked the migration of more Indigenous people to El Alto. First, a drought caused tens of thousands of peasants to leave their lands and move to El Alto, looking for means to sustain their families. Second, in 1985, neoliberal policies brought the privatization of national mines, oil and gas companies, telecommunication companies, and railroads (Postero 2006), producing: "slashed social spending, high unemployment, a disastrous pension reform scheme, and the fragmentation and destabilization of social movements" (Postero 2006, 129). Privatization meant "relocation" of workers around the country. Many unemployed workers were miners who were relocated to El Alto. The miners played an important role in the social constitution of El Alto as a city, impacting the construction and organization of the city's neighborhoods. These relocated workers also became a powerful political force. Due to this migration, El Alto became the city with the greatest migratory population (Albó 2006).

After his second re-election as president in 2002, Gonzalo Sánchez de Lozada:

> had a heavy hand in transforming Bolivia into a lab rat for neoliberal economics ... From 2000 to 2003, the income of the poorest 10 percent of the population declined by 15 percent, while that of the richest 10 percent increased by 16 percent. (Dangl 2007, 79)

By 2003, the quality of life had worsened and unemployment had risen. Sánchez de Lozada, pressured by the promise of a loan from the International Monetary Fund, proposed a "12.5% income tax on citizens with the lowest salaries in the country" (79). His plan encountered opposition from many social organizations and labor unions, but the largest protests were headed by the National Police, and supported by many union groups around the country.

Later in 2003, the government of Sánchez de Lozada decided to sell gas to the USA through a Chilean port. The gas was going to be sold raw, and would yield little profit. People protested and asked for the industrialization of the gas in Bolivian territory in order to have "cheaper access to gas related products, better local distribution and use of resources" (Dangl 2007, 122), and to have "more revenue for social programs" (127). El Alto became the "center of resistance to government control, as community organizations" (131) gave all the support to one of the most powerful uprisings in Bolivian history.

El Alto is "the site of one of the most powerful and radicalized social forces in Latin America" (Fuentes 2005). These forces are clearly visible in the social protests that Alteños led in October of 2003. The Alteños have a tradition of self-organization. The youth of El Alto create their spaces in quite a different way: "... newly urbanized *campesinos*[8] adolescents who speak Quechua, Aymara, and Spanish ... are constructing new forms of cosmopolitanism" (Goodale 2006, 634). This cosmopolitanism, explains Goodale (2006), comes from the hybridization of hip hop music and Indigenous cultural identity. This amalgamation creates the possibility of Bolivia's modernity and generates solidarity with other global youth movements in which oppression, racism, and injustice are the foci.

El Alto has become a center of rebellion and social movements. It is also the home of what Nina Uma, an Alteña hip hopper, calls the "hip hop revolution". This revolution involves music that critiques and questions social and political structure, and economic inequality, and represents what Freire (2000) calls "education as cultural action of freedom" (7). Hip hop expression is therefore both a pedagogy and a form of cultural expression. Young Alteños educate and promote change in their communities and Bolivian society at large using music. Hip hop music provides a view into young Alteños' reactions to the election of the first Indigenous president in Bolivia's history.

When Evo Morales was elected as president in 2006, industries that were once privatized became nationalized. Morales implemented anti-neoliberal policies. Moreover, policy regarding Indigenous people began to change, and led to increased Indigenous visibility and pride. Currently, Morales' government has an official discourse that aligns with Indigenous cultures and opens political and social spaces; this is a departure from any other time in Bolivian history until 2005 (Lazar 2008).

From the time I conducted this research, 2009, until this article went to press, 2012, several events tainted Morales' administration. In 2009, the Morales government was in a phase of transition from a neoliberal government to one with anti-neoliberal policies. In 2011, Bolivian citizens questioned Morales' supposed social and communitarian government principles when he planned to build a highway in the heart of a national park, which was Indigenous territory. The government refused to engage in dialogs with Indigenous communities living in these territories. This provoked a massive march that lasted for more than two months; as a result, the government lost the support of Indigenous groups, intellectuals, and old allies.

The historic events described here shaped the place that Indigenous people have in Bolivian society. In El Alto, the events that occurred in 2003 gave way to the creation of a hip hop movement that tried to break traditional anti-Indigenous or racist views by proposing new visions of an egalitarian society. Alteño youth see hip hop as a means of struggle for poor, oppressed minorities; they identify themselves with the African-American community from the Bronx who, according to the group Wayna Rap, have suffered racism, classism, and oppression, just like them. In the next section I give an overview of hip hop history in the USA. I outline how it became a global movement, and how it is used by Bolivian hip hoppers.

Hip hop revolution as cultural action of freedom

Hip hop is not just an African-American or North American cultural movement but it is, "a vehicle for global youth affiliations and a tool for reworking local identity all over the world" (Mitchell 2001, 1–2). Hip hop started in New York City as a constructive alternative for poor, minority youth who were confronted with violence, drugs, racism, and classism. Yet, hip hop now is not only a means of expression, but also a way of life, especially for young, poor African-Americans. Some scholars are critical of the movement, stating, for example, that: "young Blacks have used this access ... far too much to strengthen associations between Blackness and poverty, while celebrating anti-intellectualism, ignorance, irresponsible parenthood, and criminal lifestyles" (Kitwana 2002, xxi). Yet other scholars argue the importance of hip hop as a pedagogical tool. For example, according to Dimitriadis, citing Giroux (2009), it has: "elaborated a 'public and performative' kind of pedagogy, one sensitive to the 'shifting nature of knowledge [and] identity', one that operated in 'new spaces' outside of school" (2009, 51). Hip hop, in other words, becomes a performative and pedagogical tool for marginalized youth.

Now a global movement, young people have co-opted hip hop to critique society or the "system" that they feel oppresses them (Mitchell 2001). As a result, it can be seen that hip hop in different countries has: "been combined ... with local musical idioms and vernaculars to produce excitingly distinctive syncretic manifestations of African American influences and local Indigenous elements" (Mitchell 2001, 3). Global hip hop artists adjust art, music, and style to fit their own conditions, and to name their own circumstances.

In El Alto, Bolivia, a city created by and for people that migrated from the countryside to the city, the hip hop movement gained momentum as a result of neo-liberalism. It carves a place for Indigenous culture in the current social context. In 2003, El Alto's hip hop movement began with a group of youth that wanted to propose new social alternatives. Noticing similarities between their own unjust conditions and the African-American communities who were confronted with injustice in the Bronx in the USA, the hip hop group Wayna Rap explained:

> The first time I heard rap I felt identified with that ... I started to find more about it and I found out about all Martin Luther King's struggle in the US, a lot of struggle from the Black Panthers that looked for re-vindication because there used to be a lot of racism ... That reality happened here in Bolivia, all the discrimination, racism ...

There was a sense of solidarity in fighting racism and inequalities. Also as a pedagogic tool, hip hop required few material resources, easily lending itself to various forms of self-expression. It explains and denounces the living conditions allotted to Indigenous and poor people in Bolivia.

In addition to Bolivia, countries such as Cuba, Colombia, Brazil, and Chile have hip hop movements that reflect the situations of oppressed youth in each country, and engage issues such as race, poverty, and inequality. For example, in Buenos Aires, Argentina, a group of women hip hoppers, who are daughters of the *desaparecidos*[9] as a result of Argentina's dictatorial government of Videla during the 1970s, protest the disappearance of thousands of people using hip hop. Hip hop has been a viable and attractive means of expression for young people to organize and speak out against social injustices.

Awareness and praxis

Paulo Freire's (1993) *Pedagogy of the Oppressed* provides a lens by which to understand the young Alteños' struggle for freedom. Freire (1993, 26) argued that oppression is "not a given destiny but the result of an unjust order", created by a process of dehumanization. Mainstream education within an unjust society normalizes the idea of inferiority through "banking education" (Freire 1993), which according to Freire, is an education that sees people as machines who have to adapt to their environment and conditions as opposed to changing the situations that oppress them. The oppressed can only experience freedom through *conscientização* (concientization). *Conscientização* implies not only an awareness of the world but a call to praxis for justice and equity. This praxis needs to be an action that aims to change the conditions in the world that oppress people. Awareness and praxis are taught and performed in the Alteño hip hop movement. Drawing from Freire and Macedo (1987, viii), the Alteños have a new understanding or literacy and are "reading the word and the world" through singing, performing, and taking action.

Furthermore, Freire theorized about the, "need for not just a local liberation initiative, but an ethically grounded and politically ... unity among ... oppressed groups ... across the globe" (Roberts 2003, 460). Hip hop unites youth globally against oppressive neoliberal policies, which maintain "gross inequalities under globalisation" (462). Hip hop allows a rupture with the "common sense" (Apple 1999, 15), and it brings awareness and *conscientização* about exploitative neoliberal conditions. Free and accessible to all, this performative art is a key element in an informal education practice. The hip hop revolution, according to Nina Uma, is not a good to be purchased. This runs contrary to what education has become under neoliberal policies: a commodity only available to those who have the means to acquire it. It is a means to raise awareness, organize, and change political practices that affect the underserved.

Methods

As a phenomenological study, this project seeks "to understand the lived experiences of a small number of people" (Rossman and Rallis 2003, 94). Moreover, it uses an "in-depth, exploratory, and prolonged engagement; interactive interviews" (94) to understand the personal experiences and the personal meaning of those experiences. In the context of the Alteño hip hop movement, I wanted to understand stories people constructed in and with their music and what meanings these stories had for them.

The data collection took place in June of 2009 with the Alteño youth, and is based on 20 hours of audiotaped interviews, participant observation, field notes, and lyrics provided by participants. My commute to El Alto for the interviews was approximately an hour from the South District of La Paz where I was raised and still have family. I was born and raised in a middle-class family in La Paz and most of the City of El Alto was new for me.

My entry into the field was my meeting with the director of the *Casa Juvenil de las Culturas Wayna Tambo*, a space that is dedicated to the Alteño youth. Access was more difficult due to the recent death of Abraham Bojórquez. This event forced me to observe the movement from a different position and restructured my interests. During this time of loss and remembrance, the gains that had been made under Bojórquez's leadership in youth empowerment and the ways in which this empowerment contributes to a new sense of self-identity among the Indigenous in Bolivian society were apparent. With the help of the *Wayna Tambo* director, I contacted four hip hop artists and scheduled interviews with them. All used the Aymara language as well as Spanish in their lyrics. The *Wayna Tambo* director was a key informant; he provided information about the historical and social context, as well as an analysis of the hip hop movement in El Alto. The research, depending on participants' preference, was carried out in both public and private spaces, including community centers, parks, a singer's house, and my house. All the interviews were conducted in Spanish, transcribed, and translated into English.

Casa Juvenil de las Culturas Wayna Tambo

The *Casa Juvenil de las Culturas Wayna Tambo* is an organization that serves as both a cultural center and a radio station. Its work is strictly directed to Alteño youth and is solely in the cultural ground of El Alto. This cultural center focuses its attention on Alteño youth culture. Because the majority of the people are Indigenous, their culture mixes Indigenous traditions and modern art forms such as hip hop. This encounter creates "hybrid cultures"[10] (Rodríguez 2002, 11), which creates and recreates new identities among the youth of El Alto.

The *Wayna Tambo* pays primary attention to art forms that emphasize or reflect Indigenous concepts or practices (Rodríguez 2002), including the Indigenous Aymara language and, to a lesser extent, the Quechua language. Both languages are used in the young people's artistic production of hip hop and other music. As a result, one finds diverse forms of music, such as hip hop or heavy metal, being sung in Aymara in performances by different Alteño groups. In this way, the voice that these youth create is a hybrid of the traditional and the modern.

The *Wayna Tambo* understands young people as a critical element in the transformation of Bolivian society. Youth, explains Rodríguez (2004), provide a reference point to see and understand the cultural changes. These cultural changes are never apolitical; they are charged with political content. Rodríguez explains that youth generate and revitalize the cultural scene, and at the same time allow a view of traditional culture. The *Wayna Tambo* aims to create a political empowerment of Alteño youth through spaces of dialog where youth culture is negotiated, recreated, and identities are invigorated. The *Wayna Tambo* understands young people as agents of social change; it sees them as conscious subjects instead of static objects. The *Wayna Tambo* proposes alternative ideas and practices through the promotion and diffusion of cultural events and cultural productions. It also offers discussions about topics that concern the youth from El Alto.

The next section will analyze the data gathered. Lyrics and pieces of interviews were analyzed and grouped into two themes: self and society and the Indigenous and the system. The data provides examples of responses to neoliberal practices.

Hip hop movement and identity in El Alto

The hip hop that Alteños propose is a hip hop that instead of being aggressive, or violent, is reflexive (Bojórquez in Dosbalas 2007). Through hip hop, oppressed youth protest against the material conditions of lives and propose political agendas for change. Alteño hip hop artists also make efforts to re-establish ties with Indigenous culture, mainly through native language use. Wayna Rap and Nina Uma demonstrate an example. During a live performance at a private party I attended in 2009, Nina sang using Spanish and Aymara:

> Jallalla pachamama, ch'ama quechuas, aymaras.
> Jallalla pachammama, ch'ama pueblo guaraní.
> Toda la fuerza está en ti.[11]
>
> Long live Mother Earth, strength Quechuas, Aymaras
> Long live Mother Earth, strength Guaraní people
> All the strength is in you.

Nina Uma is able to construct a new Alteño youth identity mixing Spanish and Aymara with modern hip hop rhythms and asserting Indigenous people's relationship to nature. Both Wayna Rap and Nina Uma use native languages in their songs as a way of making Indigenous cultures visible, as well as to show that they are not ashamed of being Indigenous. Also, through the use of Aymara or Quechua, the youth demonstrate resistance towards rampant anti-Indigenous racism in a country where, ironically, the majority of the population is Indigenous.

Bolivian youth have not conceded to the dominant discourse; they construct their own identities, which reflect both Indigenous heritage and globalization:

> By refusing to accede to all of the traditional categories of Bolivian identity (campesino, Indian, Aymara, Quechua, runa, q'ara), the rappers of Wayna Tambo are part of a second revolution in Bolivia, one that is not their grandparents' revolution, even though the tires still burn at the blockades, the air is still thick with tear gas, and the

rubber bullets are all too often replaced with the real thing. This second Bolivian revolution is essentially discursive. (Goodale 2006, 635)

Historically, Bolivian revolutions were enacted by blockades, marching, strikes, and other types of public protests. Today the youth in El Alto are trying to incite a revolution using political speech (about racism, classism, or social injustice, for example) and using their traditional tongues. The following lyrics are an example:

> For the traitors, the calm ends here
> I have a wound tattooed on my heart
> From the day they shot my village
> A helicopter killing my brothers, peasants and miners
> Who were demanding their rights. (Translation belongs to Breitburg-Smith and Webb 2006)

These lyrics demonstrate the political agenda of the movement. Rather than using violence, the movement uses art to transmit thoughts and raise social awareness.

Two main themes emerged as I analyzed lyrics and interviews: self and society and Indigenous and the system. Self and society refers to identity markers that can be found in the content of the lyrics and speech of hip hop artists. These markers refer to Indigenous collective and individual identities related to being a young Aymara in El Alto. The second theme, Indigenous and the system, refers to hip hop singers' opinions about and critiques of the sociopolitical system functioning in Bolivia in general and in El Alto in particular. The system affects them both directly and indirectly economically, socially, and politically. I elaborate in the next section.

Self and society

Positionality is key to understanding the identity construction and the roles El Alto hip hop artists play in Bolivian society. In analyzing their unequal place in society, they reify an Indigenous identity that contests the colonial mind-set.

According to the director of *Wayna Tambo*, this new identity that Alteño youth are building results from two main elements: the general explosion of demands related to ethnic identities and Indigenous rights in the world in the 1990s and Bolivia's own history, tainted by colonization and globalization. He adds that the re-vindication movement in El Alto has a marked Indigenous component, especially because of the relationship that the people of El Alto maintain with the countryside. The majority of migrants stay connected to the country by maintaining land in their places of origin. However, as Llajuas, a young Alteño hip hopper in his early 30s and member of the group Ukamau Y Ke, explained to me while sitting in a plaza in the center of El Alto, young Alteños are losing the connection with their places of origin, they are used to the city and everything it brings:

> We are already used to the computer, internet, TV, etc. We go to the countryside for a field trip, to visit grandma and grandpa.

Contrary to the common idea that cultural traditions and identities are muted due to migration to a new location, these loose ties between Indigenous youth and their places of origin could be a result of the illusion of social mobility that oppressors offer to the oppressed (Freire 1993). Duncan-Andrade (2009) calls this "hope deferred". He explained this as the, "'hope' for change in its most deferred forms: either a collective utopia of a future reformed society or, more often, the [individual's] ... future ascent to the middle class" (185). Society offers the false promise of upward social mobility, and, as a result, great numbers of people move to the cities hoping for this deferred and non-existent social mobility.

During an interview with the director of the *Wayna Tambo* center he explained that:

> Colonialism has been internalized in the people. People from El Alto didn't say they live in El Alto, they were ashamed of their ethnic origins.[12]

According to Freire (1993), the concept of shame appears from the identification that the oppressed creates with the oppressor. After centuries of being placed on an inferior societal level, Bolivian Indigenous people have internalized an identity of lower class citizens. The oppressed do not see themselves as equals; rather, they see themselves as inferior to the ruling class (Bartlett 2007). Llajuas explained:

> It was embarrassing to speak in Aymara in certain places, for example speaking Aymara in public offices was terrible. The fact to wear *pollera*[13] or *sombrero borsalino*[14] or *manta*[15] ... it was a big discrimination, it was an automatic way of denigration ...

Llajuas' statement reflects the internalized shame and oppression that some have accepted and others have resisted. The Alteño youth have created their Indigenous identity from their ethnic origins, the history of their people, and the unequal conditions in which they have been raised.

In an interview with two young hip hoppers in their mid-20s from the group Wayna Rap, while sitting at a windy park next to the Public University of El Alto, one of the members stated:

> Our people, our grandparents, my mother, my grandma used to wear *pollera*, my grandpa was a migrant from the country side. When they came here it was very difficult for them because they used to suffer discrimination, exploitation, lack of education ...

The lack of resources and the experiences of exploitation are a type of violence. While not overtly physical, this is a violence directed at their humanity, and at their right to practice their culture, customs, and language. The oppressor denies them their human condition and their culture and forces them to internalize inferiority.

All the conditions explained here reached a climax in 2003, when the disenfranchised organized and demanded the resignation of President Gonzalo Sánchez de Lozada. However, this event signified more than just the overthrow of a neoliberal government, but a historical change in the Indigenous' social status, agency, and identity. As Llajuas explained and the group Wayna Rap echoed in a later interview:

> From 2003, I think that the youth, the Alteña society feel proud, because from here, from El Alto all the protest voices rose to overthrow a government. It is because of this that the Alteño and all the young people, the whole society: the *pollera*, the *sombrero* from the city of El Alto started to acquire life, value. As a result we started to create an identity of pride. We felt proud of being Alteños and Aymaras. (Llajuas)

> Before 2003 there used to be a lot of discrimination toward ourselves. The Alteño used to say 'no', I'm not from El Alto, I come from down there. However, he used to live near to us. (Wayna Rap)

The Alteños overthrew their government due to their ability to unify, learn, and evaluate their conditions; they became the main actors of this historical moment. Empowered by confronting their oppressor, they regained pride in their identity. This is a very special case, because they were not only facing White middle-class men, but a government that represented the new Bolivian *colonizador*.[16]

It is important to mention that this process is not new. Many other Indigenous uprisings have happened throughout Bolivian history. However, the change will only be lasting when subjugation is removed and power is shared. The oppressed must regain their humanity. The participation and leadership of the Alteños in many of the most important uprisings in Bolivian history have been steps toward this goal. Furthering this idea, the director of *Wayna Tambo* explained the participation of the Indigenous people during different historical events:

> El Alto was never disassociated from all the Bolivian processes ... the uprising of the Tupac Katari movement, his headquarters was in El Alto. The revolution of '52 has no explanation without the Miyuni miners that are now in El Alto.

These events show the presence that Indigenous people have had during all the major Bolivian unrests. Miners have a strong presence in any uprising because they know oppression first-hand from their dangerous work conditions. Peasants and miners are responsible for the occurrence and success of many of the Bolivian uprisings.

In 2003, a new movement began in El Alto with a group of youth that wanted to use hip hop to propose new social alternatives to neoliberal policies. Considered a powerful and effective instrument to communicate about revolution and injustice, hip hop would reach more young people. Llajuas explained:

> The truth is that we don't have any economic means; that is why we do something easy. If we would have money we would be doing music in the symphony ... you can easily buy what you need but we don't have money, this is why we have chosen hip hop.

Nina Uma echoed Llajuas:

> With hip hop you can create your own track; sometimes you don't even need a track.

The easiness and versatility hip hop has, allows hip hop artists to gain people's attention and to have more impact on their public. As Nina Uma mentioned:

> When you propose this from an artistic point of view, the impact on the people is different. I'll tell you, I can get up on a stage and say everything that I said, but if I don't do it in an artistic way people will get bored, they won't listen to me. I won't be able to touch people's feelings.

Nina Uma explained the power that hip hop has over people. Hip hop artists are able to artistically bring their word to the table. According to Freire (1993), "the word" will be the means by which the people will generate a change in society. The word is "an instrument which makes dialogue possible" (68). The word has two levels: reflection and praxis. If both levels are present then there will be a true transformation. The means by which the word is spread is not particularly important, but its convenience provides access to all. As the two members of the Wayna Rap group explained:

> Making rap in our language: Aymara, Quechua and using traditional musical instruments, mixing Afro-American hip hop and our culture, and we show it [our culture] to the world.

The hip hop movement is using the word by trying to promote reflection about the world. It also makes a call to action for this change to be possible. The way in which the word is spread is not important, as long as it inspires dialog (Freire 1993). It is important to understand that the call to action is non-violent and is an all-inclusive vision of social change. The identities of Alteño youth have been shaped by these social and historical events. Moving from an identity of inferiority to one of pride, young Alteños have asserted themselves through a fight that does not use violence, but proposes change through conscientization and dialog.

The Indigenous and the system

The discourse of Alteño hip hop artists critiques issues of globalization, capitalism, neoliberalism, imperialism, education, mass media, economy, and society. The deceased Abraham Bojórquez, during one of his presentations at a hip hop festival in Ecuador in 2007, said:

> My people of Latin America are one flag, we have to break with the vision of borders that has been sold to us.[17]

Bojórquez' vision of one united Latin America beyond borders is a recurrent idea in Alteño hip hop. The logic behind it is that all Latin American countries share a similar history and are currently undergoing similar social and political processes due to the large Indigenous population, as well as the large number of poor people in many of these countries. During the interview with Wayna Rap, one of the members explained:

> Poverty is the same everywhere in Latin America, so we are trying to make the connections to become a unified Latin America. Without divisions we'll be stronger.

His colleague further explained his view and action toward their goal, stating:

> Latin America has different cultures, we fight in the streets, we suffer social inequalities, then let's unify all together. With rap we are trying to do so, and we are uniting friends from Chile, Colombia, Ecuador, Puerto Rico ... Venezuela, so we try to show to the people that we can achieve a union between Latin Americans.

Solidarity among Latin American countries is born from the "struggle for their liberation" (Freire 1993, 33), from the solidarity among the collectivity and from the understanding of a common struggle to fight poverty and the mechanisms that create it.

It is not strange to find political similarities among poor Indigenous communities throughout Latin America. This is particularly true considering the history of

European colonization of the Americas. European colonizers brought a paradigm which believed in a division between White men, women, and other races (Kahn 2010). This system of thought permitted a bloody and oppressive conquest and subjugation of Indigenous people, as well as an idea of ownership of Indigenous people. Conquistadors believed that all the new discoveries belonged to them as a natural consequence because of their innate superiority (Kahn 2010). In this case, oppressors objectified Indigenous people, removing them from a context of humanity and subjugating them; "the situation of oppression is a dehumaniz[ing]" one (Freire 1993, 29). This relationship of power and ownership between oppressors and oppressed has a long history which, as a result for the oppressed, has produced an internalization of their "natural" inferior place in society; they believe in the place they occupy, the place of an object (not a subject) and of dependency on the oppressor. This state of dependency refers to social, mental, economic, and identity dependence. They cannot be without the oppressors, but they can never be like them either (Bhabha 1984).

Latin American countries share similar colonial histories. In addition, living conditions, such as the poverty and oppression of native people, have not changed much throughout time and persist through the current political moment (Dangl 2007). The power of Latin American natives comes from their unification. Accordingly, one of the members of the group Wayna Rap at the end of our interview began to rap in Aymara:

> There is a song that talks about how we, Aymaras and Quechuas, are rising with strength, with strength, it's called *Chamakan Sartasiri*, and it goes like this: 'Aymaras and Quechuas, we are rising up from the darkness, lighting up Latin America ... the sun will come for everyone' ...

These lyrics reinforce the importance of unity and solidarity among different groups to engender change and empowerment. Implicitly, the lyrics caution against divisiveness.

The Indigenous people of El Alto have organized to resist subjugation. Freire (1993) argued that, "the oppressor minority subordinates and dominates the majority; it must divide it and keep it divided in order to remain in power" (122). The power of the oppressors depends on the oppression and division of the people. They see any type of unification as a serious threat to their power. As a result, the actions taken to stop the unity of the powerless can take the form of physical violence.

Many of the hip hop songs talk about the repression that people suffered during different political moments. Ukamau Y Ke in their song *Tupak Katari* denounced the repression and use of military force in order to break the mobilization of mainly Indigenous migrant people in the City of El Alto in 2003:

> Here for the traitors the calm has ended ... I still remember the day my people were shot from a helicopter killing the peasant brother and the miner who were demanding their rights ... why then were my people held at gun point to the head with a machine gun ...

The organization of oppressed people is rapidly brought down by the oppressors because it is seen as a threat to the peace and prosperity of the privileged system (Freire 1993).

One of the many consequences of the colonial mentality is racism and discrimination. In Bolivia, Indigenous people are seen as inferior due to their belonging to Aymara, Quechua, or any other native group. Ukamau y Ke, in their song *El Abismo del Racismo,* rap:

> Racism here, racism there. I ask to my country when is this going to stop? ... that's right, I talk to you racist that believes that you are above people and because of that you discriminate against people calling me Indio, without noticing that you get sick with your own hate. You put me down because I'm poor, I don't have money but I have a noble heart. You discriminate against me because I'm Black, what's wrong with you? We are not longer in the time of slavery. You don't know that I feel proud of my culture? ... I talk to you racism, here all the colors are one ... race of racists ... we are poor, we are peasants, we are from the villas: your worst nightmare.

In the same way, Alto Lima, a hip hop artist from El Alto denounced racism in his song *Un Canto Liberal,* with the following words:

> Why? If we are in our home, you see the race difference as a threat? What is going on? The mentality is getting old, reproachable attitude ...

While anti-racism and anti-discrimination messages are expressed by these young artists, they also articulate messages of peace and integrity. Ukamau y Ke, in their song *Wila Masis Mayacht'asiñani,* rap:

> Revolution of our country with peace in the heart. Many years we have suffered ... the time to rise is here, stop the humiliation, stop the expulsion, is time of our vindication. Natives of these lands, let's fight for the equality, justice and equity, let's understand that together we will defeat, we can triumph together.

This rap reflects Indigenous people's desire for freedom, understanding that they will only be freed when they liberate both themselves and the oppressors from an oppressive system. The system enslaves both people in power and the powerless, and it is only through the actions of the oppressed that the enslavement will end (Freire 1993). These actions of freedom and this dialog between people must take place with an attitude of love and understanding to be fruitful. "Love is at the same time the foundation of dialogue and dialogue itself ... love ... must generate other acts of freedom; otherwise, it is not love" (Freire 1993, 70–1). Only love for humanity will bring revolution and, consequently, change. The Alteño hip hop artists spread the message of integrity and peace using hip hop. They know and understand that the only way of living is by understanding and believing that all human beings are equal and that economic or racial differences are not natural divisions, but instead social constructions that allow certain groups to maintain privileges over the exploitation of others (Johnson 2006). Llajuas explained:

> What we [the hip hop movement] wanted was to transform society, we wanted equality, equity, and because of this ... we've always preached that the art is a tool to transform, for conscientization of the people.

The group Wayna Rap took a similar position:

> We realized that they were also friends, we were all friends and that actually politics are the enemy.

The most challenging task that the oppressed have is to free themselves and to liberate the oppressors (Freire 1993). Only the power that rises from the weakness of the oppressed will be strong enough to liberate both of them, only "human beings in communion liberate each other" (133). Because hip hop artists communicate a message of integrity and equality, it can be said that they understand their art as an instrument to spread their message. In this case, hip hop is their means of expression and their means of *lucha* (struggle). Abraham Bojórquez, when interviewed for the hip hop festival in Ecuador mentioned that:

> We want to continue doing hip hop not with a fascist vision, but with a proposing vision ... to use the hip hop as a means for struggle.

Llajuas agreed with this statement, saying:

> Our art not only criticizes ... but I think it also proposes.

As seen in these two quotes, the idea of every revolution is to teach and to propose new and better lives for everyone. At its beginning, revolution has to emerge as a strong criticism from the viewpoints of the oppressed (Freire 1993). A member of the Wayna Rap group comments on the role of education in creating change:

> Education turns us submissive, turned our parents submissive, it turns us shy, afraid, now we want our education to be one that spreads the pride of being who you are, with our songs we tried to revalorize that pride. They need to go with attitude, I'm from El Alto, I'm brown, I'm Indigenous, I'm this, so what?, wherever they go. That whites, browns, mestizos, Indigenous, we can all live together. To achieve this equality we need to educate ourselves and know ourselves, we want that, we need the same opportunities.

This member processes his identity as learned by the education system; considering the power that mainstream education had on his life, he considers how it could be empowering as well. Only through "reflection ... upon their world [can they] transform it" (Freire 1993, 60). By understanding one's condition and one's position in society, the steps for creating change become more apparent. This change can only be achieved through education, an education made by the oppressed and not for the oppressed.

The Bolivian education system, like most education systems, has supported "banking education", which socializes the majority to submit and comply with the system that oppresses them. According to Freire (1993, 53), "knowledge emerges only through invention and re-invention". This means that people can change the system only if they have the opportunity to think in a critical way, to ask questions, and to propose alternatives. "Problem posing education" aims to change the world in order to provide better and more just opportunities for everyone. This revolutionary education is created by the oppressed for the oppressed; it involves awareness and activism. It looks to change the world instead of changing people to adapt to the world.

Discussion

Several events have occurred since my data collection which have compelled me to make final notes on the theory used, and on the complexity of terms like Indigenous, oppressed/oppressor, and unity. While I chose a Freireian framework to analyze my findings, this theory falls short of addressing, "the complexity of overlapping and contradictory positions in which the position of oppressor and oppressed are shifting and ambiguous" (Weiler 2003, 34). The complexity of events, relationships, and identities with which Alteño youth are confronted cannot be completely understood with critical pedagogy. An example of this complexity is the state repression that Indigenous communities suffered by the possible construction of the highway through the *Territorio Indígena Parque Nacional Isiboro Secure* (TIPNIS), which will devastate the lowland Indigenous resources. The process of change is long and complex. Even if one oppressor-leader has been removed or changes his way of thinking, to build a just system takes decades or longer of praxis and participation from all parts of civil society.

One important change supporting the empowerment of the Alteños is that the region (Latin America) is going through a process of regaining *lo indígena* (the Indigenous). Jackson and Warren (2005, 549), discuss "reindianization processes" that recuperate the cultural character of a group and with it the term Indigenous. This runs contrary to what happened in Latin America during the 1980s and the 1990s, where class consciousness contributed to Indigenous identity and social movements (Paredes in AnarchaLa 2010), encouraging them "to self-identify as *campesinos* [peasants]" (Jackson and Warren 2005, 551). This process of "reindianization" is visible in the "reinvention of the indianity with Morales' presidency" (Kunin 2009, citing Svampa). The term *campesino* is still being used hand in hand with the term Indigenous. This can be seen in phrases like Indigenous socialism, which is based on the Aymara communitarian structure. It can also be seen in the use of denominatives like Indigenous peasant (*campesino*) unions.

The Morales administration has created a discourse that aligns with Indigenous rights, Indigenous identity, and the values that being Indigenous brings to society. One of these values, which according to Morales' discourse differentiates Indigenous identity especially in the context of western-neoliberal countries, is the respect for and communion with Mother Earth. Nevertheless, in 2011, contrary to all their previous speeches on the protection of the environment, his government tried to build a highway that would have crossed and divided a national park and Indigenous territory with the discourse of bringing development to that area of the country; undoubtedly aligning himself with neoliberal politics of development at the expense of the environment and Indigenous living in that territory.

Morales' duality of behavior is a prime example of the complexity of understanding oppression. While Morales has been demonstrative in policy-making that affirms and empowers Indigenous people, at the same time, the economics of development are so profitable that his commitment to the Indigenous is compromised. Is he an oppressor or is he oppressed? This is the nuanced territory of oppression that begs further discussion.

It is clear that the discourse of unity was broken to fulfill regional ambitions at the expense of "other" Indigenous (those who are not Aymaras or Quechuas), who did not agree with government development policies. Furthermore, the discourse became invisible when Evo Morales rejected the opportunity to have a dialog with lowland Indigenous people, undervaluing their requests and concerns, and allowing them to march "over 600 kilometers for more than 60 days" (Avila 2011) to the capital City, La Paz. They suffered inclement weather, thirst, and intolerable police repression in order to meet the president. The use of the image of the Indigenous (*lo indígena*) as something that equals the protection of and respect for the Mother Earth becomes an essential part of Morales' discourse. However, Kunin (2009) astutely pointed out, "Indigenous and being Indigenous is essentialized by outsiders like NGOs who are the ones that state what it is to be Indigenous, and who are Indigenous". It is this simplistic, almost paternalistic view that envisions Indigenous as noble, kind, and one with the earth, that problematizes what is happening now in Bolivia with TIPNIS. This engenders questions as to who can claim Indigenous identity. The neoliberal interests of the current government tend to co-opt "Indigenous" and "Mother Earth" in ways that serve its "development" agenda, raising concerns about their future.

In distinguishing the term "Indigenous", it is important to question in what ways Alteño hip hop artists understand and negotiate highland Indigenous identity vs. lowland Indigenous identity. How do they negotiate their belonging to the Aymara or Quechua culture? Both are the largest Indigenous cultural groups in Bolivia and have more political representation than lowland Indigenous communities. Gustafson (2002) mentioned that, "Aymara and Quechua symbols, languages, and cultural substrates pervade Bolivian identity formations of all types and contribute to the wider imaginary of Bolivian as an 'Andean' country" (5–6). Alteño hip hoppers advocate for one Bolivia where everyone is included independently of their race, ethnicity, or group affiliation. Future research is needed to observe how the hip hop movement has evolved and what has been proposed during these times of political turmoil. Taking into consideration that "youth tend to engage in horizontal political engagements" (Kunin 2009, 6) by rejecting formal or conservative forms of politics and engaging in more communitarian and direct ways of discussion, it will be interesting to see if the Alteño hip hop movement was able to maintain its original discourse of unity and equality by creating a sense of cohesion, unity, and cooperation independently of people's different cultures, organizations, and territories.

Finally, it is important to take into account the Bolivian government's double discourse of unity vis-à-vis actions of disrespect towards minority Indigenous groups and how this can affect movements like the Alteño hip hoppers. Barclay (2009) compared Morales to Mugabe's racist government, referring to Morales as "The Mugabe of the Andes". While I do not agree, it is imperative to analyze events like the TIPNIS decision and ask how far the brotherhood among different Indigenous groups can endure if some do not share the government's views. It seems that power induces even those who are members of oppressed groups to forget their positionality. Power will transform an oppressed person into an oppressor if he or she has no true commitment to the people, or if he or she lacks a different vision of what development and community should be.

Conclusions

This study documents and analyzes how young people from El Alto use hip hop music to express their political, social, and economic concerns while asserting their Indigenous culture and history. It explains the use of hip hop as an educational instrument for the process of "healing" (Duncan-Andrade 2009). Healing is achieved through revolutionary education, and education that empowers people. As a result, people liberate themselves from the yoke of their oppressors. Hip hop is a means for ideas and identity expression and calls people to action; it is a "liberation process" (Freire 1993). Llajuas exemplified this idea as he stated,

"Our art not only criticizes ... but I think it also proposes". Through hip hop music, Alteño youth create a type of identity that reflects the significance of being Indigenous in Bolivia, and of being an urban migrant with rural ties, struggling with poverty, unemployment, and discrimination. Hip hop artists empower themselves through articulating their struggles and begin the process of healing from the act of silencing that they experience. This healing, however, can only be understood if it is carried out in a collective way, Duncan-Andrade (2009, 190) explained that we have a "collective capacity for healing". People coming together in opposition to the oppressive system will be the only way that any revolutionary change can be implemented.

These young hip hoppers are trying to spread what Freire calls *conscientização*. It is meant to reach every level of society in order to create political, economic, and social reforms, while reclaiming and empowering Indigenous identities. Llajuas explained during an interview: "we've always preached that the art is a tool for transforming, for creating consciousness in the people". One of the most important elements discovered is the young Alteños' desire to educate the people, as the members of Wayna Rap explained: "To achieve this equality we need to educate ourselves and know ourselves, we want that, we need the same opportunities." This element is based on Freire's theory, which posits that education is a tool to liberate the oppressed from the yoke of the oppressors. The oppressor may not know he is oppressing other people; he is simply occupying his appropriate position in society. This is why it is so important to educate not only the oppressed but also the oppressors. As Wayna Rap stated: "whites, browns, mestizos, Indigenous, Indians, we can all live together. To achieve this equality we need to educate ourselves and know ourselves. We want that, we need the same opportunities." To achieve this equity and equality, Freire (2000) firmly believed that the process and effectiveness of transformation wholly depended on the quality of education. Alteño youth, living in a context of material scarcity and oppression, are using what economics cannot control: their voices and their minds, to create, educate, and organize through their very political music.

Notes

1. "*Ya lo habíamos advertido el hombre Aymara es mejor que el sistema.*" The translation is mine.
2. Alteño makes reference to people from El Alto.
3. "El Alto always standing, never on their knees." The translation is mine.
4. *Altiplano*: Spanish for highland plateau.
5. *Latifundio*: a massive extension of land, which belongs to a single owner. It is associated with farming and exploitative working conditions for the peasants living there.
6. "The land is owned by the one who works it." The translation is mine.
7. *Microfundio*. De Mesa, Gisbert, and Mesa Gisbert (2001) define it as: "The small plot, with a minimum of production that is constantly divided for heritance purposes". The translation is mine.
8. Peasants.
9. Term used to name the people that were taken away by the government and never brought back.
10. Original phrase: "*culturas híbridas*". The translation is mine.
11. The translation is mine. The term *ch'ama* was translated using the definition provided by Pueblos Originarios de América (n.d.): http://pueblosoriginarios.com/lenguas/aymara.html.
12. This quote and subsequent translations throughout the paper are mine unless otherwise stated.

13. "Gathered skirt worn over several petticoats" (Lazar 2008, 286).
14. Bowler hat.
15. Wool shawl.
16. Colonizer.
17. This and the following quotes from Abraham Bojórquez were taken from: http://www.youtube.com/watch?v=-V4l5QhwJb4&feature=related, unless otherwise stated.

References

Albó, X. 2006. El Alto, la vorágine de una ciudad única [El Alto, the maelstrom of a unique city]. *The Journal of Latin American Anthropology* 11, no. 2: 329–50.
AnarchaLa. 2010. Anarcha Feminist-Bolivia. October 10. http://www.youtube.com/watch?v=R_FTZvMScLo&feature=player_embedded (accessed October 2011).
Apple, M. 1999. Freire, neo-liberalism and education. *Discourse: Studies in the Cultural Politics of Education* 20, no. 1: 5–20.
Arbona, J.M., and B. Kohl. 2004. City profile. La Paz-El Alto. *Cities* 21, no. 3: 255–65.
Avila, E. 2011. Bolivia: TIPNIS Indigenous marchers arrive in La Paz. *Global Voices*, October 20. http://globalvoicesonline.org/2011/10/20/bolivia-tipnis-Indigenous-marchers-arrive-to-la-paz/ (accessed September 2011).
Barclay, E. 2009. The Mugabe of the Andes? Why president Evo Morales's racial politics in Bolivia may backfire. *The Atlantic*, April. http://www.theatlantic.com/magazine/archive/2009/04/the-mugabe-of-the-andes/7320/ (accessed September 2011).
Bartlett, L. 2007. Literacy, speech and shame: The cultural politics of literacy and language in Brazil. *International Journal of Qualitative Studies in Education* 20, no. 5: 547–63.
Bhabha, H. 1984. Of mimicry and man: The ambivalence of colonial discourse. *Discipleship: A Special Issue on Psychoanalysis* 28: 125–33.
Breitburg-Smith, E., and M. Webb. 2006. Todos somos guerreros: Hip-hop in El Alto, Bolivia. http://www.youtube.com/watch?v=nBlTS3db8dI (accessed April 2009).
Crowder, J. 2003. Living on the edge: A photographic essay on urban Aymara migrants in El Alto, Bolivia. *Visual Anthropology* 16, nos. 2/3: 263–87.
Dangl, B. 2007. *The price of fire: Resource wars and social movements in Bolivia*. Oakland, CA: AK Press.
De Mesa, J., T. Gisbert, and C.D. Mesa Gisbert. 2001. *Historia de Bolivia* [History of Bolivia]. La Paz: Editorial Gisbert y Cia S.A.
Dimitriadis, G. 2009. *Performing identity/performing culture: Hip hop as text, pedagogy, and lived practice*. New York, NY: Peter Lang.
Dosbalas. 2007. Hip Hop Andino. December 15. http://www.youtube.com/watch?v=-V4l5QhwJb4&feature=related (accessed April 2009).
Duncan-Andrade, J. 2009. Note to educators: Hope required when growing roses in concrete. *Harvard Educational Review* 79, no. 2: 181–94.
Freire, P. 1993. *Pedagogy of the oppressed*. 20th anniversary ed. New York: Continuum.
Freire, P. 2000. *Cultural action for freedom*. Cambridge, MA: Harvard Educational Review.
Freire, P., and D. Macedo. 1987. *Literacy: Reading the word and the world*. Westport, CT: Bergin and Garvey.
Fuentes, F. 2005. Bolivia. *Zmag*, December 16. http://www.zmag.org/znet/viewArticle/4805 (accessed April 2009).
Goodale, M. 2006. Reclaiming modernity: Indigenous cosmopolitanism and the coming of the second revolution in Bolivia. *American Ethnologist* 33, no. 4: 634–49.
Gustafson, B. 2002. The paradoxes of liberal indigenism: Indigenous movements, state processes, and intercultural reform in Bolivia. In *The politics of ethnicity: Indigenous peoples in Latin American states*, ed. D. Maybury-Lewis, 267–306. Cambridge, MA: Harvard University Press.

Jackson, J., and K. Warren. 2005. Indigenous movements in Latin America, 1992–2004: Controversies, ironies, new directions. *Annual Review of Anthropology* 34: 549–73.

Johnson, A. 2006. *Privilege, power, and difference.* New York, NY: McGraw-Hill.

Kahn, R. 2010. *Critical pedagogy, ecoliteracy, and planetary crisis: The ecopedagogy movement.* New York, NY: Peter Lang.

Kitwana, B. 2002. *The hip hop generation: Young blacks and the crisis in African American culture.* New York, NY: Basic Civitas Books.

Kunin, J. 2009. Algunas notas sobre el rap politico boliviano: mucho más que un caso "exótico" de jóvenes indígenas que cantan ritmos estadounidenses [Some notes about the Bolivian political rap: Much more than an "exotic" case of Indigenous youth doing North American music]. http://bibliotecavirtual.clacso.org.ar/ar/libros/becas/2007/cultura/kunin.pdf (accessed September 2011).

Lazar, S. 2008. *El Alto, rebel city.* Durham, NC: Duke University Press.

Mitchell, T. 2001. *Global noise: Rap and hip-hop outside the USA.* Middletown, CT: Wesleyan University Press.

Postero, N. 2006. *Now we are citizens: Indigenous politics in postmulticultural Bolivia.* Stanford, CA: Stanford University Press.

Pueblos Originarios de América. n.d. Lengua Aymara. http://pueblosoriginarios.com/lenguas/aymara.html (accessed October 2011).

Roberts, P. 2003. Pedagogy, neoliberalism and postmodernity: Reflections on Freire's later work. *Educational Philosophy and Theory* 35, no. 4: 451–65.

Rodríguez, M. 2002. *Jóvenes y cultura. Una mirada desde la experiencia de Wayna Tambo* [Youth and culture. A Wayna Tambo view]. El Alto, Bolivia: Ediciones Wayna Tambo.

Rodríguez, M. 2004. *Para seguir viviendo. Reconfiguraciones en las relaciones entre juventud, sociedad y educación* [To continue living. Reconfigurations in the relationships between youth, society, and education]. El Alto, Bolivia: Ediciones Wayna Tambo.

Rossman, G., and S. Rallis. 2003. *Learning in the field: An introduction to qualitative research.* Thousand Oaks, CA: Sage.

Weiler, K. 2003. Paulo Freire: On hope. *Radical Teacher* 67: 32–5.

The play of risk, affect, and the enterprising self in a fourth-grade classroom

Steven Bialostok and George Kamberelis

As a predominant discourse of the early twenty-first century, the new capitalism (and its companion cultural system, neoliberalism) privilege flexibility, risk, emotional intelligence, and the enterprising self. New capitalist discourses exert powerful and pervasive effects across all dimensions of human experience and activity from personal decision-making to family life to school to the workplace, and they encourage, even demand, that workers become individualized, self-actualized subjects. In this article, we discuss how new capitalist discourses affected talk and social interaction in one fourth-grade classroom. More specifically, we report on how the classroom teacher encouraged students to become more deeply aware of their affective investments in relation to themes in the books they read and to connect these investments to their everyday lives. We demonstrate further that this emphasis on affective investment involved high levels of risk for the students and positioned them as enterprising selves.

Introduction

Foucault (1977, 1980) used the term "discourse" to refer to naturalized systems of meaning made up of ideas, attitudes, beliefs, practices, and ways of being/acting that systematically construct the subjects and objects of the world in specific ways. He argued further that discourses create truths about the world that become articulated with power, so that these truths seem universal, obvious, and undeniable. Finally, he showed how discourses become meta-forces in the world, seeping into and exerting their effects on many different disciplines and domains of practice. In the early twenty-first century, new capitalist discourses with their emphases on flexibility, risk, emotional intelligence, and enterprising selves exert powerful and pervasive effects across all dimensions of human experience and activity, including the reading, writing, talk, and social interaction that occur in public school classrooms. In this article, we discuss the effects of these discourses on fourth-grade students' ways of thinking, acting, and being as they read and discussed books together, encouraging, even demanding, that they become individualized, self-actualized subjects. To provide a conceptual framework for our analyzes and findings, we first present a general introduction to the new capitalism, as well as more detailed discussions of four fundamental constructs or themes within this economic system: the enterprising self, risk, affect, and emotional intelligence.

The new capitalism

Beck (1992, 2000) points to a range of new risks arising from increasingly global and complex societies – risks that the current welfare state is manifestly unable to deal with, and is constantly being stretched to accommodate. Globalization's effects infuse government policy, resulting in budget constraints caused by a diminishing corporate tax base, itself the outcome of policies enacted by the state in its attempt to compete for foreign investment and capital. With dwindling revenues, government has retreated from its traditional responsibilities concerning the welfare state, turning away from broad-based entitlements and automatic benefits, including costly public goods like education and health. The reshaping of Keynesian welfare states to forms that reflect the new social risks arising from globalization has led to the enactment of the neoliberal strategy of responsibilization, requiring citizens to assume risks by making their welfare the preserve of individual responsibility through self-provision.

To compete and adapt in the context of the disequilibrium of these global and economic shifts, both corporations and individuals have had to change in interconnected ways. "Enterprise" business models – designed for higher standards at lower costs – have replaced the rigid bureaucracies. In turn, businesses have required employees at every level to develop strategies and skills requisite for responding to rapidly changing markets. To produce this new type of workforce, neoliberal reform measures emerged under the name of "enterprise culture." Through complex strategies, political authority, and institutional arrangements, the enterprise culture seductively influenced social, political, organizational, and individual levels of thinking and being. Finally, to compete globally, businesses realized that they needed to focus increasingly on customer service.

Because the new capitalist workplace is continually in flux, a necessary characteristic of the new capitalist worker is the willingness to take risks. Indeed, risk taking has become a highly charged test of character (Sennett 1998). Similarly, risk has changed how affect functions within the new capitalist workplace as a deployable human resource (Ritzer 1999). Affect, particularly as described in the popular "emotional intelligence" literature (Goleman 1995, 1998), constitutes a reinvention of character, one that is aligned with the flexible, adaptable skills, and short-term reality of the global market place (Hughes 2005). In sum, new capitalism is constituted at the intersection of risk, affect, and the enterprising self. In the paragraphs that follow, we unpack these elements and the key relations between and among them.

Risk and the new capitalism

Economic change under industrial capitalism has always been inextricably tied to educational change and innovation. It also ushered in forms of global finance, technology, media, and merchandising that are more diffuse, unstable, and decentered than ever before. Whereas trust and confidence were constitutive of early or solid modernity, a heightened consciousness of risk and uncertainty emerged as central to late or liquid modernity (Bauman 2000). Importantly, this emergence of a risk society has been accompanied by a social press for individualization, where individuals confronting the anxieties that accompany global risk and uncertainty feel compelled to take personal responsibility for *choosing* and planning their own lives, including their education, careers, identities, and general well-being. One of the most important effects of this press for individualization is that an individual's position in a system of production affects her subjectivity (possibilities for self-hood) much less than her position in relation to the risks (to financial well-being, to material comfort, to safety, to health, and so on) that ever changing systems of exchange produce. Moreover, Beck has argued that traditional social categories, which have always been the shaping forces of subjectivity (e.g. class, race, gender, nationality), have been fundamentally transformed, thus changing the very nature and effects of risk. Take nation/nationality as an example. Economic activity has become increasingly disassociated from nation-states, as states have transformed the discrete production of goods by nations into forms that blur and even undermine national boundaries. As control over any particular economic project becomes far removed from the people most directly involved in production, individuals need to negotiate multiple boundaries and possibilities, while remaining aware of the ways that risks and the subjectivities they afford "flow" across territories. Such changes, according to Beck, are producing possibilities for self and social relations that have never before existed. In particular, people have more freedom than ever to construct what they see as meaningful lives, which obviously involves risks similar to the ones involved in corporate expansions, direction changes, and mergers.

The enterprising self

Social scientists have argued that promoting risk in the new capitalist economy shapes the new worker's subjectivity into what they have called "the enterprising self." Employees are now expected to be ambitious, self-reliant, self-reflexive, risk-taking constructors of their own work capacities, biographies, and success. Their identities are shape-shifting portfolios of skills and knowledge, which individuals must design for themselves (Gee, Hull, and Lankshear 1996). Within this ethos of enterprise, reflection has become a basic pedagogic stance for all workers because non-routine tasks have become part of everyone's everyday work activity. And, indeed, this basic idea permeates the discourses of work and workers in the new capitalist and neoliberal environment, where terms like enterprising, independent, self-motivated, creative/creativity, and problem solving/problem solvers abound. This marks a significant contrast to older formulations that emphasized reliability, standardization, repetition, mass production and consumption, and firm-based loyalty, among other attributes associated, in particular, with Fordism.

Within the "enterprise culture," all forms of conduct have become enterprising forms (Burchell 1993, 275). Individuals, for example, are expected to conduct their everyday lives in terms of quasi-management, making an enterprise of one's life. The enterprising self has become the driving identity in the new economy (du Gay 1996). To be self-regulating and self-actualized, all people – men, women, rich, and poor – are expected to make choices that further their own interests. And true self-realization can only be achieved through risk taking. Individual destiny is a matter of risk, choice, and responsibility. For example, more than ever couples are told to set goals; school children are instructed to commit to learning contracts; individuals are urged to work on themselves to seek self-fulfillment through therapy, lifelong learning, and exercise so they can be happier, healthier, and more well-adjusted.

Given the spread of the values of the enterprise culture among the population and the incorporation of the enterprising self into our subjectivities, it is difficult – if not impossible – to imagine traits such as initiative, flexibility, creativity, independence, leadership, choice, and responsibility as not only desirable but necessary. The power of the enterprising self lies in the fact that its inherent values have become common values. The broad appeal of the enterprising self is compelling because it resonates with basic assumptions of the contemporary human being in advanced liberal democracies (Rose 1998).

Affect

Perhaps the most vulnerable and highly charged dimension of human existence in which risk plays out for the enterprising self is affect. Indeed, affect is at the heart of everything from great literary works to the depths and heights of everyday experience to the development and maintenance of culturally based meanings and beliefs (Heise 2007). This social fact plays out in classrooms in myriad ways from investments in school tasks to responses to school evaluations, to stances of affiliation and resistance. Recent theory and research have suggested that affect is *not* so much about subjective feelings, but about personal investments and their effects. In this regard, inspired by philosopher-novelist Rebecca Goldstein's (1983) notion of the "mattering zone" coupled with ideas about the nature and functions of affect adapted from the work of Deleuze and Guattari (1987) and Massumi (1987), we argue that affect is fundamentally about investments that matter to us. The articulation of affect with other dimensions of our lived experience creates "mattering zones," which inform and regulate our everyday practices or ways of being-in-the-world. Importantly, however, to sustain themselves, these zones require a certain amount of reciprocity. If a person, activity, or institution matters to us, we must also matter to them. Our investments must give us something back – whether this something is another person, love, positive energy, good health, a sense of control, a feeling of being vitally alive, or whatever. These positive effects encourage us to go on, to invest in new forms of being and meaning, and to deal with new instances of pain, frustration, boredom, or whatever. When our investments stop paying off, when they no longer matter and/or when we stop mattering to them, we begin to divest ourselves of them. In other words, mattering zones guide people as they generate affective energy and project it onto what matters to them. Thus, *things that matter* have especially significant impact on daily life and on life histories and, consequently, often involve relatively high levels of risk. This is largely the case because mattering zones are relational; they require reciprocity. The connection of affect to ideology is particularly important in this regard. Shared ideology is at the heart of social relations and reciprocity. Experienced primarily as a pervasive sense of being connected to other people, activities, institutions, and so on, affect by itself cannot account for *why* things matter. Affect is legitimated by its connection to ideology. When the two are connected (which they always are), ideology helps to explain why certain things should matter and others should not, thus calibrating the risks involved (Heise 2007). The pleasure young people derive from certain kinds of music, for example, is always linked to the ideologies of the youth cultures to which they belong.

Marx's (2000) notion of surplus value is instructive here. When something matters, it has a surplus value (a payoff beyond itself) that justifies why we would invest in it. Mattering zones, then, are constructed as zones with surplus value and they are distinguished from other potential zones that do not have surplus value. The more powerful the affective investment, the more powerfully it tends to be linked to ideology, and the greater the surplus value it tends to have to differentiate it from other potential investments. The avid or fanatical reader, for example, believes that filling virtually all her leisure time with reading constitutes a much more worthy investment than, say, watching television, hanging out with friends, shopping, or traveling. Among reading's payoffs are pleasure, knowledge, self-advancement, cultural and social capital, and the like. Once ideologically constructed, surplus value takes on a sense of the real beyond ideological challenge. It becomes reified or naturalized and thus seems incontrovertibly real, powerful, and pervasive. Therefore, the more surplus value, the more risk.

Mattering zones are thus more than just predispositions toward particular kinds of emotional investments. They are centrally involved in the constitution of identities and social relations. Lived spaces are dominated by affective sensibilities and are thus centrally located in mattering zones (e.g. family, career, and friendship networks). They are key sites where people shape (and have shaped) their identities and insert themselves (and are inserted) into various circuits of power. By making certain people, objects, or beliefs matter, we invest them with power, authority, and legitimacy. Conversely, when people or things do not matter to us, they have no power, authority, or legitimacy. Mattering zones are thus fundamental to an economy of belonging. But mattering zones also connect different investments and sites of investment. They always index possibilities for moving from one investment to another. As such, they provide ways for binding identities together in the specific ways that constitute specific modes of the enterprising self.

Emotional intelligence: the nexus of risk, affect, and the enterprising self

The multiple discourses of risk, the enterprising self, and affect come together in the new capitalistic construct of emotional intelligence. Goleman (1998) borrowed the term emotional intelligence from Salovery and Mayer who described it as a form of social intelligence: "that involves the ability to monitor one's own and others' feelings and emotions, to discriminate among them and to use this information to guide one's thinking and actions" (Salovery and Mayer 1990, 189). Salovery and Mayer recognized the connection between two underlying components of personality: cognition and affect. Goleman expanded their definition of emotional intelligence to include competencies such as empathy, social competence, optimism, conscientiousness, and motivation, thus making it more about ideologically informed investments. He went on to argue that emotional intelligence is not only essential for success in the new workplace but the most significant factor in job performance and evaluation.

Emotional intelligence must be understood as a reinvention and redefinition of character, a version that attends to the short-termism and moral ambiguity of the post-Fordist, flexible workplace and that places individual discretion in the place of the Weberian iron cage (Hughes 2005). First, employers do not expect that workers' emotional intelligence is designed to perform a role in a specific employment context. Instead, they view emotional intelligence as embodied *habitus* (Bourdieu 1990), especially its affective dispositions (Zembylas 2007). Second, emotional intelligence is fundamentally about personal responsibility and knowing how to utilize one's own affective dispositions not only for self development and promotion but also for the benefit of the collective (i.e. the office, the firm, and the institution). Affect is harnessed for the interests of both labor and capital. As corporate industry leader Mike Bagshaw argued, businesses need to train people to "be affective to be effective" (Bagshaw 2000, 64). For similar reasons Goleman has developed corporate training programs to emphasize emotional intelligence, and he also believes emotional intelligence should be a central component of curricula in US schools.

Although none of Goleman's writings suggest that he is attuned directly to the *critical* sociology of the workplace, his references to family life no longer offering children a "sure footing" (Goleman 1995, 279) suggest his recognition of the endemic uncertainty and instability that Sennett (2007) attributed to the rise of the new capitalism and the increasingly prevalent function of risk within it. Like affect itself, emotional intelligence is risky business, a social fact that was brought into high relief in the classroom that is the focus of this study.

The study
Data sources
Bruce is a veteran teacher of nearly three decades who leads a very active life outside of work. His fourth-grade classroom, located in a bedroom community in Colorado, mirrors his active lifestyle. In what could easily be described as the idealization of progressive pedagogy, the 23 children in his classroom actively read self-selected novels; they share their thoughts in small group literature discussions, sometimes with Bruce facilitating and sometimes without; they participate in process writing workshops, enthusiastically inventing and sharing ideas with each other, revising and editing; they conference individually with Bruce regarding aspects of their literacy progress; they conduct science experiments; they listen to and talk about contemporary popular music; and they talk about politics and state history. Parents know, like, admire, and respect Bruce. Bruce makes a point of learning about his students' personal and family lives.

Prior to conducting this study, Steven interviewed many teachers about their instructional ideologies and practices. A striking discovery was how many of them emphasized the importance of encouraging risk taking among their students. Bruce was among the most vocal in this regard, insisting that risk taking was central to all good teaching and learning. Steven spent 1–3 mornings per week for one school year as a participant observer in Bruce's classroom, videotaping language arts-related interactions between the teacher and individual students, the teacher and the class, and among groups of students. Field notes complemented the data collection. Bruce also regularly engaged in casual conversations and interviews. Typically, Bruce would view video clips or read transcripts of the clips and then comment on what was going on in them, what his learning goals were, and how effectively he thought these goals were accomplished.

Findings
Example 1
Bruce sat with Matthew for an individual reading conference about the book *Flush* (Hiasson 2005). Matthew struggled to understand some of the book's complexities. In the novel, Noah's father is put in jail for sinking a casino boat, and his mother

plans to divorce him unless he learns to control his impulsivity. During this reading conference, Bruce attempted to help Matthew better understand the book by encouraging him to connect it to his own parents' divorce:

Bruce: When we talked yesterday. We were talking about. Why is Noah so motivated to solve the case? So remember, when we were talking about prior knowledge really depends on what you know and it influenced what you know about the book. So, why do you think ...? You talked about how you guys are so similar. Do you remember that? And – What do you think? So you were talking about the fact that what are the ways that you were so similar to Noah?

(Seven seconds of silence)

Bruce: How are you like Noah in the book?
Matthew: Because his parents are both getting divorced. And my parents are divorced.
Bruce: Okay, and how did that help you understand the book?
Matthew: It didn't really help me.
Bruce: It didn't help you? Then let's go deeper. It doesn't do you any good (interruption) So, you know that on the surface, his parents are divorced and so are yours. But that's not helping you understand, so let's go deeper in your thinking. So, and let's look at your question here. Why is Noah so motivated to solve the case?
Matthew: He's trying to figure out if his dad did sink the ship.
Bruce: Okay, and why is he so motivated and how is that like you? Because, (indecipherable), I think there are a lot of things in here that are like you.
Matthew: I don't know what's like me.
Bruce: What's that?
Matthew: I don't know anything that's like me except for his parents are divorced.
Bruce: Except his parents are what now?
Matthew: Divorced.
Bruce: Okay now. Remember. Have you ever had a situation where you've been separated from your parents?
Matthew: Once in a while?
Bruce: Once in a while? What were you having such a hard time with at the beginning of this year?
Matthew: Um, it's because I'm just like scared that they're not going to like each other. Because they usually w- They-
Bruce: They?
Matthew: When I'm like off track or something. Like if we have no school or I'm off track or something, and when they – Mom comes to pick me at Safeway or Dad comes to pick me up at Safeway, they usually yell at each other a lot.
Bruce: Okay.
Matthew: That scares me, like cuz it makes me think they're not too – like, not even be friends.
Bruce: Okay, so when you're separated. You remember at the beginning of the year when you were at your dad's, who were you missing?
Matthew: Mom.
Bruce: And when you were at your mom's, who were you missing?
Matthew: Dad.
Bruce: Dad. Remember how you – you were having stomachaches all the time? Do you remember this? This – You had – Remember this? This was two weeks you were having stomachaches. You were going home everyday. Remember

this? So how do you think Noah's feeling that his dad's in jail and he can't get to his dad?

Matthew: Pretty sad and mad mixed.

Bruce: Yeah, why sad and mad? Why do you think that?

Matthew: Because he's sad because he don't – doesn't get to see his dad. And he's mad because they won't let him go see his dad.

Bruce: Okay, okay. And you know those feelings. 'Kay, so knowing that-

Matthew: Cuz like when I'm at Mom's, I say "Mom, can I go visit Dad?" "No, cuz we have to do a lot of stuff this week."

Bruce: Right.

Matthew: And when I ask, "Dad, can we go see Mom?," it's like "No, we're going a lot of stuff this week."

Bruce: Right. Matthew, you just did an amazing job. What did you just do? What did you just do that helped you understand this book more? Because now you understand Noah a little bit more, don't ya? So now when you look at that question you wanted to know about, why does Noah so much want to solve this case?

Matthew: Cuz he's confused that people are saying Dad isn't – well, sunk the ship and then he – and then a lot of other people are saying he didn't sink the ship. Like Dus-

Bruce: You know, I just thought of another thing here – think about it. When you said that he's confused because he's hearing other things, you *really* understand things. What are *you* so confused about with your own Mom and Dad? What confuses *you* right now?

Matthew: That they don't like each other that much.

Bruce: Yeah, and remember for a while they were talking bad about each other.

Matthew: Uh-huh.

Bruce: And you were really confused, you were like-

Matthew: And I kept talking bad about Dad because he did – was – he cheated on Mom. That's why they divorced.

Bruce: (Extended laugh) I don't think he'd want you telling me that, but thanks for telling. Okay, that makes me understand, so you're confused too. (Bruce continues laughing.) So you really get this then, don't you? You're feeling the same thing. Now. What did you just do beside tell a family secret you probably shouldn't have told? What did you just do with your reading because that was really good reading? What did you do that allowed you to understand the book more? What did you do? This is really important.

Matthew: Read it deeper, like slower. A little slower. Slower.

Bruce: Yeah, deeper.

On the most transparent level, Bruce tapped Matthew's prior knowledge about his own parents' divorce to help Matthew understand the divorce in the book. However, Bruce also shared the ideology of "personalism" common to many Americans (Hill 2008), which insists that each individual has an invisible interior that is the site of beliefs and intentions and affective states. It was not enough for Matthew to use his prior knowledge to understand the book ("It didn't really help me"). Bruce problematized what may be Matthew's superficial analysis, encouraging him to "go deeper," to tap into an internal state where deep and true emotions exist. But Bruce did not just encourage Matthew to engage in a purely psychological or therapeutic exercise. Instead, he revisited Matthew's question about why Noah was motivated to solve the case, shuttling back and forth between the cognitive and affective ("Why is he so motivated and how is that like you?"). Matthew's response that, "He's trying to figure out if his dad did sink the ship" led Bruce to ask: "Why is he so motivated and how is that like you?" Never mind for the moment that Bruce's question suggests that he is using known personal information about Matthew. Bruce targeted Matthew's rational thinking and judgment while simultaneously focusing on his affective investment in the issue at hand.

Yet Matthew initially did not seem to make the connection that Bruce had imagined, so Bruce led Matthew into a confession: "It's because I'm just like scared that they're not going to like each other." Matthew's confession then comfortably cascaded with Bruce gently "colonizing" his subjectivity, as indicated by the rapid volleys between Bruce's questions and Matthew's increasingly rich and revealing responses. The positive alignment that developed here led Bruce first to compliment Matthew's newly heightened emotional reflexivity and then to make him conscious that he was using his emotions to enhance his thinking: "What did you just do that helped you understand the book more? Because now you understand Noah a little more, don't ya? ... Why does Noah so much want to solve this case?" Bruce clearly enacted a kind of "disciplinary technology" (Foucault 1977, 1980) here to stimulate Matthew's desire to talk about himself (and thus to come to know himself better). He encouraged Matthew to begin to govern himself through increased self-reflexivity about his emotions, which was one of the fundamental social norms of this classroom.

Next, Bruce reframed the interaction by recontextualizing Matthew's use of the word "confused" in relation to Matthew's life: "What are *you* so confused about with your *own* Mom and Dad?" Following Matthew's revelation that his parents do not like each other, Bruce focused on the object of Matthew's confusion, which led to Matthew's further revelation that his father had an affair.

This revelation seemed to make Bruce uncomfortable; he laughed nervously. Matthew, who had been smiling throughout, turned away from Bruce for a moment, perhaps a little uncomfortable too but also keenly tuned into the affective tenor of the moment, a central feature of emotional intelligence. Matthew was not only to be learning how to "go deeper" with his interpretations but also how to become more aware of his own affective investments in relation to literary response and to life. In Hochschild's (2003) language, Matthew's emotions are discursively "transmuted" so that his understanding is "enhanced." But there is more going on here as well. The tension of the moment has taught him that affect must be managed in ways that are appropriate to context. Indeed, one gets the sense that he was both excited to have made an affective breakthrough and a little concerned that he may have gone a bit too far. He has begun to learn that managing tensions between the personal and the collective interests is central to the work of the enterprising self.

After this text-to-life interlude, Bruce shifted back to the analysis of the book, calling attention to the relations between affect and cognition, another central feature of emotional intelligence: "What did you do [with your thinking] besides telling a family secret you probably shouldn't have?" As the conference ended, Matthew claimed to have learned the benefits of reading "deeper" and reading "slower." It is also clear that he was becoming more deeply aware of the power of his affective investments and that he was developing subjectivity with particular desires, intentions, mattering maps, and potentials characteristic of an enterprising self. Indeed, Matthew took several risks in this interaction – both with respect to the information he has disclosed and with respect to dwelling in a confusing, even scary affective space. And he has done this largely because, like the astute personnel manager in the corporate world, Bruce has valorized affective risk taking, and by default, the place of affective risk taking in the construction of the enterprising self.

Example 2

Bruce sat on his chair in front of his students who were lounging on the carpet in front of him holding their *Living Books*, a journal they wrote in at the beginning of each day. Just as the students were about to share aloud their most recent entries, Bruce addressed the class:

> What does this say about you? Is it a reflection of your life? If you do keep these, as most kids do, and you look back on this, what are you going to think about yourself as a writer? What are you going to think about yourself as a person? What are you going to think about yourself as a fourth grader? If you look in your *Living Books* right now, and I want you to be honest. I don't want any of this stuff, "Yea, it's okay." I don't want any of that garbage. If I look back at my Living Book, what does it say about me? Here's what I'm expecting ... You're going to talk to me. You're going to talk to the class. I want you to be honest. I want you to tell the class what your Living Book says about you. I want to hear real stuff. If you have your Living Book [in the future] and assess and evaluate your life, what would it say about you as a fourth grader in 2008? I expect to hear amazing things about what you are doing right now with your life. Is it worthwhile? Is it balanced? You need to commit to this classroom and the most important thing, you need to commit to yourself as a student. That's why we're here, because only the best survive. And I want you to be the best. I don't want you to be *kind* of a good veterinarian. I want you to be the best. I don't want you to be an *okay* Ford mechanic. I want to be able to take my Focus to you and you tell me what's wrong and fix it so it runs at the top. If you're going to be a bioengineer, I want you to be the best. I want you to find the solutions for gas wars. I don't want you to just be okay.

Bruce's lesson seemed intent on helping them not only to think about themselves as writers but also to develop greater reflexivity and to see their lives as having a coherent narrative and rewarding self-identity. Among other things, *Living Books* could be read in the future, helping students to reflect back upon their lives and observe their own trajectory of development (Giddens 1991). Indeed, Bruce expected them to live their lives reflexively, to answer the question that high modernity demands daily: "How shall I live?" Also, the autobiography: "is at the core of self-identity in modern social life. Like any other formalized narrative, it is something that has to be worked at, and calls for creative input as a matter of course" (Giddens 1991, 76). Bruce viewed *Living Books* as creative, reflexive tools that would allow students to look back upon their lives with no regrets. But because *Living Books* were shared publicly, they also had a "confessional" function (Foucault 1978). They brought the private into the public for viewing and evaluating. Having discovered and revealed secrets about themselves, students could more freely engage in "the care of the self" (Foucault 1986) by recognizing the different ways of producing one's subjectivity, and by taking increased responsibility for that production process.

Importantly, this process involves risk. The Social Darwinism embodied in Bruce's lecture (only the best survive) reflects his sense that the world is an unpredictable, scary, and risky place. *Living Books* provided students with strategies for actualizing particular subjectivities amidst such a world. This actualization process required that they open themselves up to each other and fashion themselves as active and self-regulating risk takers or enterprising selves. Importantly, this played out within the stability and safety of Bruce's classroom. Students could safely engage in the practices of risk taking and enterprise that they would later need to practice in more unpredictable and dangerous environments with increased downside risks.

Yet there is a tension between the individualized self-interest required to become the "best" – entrepreneurial selves who are told they have a moral duty both to "responsibilize" and to invest in themselves as rational choice actors – and Bruce's demand for a commitment to each other. The question is: what sort of "commitment" does Bruce expect? With an uncertain future now presented (they cannot just be an "okay" Ford mechanic), but with a multitude of possible selves they might become through meritorious activity, the students were asked to begin their journey toward self-determination by first turning toward each other, their immediate source of trust and commitment.

The transcript excerpt below, which is the continuation of the *Living Books* discussion, demonstrates that Bruce created a classroom environment in which the collective exploration of risky issues could be discussed, especially in relation to affective states, desires, and possible selves. Indeed, their expressions of self-disclosure stood out against the more ordinary routines and conversations that constituted a significant portion of the larger data-set from this classroom:

Kevin:	Some of the stuff that I write about, what I did, just talks about the weather.
Bruce:	So, real superficial? No going deep?
Kevin:	Yes.
Betty:	I'm finding that I'm not really talking about me. I'm more talking about what happened to me after school or what happened today.
Bruce:	Cool. So you realize you want to do more about what you are thinking about or wondering about.
Betty:	That's more what I'm talking about.
Jacqueline:	A lot of what I wrote it like what I've been doing and what happened and what I think happened and then also like when I got my new kitten.
Bruce:	Okay.
Jacqueline:	And I didn't write about what I care about. Sometimes I just write about things that don't really matter.

At some level, these students clearly seemed to understand the nature and importance of their affective investments. Yet no matter how insightful, their comments were produced under Bruce's "gaze," which demanded a particular standard of affective involvement and self-disciplining, which was cultivated in this dialog (and elsewhere in the data-set). In this regard, Hatcher (2008) highlighted how the cultivation of emotional intelligence helps to produce the idealized corporate character through the measurement of affect, thus affording "fine-grained disciplining, dividing, ranking, and tracking of improvements" (Hatcher 2008, 158), that in turn constitute a self-controlling self. In this interaction, the students confessed to not meeting Bruce's standard and consented to becoming subjects willing to take risks by "going deep" with their writing. Each child, with little intervention from Bruce, confessed that her or his writing was superficial and vowed to work on that problem.

Arguably, Betty revealed the most about identity under the new capitalism. She felt an obligation to share about *her*, not "what happened" to her or what she did, as if true affective awareness – honesty – comes only in the form of personal self-disclosure. As Jacqueline stated, focusing on "what happened" (such as getting a new kitten) is inauthentic, or at least not particularly useful for producing one's life. But what ultimately counts as "going deep"? Bruce's responses suggested that what is important to write about is what one is "thinking," "wondering," and "feeling," in self-reflexive ways. In other words, what is important is to become an enterprising self. Even though Bruce was clearly aware that his students' subjectivities were contingent on many forces not in their control, he nevertheless worked hard to cultivate autonomous, active subjects who were, "equipped with a psychology aspiring to self-fulfillment and actually or potentially running their lives as a kind of enterprise of themselves" (Rose 1996, 139). He further argued that their futures would likely be bright and successful if they heeded his advice about the importance of becoming enterprising selves: "If you're going to be a bioengineer, I want you to be the best. I want you to find the solutions for gas wars." In the new capitalism of neoliberal knowledge economies, enterprising selves are individualized, self-realized, self-actualized subjects engaged in continuous reflexive self-assessment. They are well equipped to market themselves. They are the children Bruce hopes are all children.

Example 3

In this final example, Bruce began by reading from his own *Living Book*, parts of which are excerpted below:

> I believe what your actions and what you do changes your emotions. So even if you don't *feel* it, if you *act* like it – here's what I believe. Sometimes I'll be feeling really sad. And if there's a party coming up or something, and I don't want to go to the party because I'm sad. But if I *go* to the party, and *act* like I want to be there, guess what happens? I have fun. So what *I* believe is that your actions – the things you do, and the behaviors create emotions, and change your behavior. That's what I believe.

Foucault (1986) argued that to know oneself is to care for oneself, especially one's emotional economy. Bruce's *Living Book* entry was a highly visible, even palpable, exemplar of the kind of self-reflexivity, self-examination, and self-care he hoped his students would develop. In confessing that he was a flawed human being, Bruce also acknowledged that he marshaled his own abilities and emotional resources in the service of his own development as a more self-actualized human being (Hartmann and Honneth 2006, 45). Taking responsibility for one's life in this way is derived from self-knowledge and requires risk taking, which Foucault (1978) described as "testing procedures," practices to "measure and confirm" one's "independence" when faced with potentially harmful temptations, "establishing a supremacy over oneself" (58).

Bruce had barely finished reading from his *Living Book* when Gary offered up a confession of his own:

> Gary: Mr. I conquered a fear today.
> Bruce: What?

Gary: I just remembered.
Bruce: What?
Gary: I climbed to the top of the net. When you get close to the top, it starts to get dark and I kept on going.
Bruce: How does it feel when you *do* conquer?
Gary: Everybody in the entire gym was like "YAY."

Gary seemed to take great pleasure at having climbed to the top of the net (see Foucault [1985] on the relations between truth and pleasure). During the interaction, Bruce positively evaluated Gary's conduct by highlighting the "conquer" metaphor without associating "conquering" with a specific activity or task. In fact, he seemed to disassociate it from Gary's unique accomplishment in order to universalize conquering one's fears as an important and valuable "good." This amplified the metaphor's power considerably. "How does it feel when you *do* conquer?" is more about Gary's emerging self than his specific act of conquering a particular fear, and it is even more about the value for all people of "conquering" obstacles that stand in the way of self-mastery.

Even before Gary had finished his story, many other students raised their hands, eager to tell stories of their own. Bruce sanctioned their bids, and they described overcoming fears in various arenas of their lives. Albeit unknowingly, many of them also connected their stories to what Foucault (1985) has called the discourse of self-mastery. Individuals who engage in self-mastery practices recognize that there are different ways of producing one's self and take responsibility for that production process. In doing so, they both acknowledge and respect normalizing or objectifying processes inherent in all social domains but choose whether or not to comply with them. After many students in the class had finished telling their stories, Bruce mounted a poster on the easel that contained several prepared questions for the class to discuss, which would facilitate their next *Living Book* entries:

- How is your fear of failure holding you back?
- How does the fear of holding you back impact the risks you take?
- How does the fear of failure impact your life?

To begin a conversation about these questions, Bruce read aloud another entry from his *Living Book* that described an email from a parent of a student who was worried about her son's fears about failing when taking risks. Bruce then asked the class, "You know what I mean by that?" Colton responded, "Does it mean that it kind of controls your life?" to which Bruce replied enthusiastically:

Yes! And it keeps you from doing things you know you really have to do. It doesn't do any good to pretend it's not there. Remember we were talking the other day about being strong and being afraid. You speak your opinion, even if your voice shakes.

Although "fear" is a complicated, basic, even primitive affective response, the questions that drove this interaction are framed in terms of morality and enterprise, which presuppose a particular new capitalist mindset. Recall that one of Bruce's primary goals was to help his students maximize their potential based upon assumptions about the importance of self-knowledge and the role of self-regulation in overcoming fears and other obstacles to self-actualization. Bruce's questions and goals were also shaped by his knowledge of the psychological literature on motivation such as that of Carol Dweck. Dweck (2007) described two types of minds: fixed mindsets and growth mindsets, and she claimed that the latter mindset is a requirement for happiness. The questions that Bruce has written, although not taken directly from Dweck's published work, have clearly been influenced by it. Further, because Bruce is the expert who wrote the questions, and because the questions are themselves phrased authoritatively, the children readily align themselves with the objectives of experts and the power/knowledge entailed in such alignments.

After his exchange with Colton, Bruce directed the class to the first question on the poster and with little pause or prompting, the children responded. Although we present just the first two stories that unfolded, most of the class offered very similar stories:

Marilyn: I remember my old school like I was struggling on this problem on this test, and we can have partners, but no one really liked me because I was different. I had really short hair. And so when I asked them, they would say, "No, you should know that by now I'm not gonna help. You gotta learn that all by yourself." And so I always got scared to ask people, and I always got scared to try, and I was always scared to fail.

Jacqueline: When we're doing math, I don't learn it as quickly as others do. And people around you are always saying this is easy and we learned this in kindergarten. People always say that. And I don't think it's true. And I don't say anything because I have a feeling if I say, "Um, that's not what everybody thinks," then it'll start like a fight or something. And, um, so I just think that I should open up more so if I need help I should say something.

Both girls told stories about personal fears and the self-initiative and risk taking required to overcome them. Their commitments to "open up" (Jacqueline) and "ask people" (Marilyn) for help suggest their incorporation (or at least tacit knowledge) of aspects of neoliberal ideologies where individuals are complicit in creating subjectivities that align with the "ethos of enterprise" (Du Gay 1996), where control of one's behavior can operate through "the rational reconstruction of the will" (Rose 1999, 270). Additionally, Jacqueline's recognition that she should "open up" reflects her realization that she can modulate her affect through the choices she makes.

After all children who wanted to share stories related to Bruce's first question had done so, he shifted to the second question, the one that emphasized future risks: "What will your life look like if you continue to avoid new chances to grow and learn?" Many students shared ideas:

Jacqueline: If you avoid your fears, then what are you going to do when you are ...
John: In high school?
Briana: Lots of people are bullies in high school. Overcome your fears.
Jacqueline: What's gonna happen when someone wants to do something with you that includes one of your fears and you can't because you never tried to conquer it.
John: Like grasshopper catching.
Jacqueline: When I was on the ladder I was far away. I couldn't do it. I was too scared because I wouldn't conquer it. Because I was trying to avoid it because I thought I was going to fall off the ladder. So if you avoid your

	fears, then you'll never conquer them and you'll (indecipherable) the rest of your life.
Briana:	You'll always be scared of ...
Max:	The only time you were asked to go skateboarding, and you don't know how to, and that's the only time you've been asked, then you have to come across it or in your life, you'll never have another chance to do that.
Gary:	What would my life would be like if I didn't overcome my fears? It would be a whole, yeah exactly, I feel crazy because just wait until you're in high school; you'll have about ten times as many fears as you have now.
Max:	Or you'll turn out like one of those geeks that stay in their mom's basement.

The question – "What will your life look like if you continue to avoid new chances to grow and learn?" – does not explicitly refer to some distant or not so distant future. However, John and Briana (and later Gary) immediately began talking about high school – five years away – and their potential fates if they do not learn to manage fears in the present. In this interaction, the children got wholly caught up in discourses of affect (e.g. current fears, potential fears, and overcoming fears). That they focused so intently on fear, how to manage fear, and how they planned to act upon future fears suggests that it is useful to consider risk as a form of individual rationality and not only, as Beck and others discuss, a global narrative of the risk society. As we noted earlier, affective investments are effective only to the extent to which they are articulated with ideologies into some kind of reason-affect assemblage.

Indeed, each child seemed to be quite rational as they imagined risks that might be in their futures and strategies to manage these risks. As Gary stated, "What would my life be like if I did not overcome my fears?" He and the other students revealed the way in which risk management has become simultaneously part of our cultural common sense, functioning as a form of social regulation (Besley and Peters 2007) and a form of subjectivity. As responsibilized citizens (or children learning to be responsibilized citizens), these students are learning to control their bodies, their education, their health, their relationships, and their retirements at the same time they are learning to control their fears.

Max's self-disciplining coda – recognizing what personal responsibility might entail, eschewing the culture of dependency of the post-welfare state for fear of what might happen – seemed a matter of trying to "tame chance" (Hacking 1990). Max realized that he had choices, but he thought about "choice" in neoliberal terms, where freedom necessarily entails moralization and responsibilization. Max seemed to think about his life as a series of questions rather than as a set of presupposed givens, where "reflexivity transfers from monitoring the social to monitoring the self" (Lash and Urry 1994, 41). Clearly Max monitors both, connecting in his mind the ubiquitous social with the potentially disastrous personal. Avoiding such a consequence can easily be seen as Max's personal reflexive project.

Conclusions

Using several themes from the risk literature as analytic tools, we considered how the conversations in Bruce's classroom were not isolated classroom events but events that were inscribed within the discourses of the new capitalism and neoliberalism. As such, they provided examples of "technologies of empowerment" (Cruikshank 1999) which steered these students toward subjectivities of active, self-managing, and enterprising individuals who were willing to take personal responsibility and risks within a lifestyle of choice. In relation to this claim, Beck (1992) argued that the primary affective state set into motion in the risk society is fear (or anxiety). Bruce consistently expressed confidence that his classroom provided children with opportunities to make choices, to become conscious about their decisions, and to reflect upon their actions and decisions. The most frequent and obvious way that these "empowerment" potentials circulated within classroom talk was when they were discussing their affective states and investments. But empowerment discourses such as the ones Bruce cultivated were also a means of producing "rational economic and entrepreneurial actors" (Cruikshank 1999, 68).

Conceived in this way, affect reflects a set of vocabularies that are authoritative because they derive from rational discourses grounded in political authority that act "at a distance" (Latour 1987; Miller and Rose 1990) and aim at the aspirations of individuals, families, and organizations. Knowledge is always linked to power. Affect is always linked to ideology. These discourses, then, are "the means by which government works through rather than against the subjectivities of citizens" (Cruikshank 1999, 72).

During his reading conference with Matthew, Bruce made it clear that he believed that Matthew could only understand the book they were reading if he also understood his own affective investments in the book and their relations to his affective investments in his personal life. Bruce's intensive efforts to regulate Matthew's consciousness – to get him to take risks that involve getting in touch with his affective states and investments – were not without productive effect or, in industrial terms, commercial ends. Referring to the corporate world, Cooper and Sawaf (1997) explained that, "when you are conscious of your emotional states you gain valuable flexibility of response ..." (13). In the cultural economy of this classroom, Matthew's emotions were commodified, and thus transformed into a marketable product (Fineman 2000).

Affect and affective investment, of course, exist in all areas of social life. But Bruce took this social fact as an unquestionably necessary starting point for all learning in his classroom, thus dissolving the line between affect and cognition. The primacy of affective investment was as much the grand narrative of Bruce's classroom as it is the grand narrative of the new capitalist workplace.

At one level, it might seem curious that the discourse of affect is a key narrative of the workplace at all. Non-rational dispositions have long been considered a hindrance to the progress of many organizations. The traditional view of organizations holds that the "infusion of instrumental rationality into the capitalistic bureaucratic structure leaves little room for human feeling and sentiment" (Bolton 1998, 11). Affect and its manifestations, certainly in British, American, and other western European workplaces have long been matters of privatization and individualization. Concomitantly, rationality has long been prized in western social conduct, and indeed, emotional restraint has long been the hallmark of "civility" in and beyond organizations. But the workplace under the new capitalism is a very different social space than it was under traditional capitalism – a space in which many aspects of human acting and being are being transformed under the banners of individualism and freedom, but also (and not always so transparently) in the interests of corporate success (read: profit).

Finally, it is also curious that discourses of risk were so prevalent in Bruce's classroom. It is not that these children's lives are inherently more risky than those of other children. The fact that these children are growing up in a quiet, suburban neighborhood and do not face the obvious risks of living in more explicitly "dangerous" neighborhoods is precisely the point. In liquid modernity, thinking in terms of risk and risk assessment is an ever-present enterprise, no matter who you are. The class's lively and reflexive conversation about facing their fears – falling off ladders, touching grasshoppers, and missed opportunities to learn how to skateboard and roller blade – revealed that the challenge to young children (and their parents who also live in quiet suburban neighborhoods) is to construct and reconstruct their own identities. These identities are no longer given over to them by traditional institutions and cultures. Instead, they are effects of "enterprising selves" who are not afraid to take risks (which are always affect-laden) and who are cognizant of the need to manage risk (and thus affect) in their lives efficiently and effectively. After all, who wants an identity as a "geek" who lives in his mother's basement?

References

Bagshaw, M. 2000. Emotional intelligence: Training people to be affective so they can be effective. *Industrial and Commercial Training* 32, no. 2: 61–5.
Bauman, Z. 2000. *Liquid modernity.* Cambridge: Polity Press.
Beck, U. 1992. *Risk society: Towards a new modernity.* Cambridge: Polity Press.
Beck, U. 2000. *The risk society and beyond: Critical issues for social theory.* London: Sage.
Besley, T., and M. Peters. 2007. *Subjectivity and truth: Foucault, education and the culture of the self.* New York, NY: Bruce Lang.
Bolton, S. 1998. Emotions here, emotions there, emotions, emotions everywhere. *Critical Perspectives in Organizations* 11, no. 2: 155–71.
Bourdieu, P. 1990. *The logic of the practice.* Stanford, CA: Stanford University Press.
Burchell, G. 1993. Liberal government and the technique of the self. *Economy and Society* 22, no. 3: 267–82.
Cooper, R., and A. Sawaf. 1997. *Executive EQ: Emotional intelligence in leadership and organization.* New York, NY: Perigee Trade.
Cruikshank, B. 1999. *The will to empower.* Ithaca, NY: Cornell University Press.
Deleuze, G., and F. Guattari. 1987. *A thousand plateaus: Capitalism and schizophrenia.* Trans. B. Massumi. Minneapolis, MN: University of Minnesota Press.
Du Gay, P. 1996. *Consumption and identity at work.* Thousand Oaks, CA: Sage.
Dweck, C. 2007. *Mindset: The new psychology of success.* New York, NY: Ballantine Books.
Fineman, S. 2000. Commodifying the emotionally intelligent. In *Emotions in organizations,* 2nd ed., ed. S. Fineman, 101–15. Thousand Oaks, CA: Sage.
Foucault, M. 1977. *Discipline & punish: The birth of the prison.* New York, NY: Random House.
Foucault, M. 1978. *The history of sexuality, Volume I: Introduction.* Trans. R. Hurley. New York, NY: Vintage Books.
Foucault, M. 1980. *Power/knowledge: Selected interviews and other writings 1972–1977.* New York, NY: Pantheon.

Foucault, M. 1985. *The history of sexuality, Volume II: The uses of pleasure*. Trans. R. Hurley. New York, NY: Vintage Books.
Foucault, M. 1986. *The history of sexuality, Volume III: The care of the self*. Trans. R. Hurley. New York, NY: Vintage Books.
Gee, J.P., G. Hull, and C. Lankshear. 1996. *The new work order: Behind the language of the new capitalism*. Boulder, CO: Westview Press.
Giddens, A. 1991. *Modernity and self-identity*. Stanford, CA: Stanford University Press.
Goldstein, Rebecca. 1983. *The mind-body problem*. New York, NY: Random House.
Goleman, D. 1995. *Emotional intelligence: Why it can matter more than IQ*. New York, NY: Bantam Books.
Goleman, D. 1998. *Working with emotional intelligence*. New York, NY: Bantam Books.
Hacking, I. 1990. *The taming of chance*. Cambridge: Cambridge University Press.
Hartmann, M., and A. Honneth. 2006. Paradoxes of capitalism. *Constellations* 13, no. 1: 41–58.
Hatcher, C. 2008. Becoming a successful corporate character and the role of emotion management. In *The emotional organization: Passions and powers*, ed. S. Fineman, 153–66. Oxford: Blackwell.
Heise, D. 2007. *Expressive order: Confirming sentiments in social action*. New York, NY: Springer.
Hiasson, C. 2005. *Flush*. New York, NY: Random House Children's Books.
Hill, J. 2008. *The everyday language of white racism*. London: Wiley-Blackwell.
Hochschild, A. 2003. *The managed heart: Commercialization of human feeling*. 2nd ed. Berkeley, CA: University of California Press.
Hughes, J. 2005. Bringing emotion to work: Emotional intelligence, employee resistance and the reinvention of character. *Work, Employment and Society* 19, no. 3: 603–25.
Lash, S., and J. Urry. 1994. *Economies of signs and space*. London: Sage.
Latour, B. 1987. *Science in action*. Milton Keynes: Open University Press.
Marx, K. 2000. *Theories of surplus value: Books I, II, and III*. Amherst, NY: Prometheus Books.
Massumi, B. 1987. Translators forward: Pleasures of philosophy. In *A thousand plateaus: Capitalism and schizophrenia*, ed. G. Deleuze and F. Guattari, ix–xv. Trans. B. Massumi. Minneapolis, MN: University of Minnesota Press.
Miller, P., and N. Rose. 1990. Governing economic life. *Economy and Society* 19, no. 1: 1–31.
Ritzer, G. 1999. *Enchanting a disenchanted world: Revolutionizing the means of consumption*. London: Pine Forge Press.
Rose, N. 1996. Identity, genealogy, history. In *Questions of cultural identity*, ed. S. Hall and P. du Gay, 128–50. London: Sage.
Rose, N. 1998. *Inventing our selves: Psychology, power, and personhood*. Cambridge: Cambridge University Press.
Rose, N. 1999. *Powers of freedom: Reframing political thought*. Cambridge: Cambridge University Press.
Salovery, P., and J.D. Mayer. 1990. Emotional intelligence. *Imagination, Cognition, and Personality* 9, no. 3: 185–211.
Sennett, R. 1998. *The corrosion of character: The personal consequences of work in the new capitalism*. New York, NY: W.W. Norton.
Sennett, R. 2007. *The culture of the new capitalism*. New Haven, CT: Yale University Press.
Zembylas, M. 2007. Emotional capital and education: Theoretical insights from Bourdieu. *British Journal of Educational Studies* 55, no. 4: 443–63.

"English for the global": discourses in/of English-language voluntourism

Cora Jakubiak Neisser

Drawing upon the notion of hyperglobalism and critical perspectives on English as an international language, this study examines the ways in which English language teaching via volunteer tourism (i.e. English-language voluntourism) is represented and legitimated as an altruistic practice among organizational sponsors and in the talk of current and former volunteers. Data were collected as a part of a larger, multi-sited ethnography that included interviews with program participants, fieldwork in the office of a sponsoring non-governmental organization, and a content analysis of organizational sponsors' promotional materials. Data analysis illustrates that English-language voluntourism relies on and recreates a discourse of hyperglobalism in order to construct short-term, volunteer English language teaching as a benevolent and appropriate development intervention. However, English-language voluntourism program participants often come to a new, critical awareness of hyperglobalism and its attendant ideologies by participating in these same programs.

Introduction

A 2007 *Time* magazine article entitled "Vacationing Like Brangelina: Does Volunteer Tourism Do Any Good?" poses a compelling question in reference to volunteer tourism. This is a practice in which people from the Global North[1] work on a short-term basis in fields like education, childcare, and nature preservation in the Global South as an alternative form of travel (Wearing 2001). The *Time* piece asks: "Are volunteer vacations ... merely overpriced guilt trips with an impact as fleeting as the feel-good factor? Or do they offer individuals a real chance to change the world, one summer jaunt at a time?" (Fitzpatrick 2007, 49). Given that 37% of all volunteer tourism projects fall under the category of teaching (Callanan and Thomas 2005) and that "[t]eaching [English] is one of the most common volunteer assignments" (Collins, DeZerega, and Heckscher 2002, 8), a more pointed question to ask of volunteer tourism may not be whether it works but how. Unlike volunteer tourism projects such as post-earthquake debris removal or nature trail reconstruction, the goals and outcomes of English language teaching via volunteer tourism, or English-language voluntourism, are blurry. Thus, this study explores the following questions: how is English-language voluntourism represented and legitimated? What discourses construct it as an altruistic practice? How and in what ways do English-language voluntourism program participants subscribe to or contest these altruistic discourses? In answering these three questions, I seek to expand the meaning and significance of *Time's* treatment of volunteer tourism. Whether volunteer tourism, defined broadly, ultimately "does any good" may depend not so much on what volunteer tourists actually accomplish in the field, but on the visions of success, ideas of social change, and model ways of being in the world that they (and their projects) carry forth.

Central to understanding the discourse of English-language voluntourism, I suggest, are two conceptual tools: hyperglobalism and the critical notion of English as an international language (EIL). Following a topical review of English-language voluntourism, I explicate these two theoretical concepts and explain their significance to this study.

English-language voluntourism

Volunteer tourism, or *voluntourism* (Callanan and Thomas 2005, 183; Wearing 2001), is defined as the short-term (generally one week to three months) practice of, "volunteer[ing] in an organized way to undertake holidays that might involve aiding or alleviating the poverty of some groups in society" (Wearing 2001, 1). Although the term, voluntourism, has been appropriated in the US domestic context (cf. Villano 2009), academic literature on volunteer tourism characterizes it as moving in a Global North–South flow. Volunteer tourism is a form of new tourism (Poon 1993), also called niche tourism (Novelli 2005) or New Moral Tourism (Butcher 2003), a form of alternative tourism that responds to the numerous, strident critiques issued against international mass tourism. These charges include cultural imperialism (Jaakson 2004), commodification (Wearing, McDonald, and Ponting 2005), and usurious economic practices (Urry 2002). Specific forms of new tourism include, but are not limited to, research tourism, gastronomic tourism, space tourism, and volunteer tourism (Novelli 2005).

The phenomenon of volunteer tourism has grown exponentially since the mid-1990s (TRAM 2008). Since the early 2000s in particular, researchers have noted a "volunteer tourism rush" among Global North travelers (Callanan and Thomas 2005, 183), and in response, some formerly traditional tour companies have been expanding their range of services to incorporate various forms of alternative tourism, including volunteer tourism (Swarbrooke et al. 2003; TRAM 2008).

Groups outside of the tourism sector have also contributed to volunteer tourism's growth and popularity. Unlike tourism industry operators, however, who promote the practice for its ostensibly light ecological footprint and the supposed culturally authentic encounters it can offer (Wearing 2001), non-governmental organizations (NGOs), faith-based coalitions, and state actors promote *de facto* volunteer tourism in the names of development aid and public diplomacy or "soft power" (Nye 2004). In these latter conceptualizations, volunteer tourism is referred to as *international voluntary service* or *international civic service* (cf. McBride and Sherraden 2007), umbrella terms that group together volunteer tourism with long-term service projects such as the US Peace Corps. NGO-sponsored volunteer tourism programs are often quite expensive, and fees for an eight-week trip can cost approximately $4000 (US) or more (WorldTeach n.d.).

Volunteer tourism, as a social practice, has both supporters and detractors. Although empirical evaluations of volunteer tourism's effects on Global South communities are few (for an exception, see Gray and Campbell 2007), multiple stakeholders maintain that volunteer tourism can harness civil society's power and solve long-term problems (Butcher and Smith 2010; McBride and Sherraden 2007). Other observers argue that participation in volunteer tourism projects leads to increased civic engagement (McGee and Santos 2005). Skeptics of volunteer tourism, however, claim that short-term, non-technical "aid" initiatives do little to alter the underlying causes of poverty (Simpson 2004). Other research (e.g. Heath 2007) points out that only particular people have both the time and material means to participate in volunteer tourism, making the phenomenon a means by which certain groups in society are able to consolidate and affirm their own power. By parlaying their economic capital into symbolic capital through the purchase of a volunteer vacation, already privileged people are able to appear distinctly altruistic and worldly (Heath 2007). Despite critiques of volunteer tourism, however, the phenomenon continues to garner wide public support (cf. Tergesen 2011).

I define English-language voluntourism as a form of volunteer tourism in which native speakers of prestige-variety, or inner-core English (Kachru 1997), teach language lessons in the Global South on a short-term basis. Consistent with other forms of volunteer tourism, participation requirements are minimal. Neither formal educator credentials nor familiarity with language pedagogy are generally required. In the words of Global Volunteers, a voluntourism sponsor:

> Any native English speaker can be a valuable resource in a classroom in Africa, Asia, Europe, [or] Mexico. ... Even if you've never formally taught a classroom subject, you can teach conversational English skills. All you need is enthusiasm and a desire to help adult and youth students. (2002)

As this quotation indicates, the actual settings in which English-language voluntourism takes place vary widely from place to place as well as among (and within) sponsoring organizations and programs. Still, English-language voluntourism is argued to have a consistently positive effect.

Although many faith-based organizations sponsor English-language voluntourism as mission work (cf. Snow 2001), this study focuses exclusively on non-sectarian English-language voluntourism as sponsored by corporations and NGOs. In these groups' depictions, whether "making a meaningful contribution to international education" (WorldTeach n.d.) or increasing "educational and employment prospects for people who would not normally have the opportunity to learn English" (Cross-Cultural Solutions n.d.), English-language voluntourism is beneficial for service recipients and constitutes development aid.

Despite claiming to facilitate development, however, English-language voluntourism sponsors actually engage very little with the language(s) of development. Although numerous scholars have placed the concept, *development*, under focused interrogation, charging that it is a discursive phenomenon with neocolonial effects (e.g. Escobar 1995; Sachs 1992), this work is largely absent within English-language voluntourism. Classical economic metrics of development are also missing. What is present, however, is oblique talk of "help" or "making a difference." In the words of Global Volunteers (2008, 9), to participate in English-language voluntourism is to, "[e]xtend a helping hand to ... youth and adults ... No teaching experience is required to be truly helpful!" Within English-language voluntourism, then, there seems to be an *a priori* assumption that any teaching a volunteer might do is better than none at all; thus, any intervention is helpful. To facilitate an understanding of why this is so, Dicken's (2003) notion of hyperglobalism and critical work on EIL provide useful points of departure. It is to a discussion of these theoretical frameworks that I now turn.

Hyperglobalism

Dicken's (2003) notion of hyperglobalism provides a conceptual tool for making sense of English-language voluntourism's dominant precepts. Coming largely from the western business world (and illustrated in works such as Thomas Friedman's *The World is Flat*), hyperglobalism posits that the world is truly borderless. It augurs a present/future that rings of neoliberal formations: a world in which consumer tastes are homogenized by Global North-based multinational corporations, a political system in which the primary role of the nation-state is to aid the global economic network rather than to provide social welfare services, and a life world in which market rationalities (inclusive of intensive commodification processes) prevail in public (and even private) domains. Although more nuanced conceptualizations of globalization view the phenomenon as one of multilateral, syncretic flows (Appadurai 1991), or as creating hybrid forms of cross-cultural interconnection (Holton 2000), hyperglobalist discourse frames globalization as driven exclusively by Global North-based economic, cultural, and political apparatuses. Refracted through a hyperglobalist lens, English language skills alone become the proposed solution to a myriad of complex problems in the Global South including, but not limited to, inefficient or corrupt governments, a scarcity of public resources, volatile labor markets, and massive underemployment.

Key tenets of hyperglobalism are neoliberalism and its corollary, self-regulating citizenship (Rose 1999; Ullman 2012). Harvey (2007) defines neoliberalism as a broad, often contested, political label used to describe the pro-free market, pro-corporate, anti-big government ideology that has become hegemonic among Global North nation-states and supranational financial institutions in the last few decades. Under the auspices of neoliberalism, ideas of civic engagement and what it means to be an active citizen are reframed. Concurrent with the dramatic decline of long-standing forms of collective, public action in the Global North such as political letter-writing, union membership, and protest rally attendance (Putnam 2000), there has been a rise in more private, individually-oriented forms of civic participation such as fee-requiring, "thon"-style athletic events like breast cancer walks, socially-conscious consumption, and volunteering (King 2006). These hybrid civic/private practices rely not on 1960s-style clamor to generate social change, but on what Duggan (2003, 14) calls neoliberalism's "valorized concepts": privatization and personal responsibility. "In both arenas, neoliberals have promoted 'private' *competition, self-esteem,* and *independence* as the roots of *personal responsibility,* and excoriated 'public' *entitlement, dependency,* and *irresponsibility* as the source of social ills," Duggan writes (14, emphasis in original). Thus, within neoliberalism, individuals are expected to self-regulate: to take personal, private responsibility for their own (and others') vulnerabilities, be these educational, health-related, or monetary.

English-language voluntourism's proposal that wide-scale social or economic change in the Global South can be wrought by way of individual, short-term volunteer efforts, I suggest, may be read as a reflection of broader, neoliberal shifts in state formation and the new forms of citizenship that they engender. Within a neoliberal frame, to participate in volunteer tourism exemplifies proper civic action and personal virtuosity. One can address dissatisfactory social issues through consumption (i.e. the purchase of a volunteer vacation) while ostensibly providing others with the tools for life-long learning (i.e. the English language) and personal responsibility (i.e. increased self-esteem). Concurrently, to teach English language skills as a form of development assumes that Global South people truly need these additional language skills and can put them to practical use. In the following section, I explore this framing of English as an unquestionably useful tool for self- (and economic) improvement by drawing upon critical notions of EIL.

EIL

The proffered link between English language teaching and development within volunteer tourism, I offer, finds root in the critical notion of EIL. In this perspective, English is a symbolic and material commodity, a tool with high exchange value in an ever-expanding global marketplace (Heller 2010; Pennycook 2007; Phillipson 2000, 2001; Vavrus 2002). Some scholars (e.g. Holliday 2005; Rubdy 2009) use the term, EIL, to suggest that native speakers of prestige-variety English such as American Standard English or British Received Pronunciation no longer have a special purchase on English or its use (for related work on pluralistic notions of EIL, see Seidlhofer, Breiteneder, and Pitzl 2006). However, I employ the term, EIL, here to index what Pennycook (1999) calls the modernization model of English language spread. This is the idea that prestige-variety English issues exclusively from the Global North (hence, the salience of "native speakers") and is the language of: "computers, technology, science, tourism, diplomacy, internationalization, globalization, modern financial markets, the internet, e-learning, whatever is new" (Pennycook 1999, 6). Within a critical EIL framework, English is the language of "the world," and other languages are relegated to local, often distinctly more humble, purposes such as child-rearing, gossip, and religious practice. "Learning English has become a component of an *imagined global citizenship*, one of the many ways of *imagining globalization*," Niño-Murcia (2003, 121, emphasis in original) writes, and people throughout the world (to judge by the profitable industry that is English teaching) seem to concur (Phillipson 2000, 2001).

As my data below will demonstrate, English-language voluntourism discourse takes a near celebratory (Pennycook 2000) stance toward the English language, both in its current state and in the expectation of its expansion. English-language voluntourism discourse offers continually and without question that English language skills will help people in the Global South, whatever it is that individuals might do with these skills. Heller (2010) suggests that such uncritical acceptance and promotion of English is evidence of neoliberalism. She writes that: "[F]ormer colonial powers explicitly attempt to reconstitute their former empires as economic markets and to recast the former language of empire as a neutral and equitable means for gaining access to the global economy" (105). Using her argument as a frame (and following Phillipson 2001), I offer that English-language voluntourism's celebratory promotion of English (particularly in the name of development) may be read as a mechanism through which neoliberal prerogatives are maintained, naturalized, and expanded. As Phillipson (2000) reports:

> [t]hroughout the entire post-colonial world, English has been marketed as the language of "international communication and understanding," economic "development," "national unity," and similar positive ascriptions, but these soft-shell terms obscure the reality of globalization, which is that the majority of the world's population is being impoverished, that natural resources are being plundered in unsustainable ways, [and] that the global cultural and linguistic ecology is under threat. (99)

Despite its pretensions to altruism, then, English-language voluntourism may in fact be aiding and abetting the very formations and ideologies that lead to structural inequities in the first place.

Moreover, the disconcerting reality of EIL is that English language skills alone rarely deliver on the material or social goods that the discourse around it promises. In the realm of long-term, sustained English language teaching in the Global South, broad tensions already exist at the intersection of language and development. Despite evidence that reduction in economic vulnerability (particularly among adult women) is tied to strong primary, or first, language literacy, English language education programs claim scarce resources in the Global South (Bruthiaux 2002). Other scholars point out that both quality English language education and the opportunity to use English are correlated to people's current social class positions rather than likely to change them (Niño-Murcia 2003). As Pennycook (1999) notes, *English as development* (a process in which English language learning is the development goal) is often confused with *English for development* (a process in which increased language capacities ostensibly help people to participate in development projects). In the English-language voluntourism context, EIL teaching stints are short, frequently conducted by inexperienced volunteers, and often disconnected from broader educational curricula. Consequently, it is unclear whether English-language voluntourism is *English as development*, *English for development*, or something else entirely. Sponsoring organizations and program participants themselves are often unsure, which leads to the findings of this study. Before explicating organizational and participant views, however, I detail my investigative methods.

Summer 2007 through January 2009: data collection

Data for this study were collected as part of a larger, multi-sited ethnography (Marcus 1995) that took place in three different settings. In the summer of 2007, I engaged in eight weeks of participant-observation in Costa Rica under the auspices of an NGO-sponsored English-language voluntourism program, paying approximately $4000 (US) to do so. In 2008, I worked as a program assistant for six weeks in the US organizational offices of the same NGO. From 2008 to 2010, I conducted research in the virtual world, where I examined over 20 programs' websites and promotional literature.

Thirty-four interview transcripts and 21 organizational websites formed the primary data corpus for this study. While engaging in participant-observation in Costa Rica, I conducted 14 open-ended, semi-structured interviews with 12 of the other 20 American volunteers in my cohort (two participants were interviewed twice). The other 20 interviews were conducted with former program participants in 2009 in the northeastern US city where my study's focal NGO is based. Purposeful sampling (Patton 2002) was used to identify and contact NGO program alumni who currently resided near the city and had volunteered in the past two years.

All 34 interviews lasted between 30 and 75 min, were audio-recorded, and later transcribed for analysis. An interview guide was used to prompt participants to discuss certain topics, including, but not limited to, their impressions of the volunteer experience, their motivations for having participated, their understandings of the role of English language teaching/learning in the communities in which they were serving (or had served), and their understandings of international development in education (the NGO's stated mission). Thirty-one of the 34 participants were between the ages of 18 and 22; the others were 25, 27, and 35, respectively. The youthful tenor of my interview participant group was consistent with broader demographic trends in volunteer tourism (TRAM 2008).

I also examined 21 organizational sponsors' websites and promotional literature. I used a process of purposeful sampling (Patton 2002) to identify organizations that: run 1–12-week English-language voluntourism programs; do not require program participants to have prior teaching experience; are non-sectarian; and are based in the USA or UK.

Both interview transcripts and sponsoring organizations' promotional materials were analyzed using a constructivist, grounded theory approach (Charmaz 2006). Key themes were developed deductively (based on ideas and categories implied in the academic literature or in the interview questions) as well as inductively (based on ideas and categories presented by participants' comments or in promotional material). In the next section, I discuss these themes, which illustrate the varying ways in which English-language voluntourism discourse relies on and recreates hyperglobalist and EIL concepts.

English for a myriad of purposes

English for the global

The language used in English-language voluntourism promotional materials frequently characterizes English language proficiency as part of a "global skill" set (GeoVisions n.d.), a component of a tool-kit from which users can ostensibly draw in order to access a global imaginary, or "world stage," as one organization calls it (Global Volunteers 2008). This discourse, what I call *English for the global*, suggests that unlimited opportunities exist on the so-called world stage and that English skills alone permit admittance. Projects Abroad (n.d.), a voluntourism sponsor, frames this idea as follows: "Brazilians are discovering that learning English is an important way to improve their lives and gain access to this increasingly globalized world." Similarly, Global Volunteers invites prospective applicants to: "[H]elp Chinese students and teachers prepare for work in the global arena, where English serves as the universal language of commerce, technology, and opportunity" (2002). Whether described as a "stage" or "arena," *the global* in *English for the global* is presented as terra firma, a locality set apart from or outside the purview of Global South peoples' current day-to-day lives. English is presented as the *lingua franca* of this imagined global terrain, and it is primarily through English language skills that people are allowed access to it (though through which modality, speaking, listening, reading, or writing, is unclear).

Program participants also used *English for the global* discourse in their explanations of English-language voluntourism's broader purpose. "I don't know if this is [the NGO's] goal," Scott, an in-service program participant said, "but it'll probably end up – if it at least succeeds in teaching English – in getting [local people] involved in their world" (7 July 2007). Another program participant, Heather, reflected on her service purpose in this way: "We're really just ... helping with the globalization needs of countries. You know, to sort of give these kids a foundation for a world that is becoming vastly more global" (27 July 2009). Here, we see *English for the global* as well as a confluence of individual and national interests. It is implied that if a nation-state's people possess English language skills, nation-states, by extension, can enter the global arena.

English for the local

Its promotion of a global imaginary notwithstanding, English-language voluntourism discourse also presents the need for English language skills as patently local. What I call *English for the local* discourse suggests that people of all ages throughout the world require English language skills right where they are, in place, to maintain their current standards of living or to make incremental progress toward the future. Volunteer Adventures (n.d.), a voluntourism sponsor, illustrates *English for the local* in claiming: "In an increasingly global society, English is rapidly becoming a basic requirement for economic and social progress." Here, the global is not a geographically distant place to which English language skills are essential for access. Rather, it is offered that the global has subsumed the local, rendering English language skills necessary for any and all people at multiple scales of life.

English for the local discourse, however, augurs more modest uses of the language than does *English for the global*. The latter is largely optimistic and often centers on expanding people's professional career prospects. WorldTeach (n.d.), for example, states that: "To access opportunities in an increasingly international economy and society, China's younger generation will need English language skills." Or, as Edward, an in-service program participant, commented, greater English language proficiency among rural Costa Ricans: "would allow for great opportunities for those kids as they begin to move into both tourism in Costa Rica and worldwide business as a whole" (3 July 2007). In contrast, *English for the local* discourse often ties English language skills to minimum quality of life issues at a local scale. The fact that many people in the Global South live without running water or in homes with dirt floors, for example, is framed as imminently addressable through *English for the local*. In the words of Projects Abroad:

> Costa Rica is attracting ever-increasing numbers of visitors, but many local people still live in very basic conditions. Knowledge of English is vital in order for them to make the most of growing opportunities for work in tourism and commerce. (n.d.)

Within *English for the local* discourse, "basic conditions" of life in the Global South are not the consequences of structural poverty, inequitable resource distribution, or the legacy of colonial policies. Rather, low standards of living are framed as the result of local people's current lack of English language skills, a deficiency that renders them unable to access the global that has now come to them. One volunteer tourism sponsor takes this idea so far as to suggest that the broad-scale provision of English language skills in Mexico might help to solve a particularly sticky problem there vis-à-vis people and place:

Our university host partners report that becoming fluent in English is a priority for their students, who laud volunteers' help in their career development. Your efforts will help Mexican university students gain the skills to find good jobs and prosper in their homeland. (Global Volunteers 2008)

It merits stressing that the local employment for which voluntourism sponsors claim English language skills are necessary bears little resemblance to the career tracks that supposedly exist in the global imaginary. *English for the global* discourse generally characterizes English language skills as providing entrée to greater, more expansive life options: e.g. "[Volunteers] help students master the English skills that open doors to better career opportunities" (Cross-Cultural Solutions n.d). Although what these "better career opportunities" actually are remains unstated, there is a suggestion that work in the global imaginary is well-paid and even white-collar. In contrast, *English for the local* portends distinctly more humble outcomes. As Global Service Corps (n.d.) states: "Our EFL program aims to improve students' conversation skills in English and prepare students to gain employment in Local and Internatonal NGOs, companies, and garment factories." Similarly, United Planet (n.d.) suggests that volunteers on its Peru program can: "work with a local Peruvian organization by ... helping with leather purse-making workshops, teaching English (which is an essential work skill in Cusco), and organizing activities for street children." Within *English for the local* discourse, then, English language skills no longer provide access to a global imaginary in which professional career opportunities abound in the knowledge economy. Characterized instead as a "work skill," English language proficiency becomes the means by which local people can find employment making mass-produced clothing or, perhaps, selling hand-hewn purses on the street.

English for competing/escaping poverty through employment

English-language voluntourism discourse also offers that English language skills can make people more competitive and thereby able to evade vulnerability. This discourse, what I call *English for competing/escaping poverty through employment*, offers that English language skills will provide people in the Global South with a value-added edge, a means of breaking free of meager material or social circumstances. This idea of movement or escape through English language skills is captured in the words of GeoVisions: "English is a much sought-after skill in Thailand and one that can lead to otherwise unattainable upward social mobility" (2011). Similarly, Global Volunteers explains that "[i]n many places, knowing English provides a passport out of poverty through employment" (2002), a metaphor that explicitly links English language skills to movement.

In conjunction with this notion of escape, the discourse of *English for competing/escaping poverty through employment* also intimates that possessing English language skills differentiates certain people from others, availing these marked individuals of wage-earning possibilities that are unavailable to the broader collective. Per Cross-Cultural Solutions, "in many of the communities where we work, language barriers can make it difficult to compete for sought-after opportunities" (n.d). This comment suggests that though scarce, job opportunities exist for those with English language skills.

The discourse of *English for completing/escaping poverty through employment* is productive in multiple ways. For one, it unhinges broad-scale sociopolitical problems from human creation or intervention. Volatile labor markets, insufficient employment opportunities, and minimal public safety nets are characterized not as structural problems in need of human-directed remedy, but as permanent conditions from which individuals can and should escape through the acquisition and use of English language skills. Second, unaddressed in *English for competing/escaping poverty through employment* is the fate of the remaining residents of resource-poor, Global South communities as more competitive, escape-minded English language learners earn their "passports out of poverty" and leave, be it figuratively or literally. The discourse makes no provisions for individuals who cannot or do not learn English, except, perhaps, to frame their poverty as an indictment for failing to do so. Moreover, as *English for competing/escaping poverty through employment* does not address the root causes of poverty, it offers little in the way of long-term, substantive change for the most vulnerable or greatest number of people.

Finally, *English for competing/escaping poverty through employment*'s consenting nod to individualism naturalizes life as a zero-sum game in which people are more rivals for scarce resources than they are members of larger, often symbolic and identity-affirming, communities. This discourse encourages people to differentiate themselves from the crowd and adopt new ways of being through English language learning, and whether such a goal is politically inflected or even culturally appropriate in particular contexts remains largely unexamined. As Heller (2002) notes in reference to the commodification of language, "the popularity of the view that language skills are [strictly] technical ... fails to account for the reality of the social categories which are at play" (62). Language use is often tied to identity, to new ways of thinking and being (Block and Cameron 2002); yet, English-language voluntourism discourse frames English language use as solely a skill, as something to be used or removed akin to a tool belt.

English for competing/escaping poverty through employment discourse did not go uncontested among study participants, however. Meaghan, interviewed in Costa Rica, noted that English-language voluntourism seems to pay little attention to the broader, cultural politics of its goals and work. She explained:

[W]hat [English-language voluntourism] is doing is, like, providing and, and spreading English as sort of the international language without necessarily much ... awareness of, like, the deeper meaning of all of that ... [L]ike, power-wise. Like ... "You, you can get so far with your native language, with Spanish, but, like, if you REALLY want to succeed, you need to speak the language that, like, they speak in the United States and England" ... [W]hat are the political implications of, like, teaching English in a country that's considered developing by, by other countries that consider themselves to be developed? So what are the politics of that? (9 June 2007)

Meaghan's commentary highlights some of the unchecked assumptions of *English for competing/escaping poverty through employment*. First, the discourse presumes that Global South people want to leave or separate themselves from their communities, especially if those communities are poor. Second, the discourse takes as *a priori* that for people in situations of vulnerability, taking on the language of a more powerful, outside group is both desirable and unproblematic.

English for leaving the rural

What I call *English for leaving the rural* is another discourse that circulates within English-language voluntourism. T*he rural* in English-language voluntourism is often presented as a constraining factor in people's lives; small or remote villages are frequently characterized as decreasing people's economic security, limiting their present and future happiness, and reducing their overall prospects. *English for leaving the rural* discourse proposes that traditional communities (while fun or exotic for visiting volunteers) are places to be vacated by permanent residents and that English language skills can grease the wheels of such movement. WorldTeach exemplifies this discourse in saying:

> [Our] volunteers have been able to provide rural students with more than just English education. They are also offering them access to greater economic opportunity. Graduates of the *Liceo Rural* program [the summer program on which volunteers worked in 2009] enter a professional network that offers them contacts and opportunities beyond their home village. (n.d.)

Here, it is offered that the rural must be transcended if one is to make the most of one's life, and English language skills can lead the way.

Program participants' commentary also reflected *English for leaving the rural*. Catherine, interviewed in Costa Rica, asserted that the rural students she was going to be teaching: "are going to be so thankful to have learned something ... they can maybe go out into a city in Costa Rica and practice [English], like, make more of a life for themselves" (5 June 2007). Relatedly, but in a more critical vein, many program participants noted that there had been few immediate applications for English language skills in the sites in which they had volunteered. Shrushti, a former volunteer in Costa Rica, observed that English language skills had been irrelevant to many of her host community's residents:

> [N]o one really spoke very much English ... [T]he people that learned and spoke English went ... into Quepos/Manuel Antonio ... [S]ome of [my students] ... really wanted to learn English, but a lot of them didn't because they were like, "Well, we're just gonna, like, grow up and work in the *cooperativa*, like, doing some kind of, like, field work with the vegetables or, like, the animals, so, like, what's the point of English?" (29 January 2009)

As Shrushti points out, *English for leaving the rural* implies that English language skills are linked to relocation. For people who find the idea of leaving their rural communities unappealing or not germane to their future life plans, English can hold little purpose.

English for personal empowerment

Another discourse reflected in English-language voluntourism is what I call *English for personal empowerment*. In this discourse, English language teaching and learning are linked to western, pop-psychology style, self-improvement traits such as self-esteem, confidence, and motivation. *English for personal empowerment* offers that through the process of memorizing English words, learning simple phrases, or practicing one's pronunciation, individuals can increase their cache of self-confidence, be filled with hope for the future, and build the positive feelings that ostensibly translate into personal agency. Global Crossroad (n.d.), a voluntourism sponsor, demonstrates *English for personal empowerment* in this description of one of its programs: "[P]articipants will work in an orphanage – sharing their love and time with the needy children, teaching them basic conversational English and encouraging them to face the challenging world where English is becoming more and more of a necessity." Here, teaching English is equated with life-coaching; offering "basic conversational English" is akin to preparing others to "face the challenging world."

Implicit in *English for personal empowerment* discourse is the idea that Global South people currently lack (and that Global North people possess the means of fostering) self-management traits such as positive thinking and personal responsibility. A key facet of *English for personal empowerment*, then, is the promotion of self-help characteristics redolent of Steven Covey's "Successories" line of motivational products. i to i Volunteering, a voluntourism sponsor, illustrates *English for personal empowerment* in this message to prospective volunteers: "Helping the children with special needs on [our] project[s] will undoubtedly bring you the biggest smiles possible when you sing, dance and help to enrich their lives with your enthusiasm" (n.d.). Suggested here is that life enrichment can occur not through the building of language skills alone, but through song, dance, and the elicitation of transnational smiles.

Program participants' talk also reflected *English for personal empowerment*. English language teaching was often characterized as more an exercise in offering personal support to Global South people than an instructional endeavor aimed at building additional language capacity. Morgan, interviewed in Costa Rica, expressed this view in an explanation of her volunteer role:

> I see, like, a lot of who I am as ... encouraging people in different ways. Like, just loving them and just supporting them, and I feel like I say "Good job!" in my class, like, at least 20 times. Like, I'm always like, "Good job! Good job!" Like, "You're doing well" – even if the sentence is completely wrong. 'Cause so much of, I feel like it's important – people just need encouragement. ... So. ... that legacy would be fantastic, if I could just leave them with the encouragement and just the will to love themselves and be better. (1 July 2007)

In the perspectives of some volunteers, then, whether students feel loved or encouraged under a volunteer's tutelage takes precedence over whether students learn any English. This view is epitomized by Morgan's admission that she offers students enthusiastic praise even if their language productions are incorrect. Rather than focusing on the effectiveness of their instruction or concerning themselves with how students might continue language learning at the end of their volunteer tenure, many participants were primarily focused on promoting student's self-esteem by way of English language teaching.

English-language voluntourism, then, is often more an exercise in promoting people's positive self-concepts than one in which focused, guided language study is central. This reflects a curious component of *English for personal empowerment* discourse: there is imagined to be a social domino effect following from the mere presence of an enthusiastic, visiting volunteer. Through transmitted energy and encouragement, people in the Global South can ostensibly increase their own levels of self-confidence and take on more personal responsibility; they can acquire the "soft skills" requisite for making their own life changes. Per Josie, a former program participant: "[If] I, for instance, volunteer – go to ... Ecuador, interact with those people, [it] maybe inspires them even in a little way ... that could, you know, move them forward to do something" (27 January 2009). Reflected here is the neoliberal idea that poverty, unemployment, and other dissatisfactory social problems are due to a lack of individual initiative and imagination; Josie frames the inhabitants of the Global South as needing "inspiration" to "move forward to do something."

To Josie's credit, language in English-language voluntourism promotional literature also frequently suggests that the motivational presence of a Global North volunteer does as much, if not more, for those in the Global South as any direct language instruction. Participants mimic the language they read on promotional websites and in brochures. In the words of Cross-Cultural Solutions:

> Your fluency in English motivates working adults and recent graduates to practice their English and improve career options. Your stay may be short, but ... [y]ou can bring new energy and enthusiasm to community members who are dedicated to social change. Your personal and professional path offers local people new insight into life, education, and careers overseas. (n.d.)

English language study within English-language voluntourism, then, is in large part *English for personal empowerment*. The classroom, more than a site of language study, is constructed as a contact zone in which people from the Global South can meet and be influenced by visiting volunteers from the Global North, people whose presence alone ostensibly provides motivation, inspiration, and heretofore unimagined life insights. Within English-language voluntourism, Global South language learners are constructed as entrepreneurial subjects – people who are "expected to adapt perpetually to constantly changing education and workplaces through the individual qualities of innovation, self-reliance and flexibility" (Nairn and Higgins 2007, 265), and it is the charge of visiting volunteers to encourage this adaption.

The discourse of *English for personal empowerment*, however, was also challenged by some program participants. Joanne, interviewed a year and a half after her service time in Costa Rica, expressed discomfort with English-language voluntourism in large part because of what she felt were the numerous, naïve assumptions behind *English for personal empowerment*. The extent of her criticism was such that she reported not wanting to participate in any similar volunteer programs in the future. She explained:

> [M]y criticism ... is couched in the broader criticism of, like, what international development work is currently ... it operates under an attempt to sort of ameliorate the situation of a lot of people materially ... with this word, like, "empowerment," but it doesn't change the structures at all ... .[I]f I was thinking like this two years ago, I probably wouldn't have gone and done it, because I currently, like, wouldn't go and do it again ... I realize how little I understand what I'm doing. And I would rather spend the next phase of my life understanding better before I go and, you know, participate in microfinance and "empower women" and all this stuff without knowing, like – having no idea what that means. (30 January 2009)

Joanne's clear identification of the concept, empowerment, as one that permeates English-language voluntourism and similar, intervention-type programs suggests the preeminence of this discourse. Further, that Joanne would not feel comfortable participating in English-language voluntourism again because of her reticence toward *English for personal empowerment* reveals not only the limited space that exists for challenging this discourse, but also the few opportunities program participants ever have for exploring its underlying precepts.

Conclusion

As noted above, volunteer tourism is becoming a visible enough social phenomenon that critiques of it have begun to appear in the popular media. However, these critiques are often restricted to themes around *cui bono*: i.e. who benefits more from volunteer tourism, volunteers or the recipients of their service? In this study, I sought to widen the scope of this discussion by investigating a different set of questions. The answers to the first two, "How is English language voluntourism represented and legitimated?" and "What discourses construct it as an altruistic practice?" reflect and provide some insights on the current historical moment.

The findings of this study suggest that English-language voluntourism is constructed as an altruistic practice because within English-language voluntourism discourse, English is a magical cure-all. It has the allure of symbolic capital (*English for the global*) and ostensible pragmatic use (*English for the local*). It is claimed to facilitate human capital (*English for competing/escaping poverty through employment*), and it supposedly allows one to follow a well-trodden development trajectory (*English for leaving the rural*). Finally, it offers, in the learning, the chance for one to develop personal responsibility (*English for personal empowerment*). Although these discourses are quite disparate (they even contradict one another at times), the fact that they cover so much ground makes them very difficult to contest. Additionally, when viewed as a whole, these five discourses together comprise a very specific version of the world.

English-language voluntourism's discursive framing of the English language as simultaneously global, local, a requisite commodity of a twenty-first-century shape-shifting portfolio, a tool for urbanization, and a means of accruing personal responsibility has real material effects. In essence, it relies on and recreates a discourse of hyperglobalism, along with its attendant ideologies. English-language voluntourism, then, in its ostensible provision of English language skills, bolsters ways of being in the world (e.g. people in constant motion, people as competitors, people as individually responsible for all aspects of their lives) that reflect neoliberal prerogatives as well as new forms of governmentality (Rose 1999).

The answer to my study's third question, however, suggests some alternative possibilities. In asking, "How and in what ways do English-language voluntourism program participants subscribe to or contest these altruistic discourses?", my study suggests that by virtue of participating in these programs, some people come to a critical awareness of the same ideological foundations on which English-language voluntourism is based. In the experience of volunteering, some facets of hyperglobalism and the fallacies of EIL become legible to program participants in a way they never were previously. Thus, English-language voluntourism programs may constitute nascent sites of resistance: spaces in which program participants are able to develop critiques of the dominance of hyperglobalism and EIL.

According to McMillon, Cutchins, and Geissinger (2003), "volunteering is one of the best ways to halt the tide of the nastier effects of globalization, and instead promote the benefits of international understanding and cooperation" (xxi). I take their comment one step further. In the case of English-language voluntourism, the aforementioned tide of globalization may not be halted by the actual volunteering. Instead, the hope for stemming this tide might come through participants' experiences: their reflections, in the final instance, of what "good" means to whom, and how we get there.

Note

1. The use of this term, *Global South*, indexes work in anthropology and critical geography that upsets the notion that industrialization indicates progress, and contests the idea that nations can be hierarchically ranked to indicate their economic, social, or cultural progress. Although "North" generally refers to the part of the world above the equator and "South" tends to identify nations below the equator, the terms Global North and Global South distinguish between social, technological, and economic differences rather than geographic location. These terms conceive of nation-states as existing in both present and historical relation to one another, and implicates the actions of the Global North in political, economic, and social problems arising in the Global South, such as: Belgium's exploitation of mineral and agricultural resources in its colony of the Congo and its accompanying "Dominer pour servir" (dominate to serve) policy toward the indigenous population; the US corporation Union Carbide India Limited's role and lack of accountability in the Bhopal Chemical Disaster; Royal Dutch Shell Oil's degradation of Ogoni land in Nigeria for the exploitation of oil reserves; and other actions taken by Global North nation-states that exacerbate global inequity and contribute to localized economic, political, and social problems in nation-states historically or currently under colonial rule.

References

Appadurai, Arjun. 1991. Global ethnoscapes: Notes and queries for a transnational anthropology. In *Recapturing anthropology: Working in the present*, ed. R.G. Fox, 191–210. Santa Fe, NM: School of American Research Press.
Block, David, and Deborah Cameron, eds. 2002. *Globalization and language teaching*. London: Routledge.
Bruthiaux, Paul. 2002. Hold your courses: Language education, language choice, and economic development. *TESOL Quarterly* 36, no. 3: 275–96.
Butcher, Jim. 2003. *The moralization of tourism: Sun, sand ... and saving the world?* London: Routledge.
Butcher, Jim, and Peter Smith. 2010. Making a difference: Volunteer tourism and development. *Tourism Recreation Research* 35, no. 1: 27–36.
Callanan, Michelle, and Sarah Thomas. 2005. Volunteer tourism: Deconstructing volunteer activities within a dynamic environment. In *Niche tourism: Contemporary issues, trends, and cases*, ed. M. Novelli, 183–200. Burlington, MA: Elsevier Butterworth-Heinemann.
Charmaz, Kathy. 2006. *Constructing grounded theory: A practical guide through qualitative analysis*. Los Angeles, CA: Sage.
Collins, Joseph, Stefano DeZerega, and Zahara Heckscher. 2002. *How to live your dream of volunteering overseas*. New York, NY: Penguin.
Cross-Cultural Solutions. n.d. New Rochelle, NY: Author. http://www.crossculturalsolutions.org (accessed May 6, 2009).
Dicken, Peter. 2003. *Global shift: Reshaping the global economic map in the 21st century*. New York, NY: Guilford Press.

Duggan, Lisa. 2003. *The twilight of equality? Neoliberalism, cultural politics, and the attack on democracy.* Boston, MA: Beacon Press.
Escobar, Arturo. 1995. *Encountering development: The making and unmaking of the third world.* Princeton, NJ: Princeton University Press.
Fitzpatrick, Laura. 2007. Vacationing like Brangelina: Does volunteer tourism do any good? *Time* 170, no. 4: 49–51.
GeoVisions. 2011. *Help instill confidence and skills to allow these children to be self-sufficient and productive members of society.* Chesterfield, NH: Author. http://www.geovisions.org/pages/557_community_work_at_an_orphanage_in_kanchanaburi.cfm (accessed January 23, 2011).
GeoVisions. n.d. Chesterfield, NH: Author. http://www.geovisions.org/pages/418_our_aims_for_sustainability.cfm (accessed May 23, 2009).
Global Crossroad. n.d. Irving, TX: Author. http://www.globalcrossroad.com (accessed January 23, 2011).
Global Service Corps. n.d. San Francisco, CA: Author. http://globalservicecorps.org (accessed May 6, 2009).
Global Volunteers. 2002. St. Paul, MN: Author. http://www.globalvolunteers.org (accessed May 8, 2009).
Global Volunteers. 2008. *Adventures in service.* St. Paul, MN: Global Volunteers.
Gray, Noella, and Lisa M. Campbell. 2007. A decommodified experience? Exploring aesthetic, economic, and ethical values for volunteer ecotourism in Costa Rica. *Journal of Sustainable Tourism* 15, no. 5: 463–82.
Harvey, David. 2007. *A brief history of neoliberalism.* Oxford: Oxford University Press.
Heath, Sue. 2007. Widening the gap: Pre-university gap years and the 'economy of experience'. *British Journal of Sociology of Education* 28, no. 1: 89–103.
Heller, Monica. 2002. Globalization and the commodification of bilingualism in Canada. In *Globalization and language teaching,* ed. D. Block and D. Cameron, 47–64. London: Routledge.
Heller, Monica. 2010. The commodification of language. *Annual Review of Anthropology* 39: 101–14.
Holliday, Adrian. 2005. *The struggle to teach English as an international language.* Oxford: Oxford University Press.
Holton, Robert. 2000. Globalization's cultural consequences. *Annals of the American Academy* 570, no. 4: 140–52.
Jaakson, Reiner. 2004. Globalization and neocolonialist tourism. In *Tourism and postcolonialism: Contested discourses, identities, and representations,* ed. C.M. Hall and H. Tucker, 169–83. London: Routledge.
Kachru, Braj. 1997. World Englishes 2000: Resources for research and teaching. In *World Englishes 2000,* ed. L.E. Smith and M.L. Forman, 209–51. Honolulu, HI: University of Hawaii Press.
King, Samantha. 2006. *Pink ribbons, Inc.: Breast cancer and the politics of philanthropy.* Minneapolis, MN: University of Minnesota Press.
Marcus, George. 1995. Ethnography in/of the world system: The emergence of multi-sited ethnography. *Annual Review of Anthropology* 24: 95–117.
McBride, Amanda M., and Michael M. Sherraden. 2007. *Civic service worldwide: Impacts and inquiry.* Armonk, NY: M.E. Sharpe.
McGee, Nancy G., and Carla A. Santos. 2005. Social change, discourse and volunteer tourism. *Annals of Tourism Research* 32, no. 3: 760–79.
McMillon, Bill, Doug Cutchins, and Anne Geissinger, eds. 2003. *Volunteer vacations: Short-adventures that will benefit you and others.* 8th ed. Chicago, IL: Chicago Review Press.
Nairn, Karen, and Jane Higgins. 2007. New Zealand's neoliberal generation: Tracing discourses of economic (ir)rationality. *International Journal of Qualitative Studies in Education* 20, no. 3: 261–81.
Niño-Murcia, Mercedes. 2003. "English is like the dollar": Hard currency ideology and the status of English in Peru. *World Englishes* 22, no. 2: 121–42.
Novelli, Marina, ed. 2005. *Niche tourism: Contemporary issues, trends, and cases.* Amsterdam: Elsevier.

Nye, Joseph. 2004. *Soft power: The means to success in world politics*. New York, NY: PublicAffairs.

Patton, Michael Quinn. 2002. *Qualitative research and evaluation methods*. 3rd ed. Thousand Oaks, CA: Sage.

Pennycook, A. 1999. Development, culture and language: Ethical concerns in a postcolonial world. Paper presented at the fourth international conference on Language and Development, October 13–15, in Hanoi, Vietnam. http://www.clet.ait.ac.th/hanoi_proceedings/pennycook.htm (accessed March 7, 2006).

Pennycook, A. 2000. English, politics, ideology: From colonial celebration to postcolonial performativity. In *Ideology, politics and language policies: Focus on English*, ed. T. Ricento, 107–20. Amsterdam: John Benjamins.

Pennycook, A. 2007. *Global English and transcultural flows*. New York, NY: Routledge.

Phillipson, R. 2000. English in the new world order: Variations on a theme of linguistic imperialism and 'World' English. In *Ideology, politics and language policies: Focus on English*, ed. T. Ricento, 87–106. Amsterdam: John Benjamins.

Phillipson, R. 2001. English for globalization or for the world's people? *International Review of Education* 47, nos. 3–4: 185–200.

Poon, A. 1993. *Tourism, technology, and competitive strategies*. Wallingford: CABI.

Projects Abroad. n.d. New York, NY: Author. http://www.projectsabroad.org (accessed January 23, 2011).

Putnam, Robert. 2000. *Bowling alone: The collapse and revival of American community*. New York, NY: Simon and Schuster.

Rose, Nikolas. 1999. *Powers of freedom: Reframing political thought*. Cambridge: Cambridge University Press.

Rubdy, Rani. 2009. Reclaiming the local in teaching EIL. *Language and Intercultural Communication* 9, no. 3: 156–74.

Sachs, Wolfgang, ed. 1992. *The development dictionary: A guide to knowledge as power*. London: Zed Books.

Seidlhofer, Barbara, Angelika Breiteneder, and Marie-Luise Pitzl. 2006. English as a lingua franca in Europe: Challenges for applied linguistics. *Annual Review of Applied Linguistics* 26: 3–34.

Simpson, Kate. 2004. "Doing development": The gap year, volunteer tourists and a popular practice of development. *Journal of International Development* 16, no. 5: 681–92.

Snow, Donald. 2001. *English teaching as Christian mission: An applied theology*. Scottdale, PA: Herald Press.

Swarbrooke, John, Colin Beard, Suzanne Leckie, and Gill Pomfret. 2003. *Adventure tourism: The new frontier*. Oxford: Butterworth Heinemann.

Tergesen, Anne. 2011. Saving the world – one vacation at a time. http://online.wsj.com/article/SB10001424052970203503204577039980243232616.html (accessed December 24, 2011).

TRAM. 2008. *Volunteer tourism: A global analysis*. New Amsterdam: Atlas.

Ullman, Char. 2012. "My grain of sand for society": Neoliberal freedom, language learning, and the circulation of ideologies of national belonging. *International Journal of Qualitative Studies in Education* 25, no. 4: 453–70.

United Planet. n.d. Boston, MA: Author. http://www.unitedplanet.org (accessed May 7, 2009).

Urry, John. 2002. *The tourist gaze*. 2nd ed. London: Sage.

Vavrus, Frances. 2002. Postcoloniality and English: Exploring language policy and the politics of development in Tanzania. *TESOL Quarterly* 36, no. 3: 373–97.

Villano, Matt. 2009. Silver-spoon voluntourism: Luxury hotels offer day trips to help vacationers connect with communities. *Time* 174, no. 19.

Volunteer Adventures. n.d. Denver, CO: Author. http://www.volunteeradventures.com/projects_teaching.htm (accessed May 22, 2009).

Wearing, Stephen. 2001. *Volunteer tourism: Experiences that make a difference*. Wallingford, CT: CABI.

Wearing, Stephen, Matthew McDonald, and Jess Ponting. 2005. Building a decommodified research paradigm in tourism: The contribution of NGOs. *Journal of Sustainable Tourism* 14, no. 5: 424–39.

WorldTeach. n.d. Cambridge, MA: Author. http://www.worldteach.org (accessed May 12, 2009).

"My grain of sand for society": neoliberal freedom, language learning, and the circulation of ideologies of national belonging

Char Ullman

> This article explores the ways in which neoliberal discourses of individual freedom and choice come to typify Mexican migrants' talk about what it means to be living in the USA and about themselves as learners of English. Interviews with migrants about the English language program *Inglés Sin Barreras* [English without Barriers] provide the context for these discursive displays. *Inglés Sin Barreras* is advertized repeatedly throughout the day on Spanish language TV, and it is an English language program that comprises 12 books, workbooks, CDs, and DVDs. *Inglés Sin Barreras* acts as a storehouse for ideas about personal freedom, citizenship, and the importance of English in belonging to the USA as a nation.

Introduction

> Unfree subjects ... have to be *made* free in a process that entails the transformation of educational practices to inculcate certain attitudes and values of enterprise, changes in television programmes ranging from soap operas to game shows to implant the desire for wealth creation and personal enterprise ... (Rose 1999, 68)

How do neoliberal discourses of individual freedom and choice come to characterize the ways in which Mexican migrants living in Arizona talk about themselves as learners of English and as people who live in or belong to the USA? I explore this question through analyzing interviews with Mexican transmigrants about a particular and peculiar commodity whose presence is persistently ubiquitous in the lives of Spanish-speaking migrants[1]: *Inglés Sin Barreras* [English without Barriers]. *Inglés Sin Barreras* is an English language program for Spanish speakers who want to learn English, and it comprises 12 books, workbooks, CDs, and DVDs. Award-winning commercials for *Inglés Sin Barreras* air continually on both Univisión and Telemundo. The program usually costs anywhere from $1200 to $3000, depending on how well one negotiates with the company's skilled salespeople (Ullman 2010a). *Inglés Sin Barreras,* the commodity, along with its television advertising, act as repositories for ideas about personal freedom, citizenship, and the importance of English in belonging to the USA as a nation (Warriner 2004, 2007a, 2008). Indeed,

Inglés Sin Barreras, whether people use it or not, is a node through which Spanish-speaking migrants are inculcated with discourses of personal enterprise and where they grapple with their own brand of self-making.

Neoliberal discourses

As Harvey (2005) notes, in order for any idea to find political purchase, it must be embedded in a "conceptual apparatus" that speaks compellingly to the hearts and minds of a populace. Neoliberalism has such an apparatus. Its key ideas are those of individual freedom and choice, and they are quite saleable. These concepts must be protected not only from, "fascism, dictatorships, and communism, but ... [from] all forms of state intervention that substitute[d] collective judgements for those of individuals free to choose" (5). Neoliberalism vilifies state-sponsored programs for education and healthcare, framing them as invasions of personal freedom. Also known as advanced or late capitalism, neoliberalism represents a move away from the Keynesian solution to the problem of the liberal state. Keynes (2009) argued that the inevitable conflict between the owning class/government and its laborers could be forfended by government supported educational and healthcare benefits to be made available to the working class.

Advocates of neoliberalism reject this idea as an infringement on the choice and freedom of the citizen, which they see as sacrosanct. The role of the state, in their view, is purely to maintain law and order. That is, the wealth that has been generated by the elite, thanks to the neoliberal model, is understood to be the result of creating a protected space in which talented individuals can "use their abilities for their own purposes" (Rose 1999, 63). Bansel (2007) describes neoliberalism as a philosophy that disconnects government from the social realm, and more closely connects the individual to the market.

Davies (2005) argues that neoliberal discourses remove the social realm, replacing it with "the dream of possessions and wealth for each individual who ... gets it right" (10). Davies identifies the key themes of the neoliberal worldview as consumption, individual responsibility, the self adrift from values, surveillance, and autonomy. In the neoliberal political world, citizens must take responsibility for their own conduct and consequences, and that means previously state-run institutions, such as education, healthcare, welfare, and security come to be seen as individual responsibilities.

Bansel (2007) sees neoliberalism as referring: "to historically specific and variable ways of talking that are produced both in the apparatuses through which everyday lives are governed and the discourses through which lives are constituted" (285).

The issue of governing, or more specifically, Foucault's notion of governmentality is crucial to understanding neoliberal regimes. Governmentality, or "the conduct of conduct" (Burchell, Gordon, and Miller 1991, 48), emphasizes a variety of control techniques, including control of the self and of populations. Lemke (2000) notes that Foucault (1988, 1994) was concerned with the ways in which autonomous individuals come to learn self-control, and how this is connected to systems of political power and the exploitation of working people. Governmentality can be understood as the process through which a form of government with particular goals (and those goals always include a perdurable social order) maintains itself through the creation of security (i.e., surveillance), the production of a particular type of political economic knowledge, and the creation of citizens who allow governments to realize their policies.

Neoliberalism is merely one form of governmentality. While there are great similarities in the practices engaged in by various neoliberal regimes, neoliberalism is not reducible to a set of practices. Rather, neoliberalism is a historically particular mode of government, and when it is articulated through technologies of the self, these modes and techniques become one version of Foucault's notion of governmentality. According to Foucault, governmentality involves structuring "the possible field of action of others" (Foucault 1994, 341). This includes both the policing of the state and the policing of the self.

As the state is relieved of the responsibility to care for its people through the neoliberal mode of governmentality, the role of the neoliberal subject expands. Key to neoliberal regimes is the role of the market in constituting and regulating subjects. It is characterized by a constantly changing relationship between "the state, the economy, civil society, government, the market, and the subject" (Bansel 2007, 285). The subject of the neoliberal world must become, as Nikolas Rose puts it, "an entrepreneur of the self" (Rose 1999, 142).

Brown (2006) argues that:

> what we have in neoliberalism and neoconservatism, then, is a market-political rationality and a moral-political rationality, with a business model of the state in one case and a theological model of the state in the other. (698)

She uses the term "political rationality" in a Foucauldian sense, noting that it is, "a specific form of normative political reason organizing the political sphere, governance practices, and citizenship" (693). *Inglés Sin Barreras* works to produce the good, neoliberal subject by making individuals into the right kind of citizens through the consumption of an expensive English language program. A technology of the self, *Inglés Sin Barreras,* focuses on the individual. The state, on the other hand, has used anti-immigrant laws such as State Bill (SB) 1070 (the Arizona law that requires all people who might appear to be undocumented to carry legal documents with them at all times) and SB 2281 (the Arizona law that prohibits ethnic studies, or any studies that treat people as members of groups and not as individuals) to strengthen a neoconservative idea of the "right kind" of White state. Both *Inglés Sin Barreras* and these controversial pieces of Arizona legislation work to create citizens who are concurrently racialized and de-racialized. That is, migrants must disavow their status as migrants through the kind of consumption that is associated with becoming a US citizen who speaks English, while at the same time they are surveilled by the state, based on racialized identity markers that may or may not signal their legal status. There is a powerful tension between resistance and regulation in the production of the neoliberal subject.[2]

The production of the entrepreneurial subject

How is it that neoliberal subjects are formed? Davies and Banks (1992) argue that it is vital to consider how subjectivities are produced, made material, and given "pattern through storyline" (3). Along with the importance of storyline, the continual repetition or iteration of identity is key to subject formation (Butler 1997).

For Foucault, governmentality includes the history of statecraft, but is inextricably entwined with "technologies of the self" (Martin, Gutman, and Hutton

1988), or the personal internalization of the norms of the neoliberal subject. He argues that self-inhibition is key, and that schools, textbooks, and teachers (among other contexts) have been central to its development (Foucault 1977). It is through the process of self-policing, continually regulating one's thoughts and behaviors in relation to particular social norms, that people come to be neoliberal subjects.

The ways in which these ideas of neoliberalism have played out in New Zealand, a particularly neoliberal educational context, have been provocatively explored in a 2007 special issue of this journal (Bansel 2007; Davies and Bansel 2007; Duncan 2007; Nairn and Higgins 2007; Watkins 2007). But how might neoliberal subjects both embrace and resist these powerful norms in other contexts? For people who have migrated to the USA from Mexico, and whose presence in the new nation is often disparaged (Chavez 2008), this need to become the right kind of subject/citizen can be especially powerful.

Most Mexican migrants in the USA are economic migrants, migrating not for ideological reasons (as some Cuban migrants have) but out of economic necessity, with the will to improve a family's life chances for the next generation. As such, economic migrants have been characterized as being more entrepreneurial than their counterparts who stayed home (Chiswick 2000). Does that make Mexican migrants better neoliberal subjects? Perhaps one of the important differences between the neoliberal discourses in Mexico and the USA is that in Mexico people who cannot afford to go to school go to work, usually in manual labor. Because public schools in Mexico require that families buy uniforms and pay *útiles* (a fee for school supplies), many working people, especially in rural areas, cannot attend school through graduation. People who leave school in the elementary years usually stay in manual labor throughout their lives. While there is an adult education system in Mexico, the Instituto Nacional de Educación para los Adultos, the concept of lifelong learning (Bansel 2007) is less institutionalized for working people in Mexico than it is in the USA. This means that the concept of funding one's own lifelong learning is a new discourse for many Mexican migrants. As these data make clear, the discourse of self-funded language learning is an idea that all the participants in this study have adopted.

Regardless of a person's social position, the neoliberal state imposes the idea of self-reliance and individual responsibility on its citizens, and this is especially true for migrants. Rose (1999) notes:

> No longer is there a conflict between the self-interest of the economic subject and the patriotic duty of the citizen: it now appears that one can best fulfil one's obligations to one's nation by most effectively pursuing the enhancement of the economic well-being of oneself, one's family, one's firm. (145)

Rose recommends that citizenship be understood not solely in terms of formal legal belonging to the nation-state, but also in terms of practices, technologies, and habits of mind. Ong (2003) sees modern citizenship similarly, suggesting that it involves "the everyday processes of being made and self-making" (xvii), and that freedom, autonomy, and security are the concepts with which all migrants must grapple. Part of this self-making involves becoming the right kind of citizen, and the good neoliberal citizen is a consumer.

Consumption

Canclini (2001) suggests that the nation can no longer be understood as a territorial delineation or even as people who share a particular political history. Rather, the nation is now "an interpretive community of consumers" (43). Noting that working people in one country may have more in common with working people in another country than they do with the elite from their own nation, Canclini stresses that participating in consumption is the foundation of identification. That is, transnational circuits of consumption have come to replace more narrow notions of the nation.

Anthropologists have long been critical of simplistically conceptualizing consumption as naive consumers being duped by clever advertisers (Appadurai 1986; Douglas and Isherwood 1979). Consumption is better understood as a social process that is as much about communicating symbolic needs as it is about the things themselves. Because objects only gain value through their social use, consumption is never an isolated, individual act. As the neoliberal state relinquishes its role in the domains of education and social welfare, the symbolic value of commodities like *Inglés Sin Barreras*, in both expressing national belonging as well as distinction from others, becomes central.

Inglés Sin Barreras

How is it that *Inglés Sin Barreras*, a seemingly modest English language program, has become a nexus of neoliberal discourses for Mexican migrants? *Inglés Sin Barreras* is the most advertised product on Spanish language television, more advertised in fact, than Coca Cola or McDonald's. Ads for the program appear all day on both Univisión and Telemundo. *Inglés Sin Barreras* is mentioned in the lyrics of Spanish rap songs; it is joked about on the popular variety show, *Sabado Gigante*; and it was featured in the film *Spanglish* (Porter 2002). When I conducted a survey of 300 Spanish-speaking migrants in 2006 at an adult education center in Tucson, Arizona, 99% of participants knew about the program, even people who had been in the USA for fewer than two days. The one percent who did not know about the program was comprised of people who did not have Spanish literacy, so they could not complete the survey.

It is important to note that *Inglés Sin Barreras* can cost up to $3000, and most people buy it at 21% interest. As I have argued elsewhere (Ullman 2010a, 2010b), *Inglés Sin Barreras* operates as a kind of symbolic citizenship. The program is a commodity that comes to stand in for national belonging for some migrants, especially for unauthorized workers for whom the possibility of legal citizenship has been foreclosed. Buying *Inglés Sin Barreras* represents an investment in one's US identity, regardless of whether one attempts to use it to learn English. *Inglés Sin Barreras* also operates as a status symbol among Spanish-speaking migrants, many of whom conspicuously carry the brightly colored books to their English for speakers of other languages (ESOL) classes or wear the iconic tiny spelling dictionary on a key chain on their belt loops or purses. One woman told me that she matched her clothes to the red, white, blue, and gold logo on the key chain, because it was like a piece of expensive jewelry. *Inglés Sin Barreras* is, without a doubt, a pop-culture phenomenon.

Inglés Sin Barreras presents basic English to Spanish speakers, beginning with most of the talk in Spanish, and moving gradually to a bit more of the talk being in English. Employing an audio-lingual approach to language learning, the program focuses on learners producing perfect English sentences. While *Inglés Sin Barreras* is organized around themes such as going to the doctor, going to the grocery store, etc., it is an amended version of the situational approach (Hornby 1950), because the grammatical structures are only minimally controlled.

The 11th volume of the 2007 revision of *Inglés Sin Barreras* deals with the process of becoming a naturalized US citizen. Focusing on the naturalization interview, which includes a test of speaking, reading, and writing in English, as well 100 questions that are part of the civics test, this text zeroes in on the details of the citizenship process for those who are eligible. It includes a list of the 50 states and their capitals, as well as advice about the need to practice English conversation. Terrill (2000) notes that while some people still think of citizenship study as memorizing answers to test questions (the approach taken in *Inglés Sin Barreras*), most contemporary educators think of citizenship content as a way for students to continue practicing English and learn to function well in the USA.

The data I discuss in this article are part of a larger ethnographic project that looks at the ideologies and identities that Mexican migrants produce in relationship to *Inglés Sin Barreras*. I have found that of the more than 140 people I spoke with about the program, most people have looked only at the first volume and few people have gotten past the third. Many people told me that *Inglés Sin Barreras* was boring. Some people said the program was too difficult while others deemed it overly simple. Only two people, a married couple from Cananea, Sonora, Mexico, reported actually completing the 12-volume series. Soon after their triumph, the couple were tested at the community center where I conducted this research and they placed into the most basic level of English offered at the school, level one.

The state of the migrant in the state of Arizona

In April 2010, Arizona, a US state that borders the Mexican state of Sonora, distinguished itself by enacting what was then the harshest anti-immigrant legislation that the nation had seen in more than two decades, SB 1070. This bill required police to request legal documentation of anyone they might imagine to be in the USA without authorization during any lawful stop, detention, or arrest. SB 1070 made it a state misdemeanor, a crime, for migrants to be in Arizona without carrying the necessary documents at all times. The bill was amended soon after its introduction, morphing into House Bill (HB) 2162, which was intended to address concerns about racial profiling. HB 2162 merely lessened the fines and length of incarceration initially proposed in SB 1070. But while protests against the Arizona law were held in more than 70 cities across the country, and the US Department of Justice filed a federal injunction against the legislation, other states continue to propose similar legislation. As of late 2010, 25 of the 50 US states were working on legislation that in some way resembles SB 1070 (Immigration Works 2010).

At the same time that SB 1070 dominated the news cycle, SB 2281, the Anti-Ethnic Studies legislation passed the Arizona legislature. This law prohibits publicly funded classes, from the elementary school level through university, that are designed for students of a particular ethnic group. Particularly targeted was Tucson Unified School District's Mexican American/Raza Studies program, an innovative curriculum that has become a site of intense political struggle (Cammarota 2009). SB 2281 states that students should be taught to interact as individuals and not as members of races or classes, in essence outlawing culturally responsive teaching throughout the state (Gay 2000; Ladsen-Billings 1995). SB 2281 is a clear attempt to produce the illusory de-racialized citizen. The law explicitly prevents the teaching of any subject that might promote ethnic solidarity, again focusing on the individual, with anything related to group identity framed as an infringement on individual rights.

However, anti-immigrant sentiment had been brewing in Arizona for years before SB 1070 and SB 2281 made international headlines. In 2000, Proposition 203 was passed and it outlawed bilingual education in the state. At the time, Arizona was 25% Latino, and by 2011, that number was up to 30% (US Census 2010). In 2006, Proposition 103 made English the official language of Arizona (similar legislation that had been proposed in 1986 was found to be unconstitutional) and Proposition 300 was passed that same year. Proposition 300 restricted the use of family literacy and adult education programs to people with valid visas, which has led to the eventual decimation of adult education in Arizona.

Methods of data collection

The data I discuss in this article are part of a larger ethnographic study about the ideologies and identities that Spanish-speaking migrants produce in relation to *Inglés Sin Barreras*. I began the study in 2006 with a survey of 300 Spanish-speaking migrants at three adult education centers in Tucson, Arizona, and I found that 13% of the 300 people interviewed owned or had access to *Inglés Sin Barreras*. That led to interviews with 40 people (13%) who had the program. I also conducted an ethnographic study with employees of the Lexicon Corporation, the company that produces *Inglés Sin Barreras,* and I conducted a reception study with 100 migrants about how they interpret the ads for *Inglés Sin Barreras*. I had planned to conduct ethnographic work with three families who owned *Inglés Sin Barreras,* but this work was interrupted by three seismic events. The first was the economic downturn of 2007 which led many people involved in the study to leave Arizona, because employment, especially in the construction industry, had become scarce. Secondly, Proposition 300 was passed at the end of 2006, and that legislation limited access to adult education for migrants, requiring participants to have a valid visa in order to attend classes. The increased surveillance of Mexicans and Mexican Americans led people with and without legal documents to retreat into the shadows. Hostility towards immigrants in Arizona that had been building for at least 10 years increased exponentially. The third event was the passage of SB 1070 in 2010. I found that people I had identified to participate in the final stage of the study were moving to other US states or were returning to Mexico. This made it impossible for me to complete in-depth ethnographic work with three families, which I had scheduled for the final phase of the study (Table 1).

Table 1. Project overview.

Research activities	Participants	Location	Dates
Survey	300	Tucson, AZ	2005
Interviews	40	Tucson, AZ	2006–2008
Ethnographic study at the Lexicon Corporation	26	Beverly Hills, CA; Tijuana, Mexico	2007
Reception study	100	Tucson, AZ	2008–2011
In-depth ethnographic work	3 families	Tucson, AZ	Interrupted

The participants and the researcher

The data discussed in this article come from interviews I conducted with Mexican migrants living in Tucson, Arizona between 2006 and 2008. The people who participated in the interview phase of this study were taking English classes at an adult education center in Tucson, Arizona, and they all had access to *Inglés Sin Barreras*. Some of them had bought it, others had borrowed it from a family member or friend, and still others had borrowed it from the public library. I solicited interview participants by attending ESOL classes (with the teacher's permission) and using the final few minutes of class to explain the project in Spanish. I asked people who were interested to talk with me individually after class. All interviews were conducted in Spanish, and I have translated them here.

I had been an ESOL teacher at this adult education program for five years prior to conducting this research, and during my time as a teacher in the program, I had been part of an informal network of educators who advocated for the rights of unauthorized students. These two aspects of my history facilitated the study. Indeed, the political climate in Arizona had become so hostile in recent years, that if I had not begun this work with a level of trust already established, it would have been impossible for me, as a white, non-immigrant woman to have gained entrée into this community. Being explicit about my history at the school helps to contextualize the fact that a significant number of study participants openly spoke with me about their unauthorized status in the USA.

Hedging his bets: Angel

Rose notes that modern individuals are not merely "free to choose," but are obliged to "be free, to understand and enact their lives in terms of choice" (Rose 1999, 86). That sense of obligation was powerfully present in all my interviews with people whom I asked to talk about their experiences with *Inglés Sin Barreras* (see Appendix 1, question protocol). Angel[3] was 27 when we spoke, and he is from Sonora, Mexico. He had been in the USA for four months, and was working in maintenance at a large apartment complex on the city's west side. He had completed some high school in Mexico, and had borrowed *Inglés Sin Barreras* from his sister. He had had the program for two years when we talked (Table 2).

Table 2. Angel (Excerpt 1 – see Appendix 2 for transcription conventions).

1	Si cambio de trabrajo	If I change my job
2	y no puedo assister a la escuela	and I cannot come to school
3	o si no haiga clases	or there are no more classes available
4	que se haga con mi horario	that can go with my schedule
5	((tos))	((cough))
6	Aunque deberI:A de posible asister a la clase	And even though I SHOU:LD come to class
7	((tos))	((cough))
8	Y mirar el *Inglés Sin Barreras*	and watch *Inglés Sin Barreras*
9	No pero pues, no lo hago.	But I, I do not do it.
10	A veces lo hago	I sometimes try to do it
11	A veces lo hago	I sometimes try to do it
12	Pero pues llega uno cancado a su casa.	But then one gets home so tired.

Angel talked about using *Inglés Sin Barreras* as a back-up plan, in case he was to change jobs and/or was no longer able to attend school. Acknowledging the instability of work for migrants, Angel also pointed to the transportation barrier that many migrants in Tucson faced at the time, as busses ran during the day, and adult education classes were offered at night. Angel attended ESOL classes 20 hours a week when we spoke, and he was right to be nervous that publicly funded classes might disappear, because they did. Before the passage of Proposition 300 in 2006, there were 3000 ESOL students at the adult education program in Tucson. Governor Jan Brewer's 2011 budget eliminated ESOL and General Educational Development (GED) programs across the state. Currently, a limited number of community college classes are available (supported by other funding sources), and there are ESOL classes sponsored by the non-profit organization, Literacy Volunteers of America. The once vibrant adult education offerings throughout the state have paled significantly. It is evident that learning English is now an endeavor that must be privately funded.

Everything in Angel's statement speaks to his sense of personal responsibility to educate himself in English, and to prepare for economic and political uncertainty. Bansel (2007) notes that "self-funded lifelong learning" (288) is part of life for the neoliberal subject. At the same time, Angel framed his narrative in terms of failing to succeed as a neoliberal subject. He tried to take English classes and use *Inglés Sin Barreras,* but he was too tired to do so. It is significant that he switched from *I* to the proform *one,* distancing himself from the action, when he admitted that he comes home and does not use *Inglés Sin Barreras.* Angel has determined that his self-management is lacking, emphasizing what he SHOULD/deberI:A do, but is unable to accomplish.

The language imperative: María

María is also from Sonora, Mexico, and was a stay-at-home mother of three when we spoke. At 31, she had completed some high school in Mexico, and had been in the USA for five years. She convinced her husband to buy the program three years before we spoke. She told me that buying *Inglés Sin Barreras* was a crucial investment in her family's future. She reiterated the official discourse that migrants need

Table 3. María (Excerpt 2).

1	La gente que realmente quiera aprenderse tiene que dedicarles.	People that really want to learn need to dedicate themselves.
2	Y es otra actividad importante	And it is another important action
3	que uno TIENE QUE hacer	that one NEEDS to do
4	para poder vivir en este país, TIENES que hablar el inglés dondequiera!	in order to live in this country, you NEED TO speak English everywhere!
5	No estas en tu país.	You are not in your country.
6	TIENES QUE aprender a hablar con la gente de aqui.	You NEED TO learn how to speak with people from here.
7	Cada quien tiene sus necesidades	Everybody has their desires for learning
8	No de aprender y va a aprender en el momento que uno	And one will learn in the moment that one
9	disponga de su tiempo.	puts one's time into it.
10	Y su meta y a lograr algo.	And they have a goal and want to accomplish something.
11	Pues, TIENES QUE hacerlo	Well, you HAVE TO do it

to learn English, and interestingly, she told me this in Spanish. Notice the modal *have to*, as well as *want to* and *need to* (tenir que, querer, and deber que). Her word choice resonates with Angel's self-admonition that he SHOULD go to English classes along with watching *Inglés Sin Barreras* (Table 3).

María distanced herself from this vision of what migrants must do in order to belong in the USA by using "People/La gente; one/uno; everybody/cada quien, and you/tu." She very consistently avoided any statements with the first-person singular form. At the same time, María made clear that living on US soil means that one is obliged to learn English and to use it in a variety of settings. Indeed, María's dedication to this language ideology of speaking English everywhere was striking. She told me about her view in Spanish, and right around the time that we spoke, Proposition 103 had made English the official language of Arizona. It is significant that María talked about the norms of how one must act while living on US soil (use English everywhere), but her references to US citizens were vague. After I stopped recording, María told me that she and her husband were unauthorized, but that all of their children were US citizens. At that point, I asked her to tell me more about her belief that people need to speak English everywhere. She explained that her goal was to learn English and to speak English as well as her children did, but she still hoped there would be a place for Spanish somewhere in her family. As I asked more questions, her stance softened a bit.

In the last section, María focused assertively and quite generally on migrants needing to have the will to study English and to accomplish their goals. María's utterance aligns resoundingly with Bansel's (2007) description of the neoliberal discourse of freedom that, "individuals succeed or fail by dint of their own self-discipline, hard work, personality, ambition, and effort" (298). Bansel goes on to say, and I concur, that this view erases the constraints of the labor market, as work is not equally available to all. This is especially the case for someone like María, who is an unauthorized worker.

Self-management and personal responsibility: Raul

Some people talked about there being a correct way to use *Inglés Sin Barreras*, implying that if they had in fact used it the right way, they would not have had to have attended a publicly funded school. Raul was 48 when we spoke, and had lived in the USA for 21 years. For the past 10 years, he had run his own construction business specializing in stucco work. Increasingly, he found the work too physically demanding and he was learning English in order to find a more sedentary job. Hav-

Table 4. Raul (Excerpt 3).

1	Mire, de hecho	Well, the truth is
2	a mí me lo pasó un amigo a mí, *Inglés Sin Barreras*.	that a friend passed *Inglés Sin Barreras* onto me.
3	Ahí aprendió inglés.	He learned English from it.
4	Pero si 'staba, pues si lo estudió todo bien a como era	But he used it the way he was supposed to
5	y no hubo necesidad de que viniera a la escuela.	and there was no need for him to go to school.
6	Pero yo, No.	But not me.
7	Aquí estoy en la escuela.	Here I am in school.

ing migrated from the Mexican state of Jalisco, Raul had to quit school in Mexico after third grade, so that he could work to support his family. He bought *Inglés Sin Barreras* four years before we spoke, and he stressed that he did not buy it from the company, but from a friend, and he got a bargain: he paid $500 for it (Table 4).

Raul represented going to school as a result of his not having used *Inglés Sin Barreras* correctly. It is significant that he framed going to a publicly funded school as a kind of embarrassment, something that must be done when one does not, as Davies suggests, "do the right thing" (Davies and Bansel 2010, 11). That is, the personally responsible thing to do is to purchase *Inglés Sin Barreras* and use it correctly. Even though Raul was a good consumer, in that he bought *Inglés Sin Barreras*, he understood himself to have failed at being an "entrepreneur of the self" because he did not use the product as it should have been used.

I asked Raul how he used the program and what was "incorrect" about it. He evaded my questions until finally, he confessed that he had watched little more than an hour of the first volume of the program. He could not make himself use it, because it was boring. He talked about his not using the program as "a failure of the will/una falta de voluntad." This interpretation takes the program itself, its quality and the effectiveness of its pedagogical approach, out of the conversation, and makes learning English solely an individual responsibility. This perspective aligns seamlessly with Bansel's (2007) description of the neoliberal mantra, that individual subjects are imbued with the need to be responsible and that "collective responsibilities are anathema" (289). Raul seems to be saying that having to attend the school and learn English in a collective environment is a failure and an embarrassment. This undesirable outcome occurred because of a failure of his own will.

The distraction of parenting: Mirna

Mirna echoed the same sentiment, that people who do not have success with *Inglés Sin Barreras* have somehow used the program incorrectly. Mirna had been in the USA for 18 years when we spoke. She owned a small cleaning business and had come to Tucson from the nearby border city of Agua Prieta, Mexico. She was 37 at

Table 5. Mirna (Excerpt 4).

1	Yo creo que el programa es muy bueno.	I believe the program is very good.
2	Nada mas que a veces	It is just that sometimes
3	uno no lo usa debidamente	one doesn't use it
4	como, como debe.	the way it is supposed to be used.
5	Pero para mí	But for me
6	el programa es bueno.	the program is good.
7	La única razón	The only reason
8	por la que yo no he aprendido inglés	that I have not learned English
9	con el programa	with the program
10	es porque en la casa	is because at home
11	esta uno	it is just you
12	si me propongo una hora	if I try to do something for an hour
13	cada día los niños como ellos saben	every day it seems like my kids know
14	y 'stoy en	and I'm there and it is
15	"MAMI, necesito un vaso de leche"	"MOMMY, I need a glass of milk"
16	Necesito	I need
17	Necesito	I need

the time of our interview, and was a single mother with three children. Divorced, she had gotten "custody" of *Inglés Sin Barreras* when she and her ex-husband had divided up their belongings. She told me that her husband had gotten the car and she had gotten *Inglés Sin Barreras*. One of the few things they had agreed upon was that their used car and *Inglés Sin Barreras* had roughly the same value (Table 5).

Like Raul, Mirna understood there to be a right and a wrong way to use *Inglés Sin Barreras*, and if one has to attend school to learn English, the program must have been used incorrectly. Again, the program itself, its pedagogy and significant shortcomings (i.e. its dullness, pedagogical limitations) are erased, and learning English becomes solely a question of personal will. This discourse of language learning, "It's a good program, I'm a bad language learner" was mentioned again and again by study participants. Perhaps the social/economic value placed on the program, through its high cost and high value in trade (e.g. through mutual agreement, this divorcing husband and wife determined that the program's value was comparable to that of a used car), makes it difficult to critique the program. Indeed, suggesting that the program might be less than stellar calls into question the powerful discourse of the autonomous individual who is responsible for consuming wisely. If people must manage themselves as entrepreneurs (Bansel 2007), the free subject is "responsibilized" (288), and the program (or a school, for that matter) loses importance. It is the consumer, not the commodity consumed, that matters.

It appears that for Mirna, like Raul, the way to "get it right" is to have uninterrupted time to dedicate to using *Inglés Sin Barreras*, and to have the will to sit through a boring program. The wrong way is to have other obligations, such as parenting, that infringe upon the time one can spend working on the program, and becoming a neoliberal subject.

Mirna started out by distancing herself from personal responsibility for using *Inglés Sin Barreras,* by using we to refer to migrants, noting that migrants do not always do what "we are supposed to do," perhaps referencing the social pressure to belong to the USA through the mastery of English (Warriner 2007b). It is significant that she speaks of what migrants are "supposed to do," aligning herself with norms of behavior that involve self-policing. It seems that Mirna is deeply engaged in the process of self-making, and is acutely aware of the discourse that says migrants must learn English in order to succeed. But quickly, she switched from the distanced we = migrants to personalized *I* statements when she spoke of being a mother. Inhabiting her identity as a mother in the first person, it seemed that the parental role was embodied and perhaps in conflict with the more abstract category of the neoliberal subject.

She made it clear that her time to study was truncated, and that her role as a mother and primary caretaker of her children made it difficult for her to be that profit-maximizing, neoliberal subject. Giddens (1991) offers the reminder that while economic and social barriers based on aspects of identity such as gender, age, ethnicity, race, and class were once thought to have been significant, these inequities are now seen, through the neoliberal lens, to be remnants of an almost forgotten past. When Mirna recounted the barriers to her becoming a good neoliberal citizen, she highlighted her children's cries of, "I need, I need …" Having to respond to her children's needs makes Mirna a compromised neoliberal subject. Hondagneu-Sotelo (1994) critiques the alleged equality of this neoliberal view, offering the reminder that people live in specific social contexts, "not in a vacuum outlined only by huge structures" (187). However, both Mirna and Raul have framed their experiences of using *Inglés Sin Barreras* as stories of failure, even though both of them were putting significant work into learning English, as was evidenced by their 20 hours a week studying English at the adult school. But through the neoliberal lens, their failures were: (1) a lack of the will to learn on their own; (2) allowing parenthood to impede being "an entrepreneur of the self"; and (3) having to resort to using publicly funded ESOL programs to learn English, a collective endeavor which compromises one's personal freedom. Perhaps their sense of failure also came from being embedded in their social worlds, and not being able to uphold the illusion of being free subjects who wholly choose their own destinies.

"My grain of sand": Magdalena

The final piece of data I consider comes from Magdalena, a 42-year-old woman who has gone back and forth between the border town of Agua Prieta and Tucson for three years. She is married and has two grown children. Although she was unemployed when we spoke, she was looking for a job as an office cleaner. She told me that she had previously worked for a small company that was contracted to clean the offices of the immigration and customs enforcement (ICE) agency, even though she did not have legal documents to work in the USA. She borrowed *Inglés Sin Barreras* from a friend of the family, and she had just recently viewed an hour of the first volume. In Mexico, she had completed one year of high school. Like María, Magdalena spoke about learning English as a responsibility, but she took this idea beyond the level of political slogan, and incorporated it into her sense of destiny as a citizen, a woman, and perhaps even as a spiritual being (Table 6).

Magdalena spoke explicitly about learning English as the responsibility of US citizens. She very clearly stated everything in the first person, a way of taking responsibility grammatically, something that none of the other participants did as forcefully or as consistently as she did. Magdalena explained to me that she had a border crossing card, which allows Mexican nationals who live near the US border to cross into the USA for limited periods of time, in order to shop. While a border

Table 6. Magdalena (Excerpt 5).

1	No me gustaría que se me pase la vida.	I don't want my life to pass by.
2	Si estoy viviendo en este país,	If I am living in this country,
3	y después siento que es una responsabilidad aprender el inglés	and after, I feel it is a responsibility to learn English
4	Para ser una mejor ciudadana.	To be a better citizen.
5	Para, porque no he perdido las esperanzas en un futuro	Because, I have not lost hope for the future
6	estudiar algo y prepararme.	to study something.
7	Siento que sería un desperdicio.	I feel like it would be a waste.
8	hacerme vieja en la cocina, cocinando	for me to get old in the kitchen, cooking
9	aprendiendo nada más de cocina de como llevar una casa	learning nothing more than cooking and keeping house
10	TENGO QUE aprender	I NEED TO learn
11	Cuando Dios nos dió cerebro	God gave us a brain
12	Y lo, pudo aprender algo más	I can learn something more
13	Y aportar.	And to contribute.
14	MI granito de arena	MY grain of sand
15	para la sociedad.	for society.

crossing card does permit commerce in the USA, it does not allow one to live and work legally in the USA, so her presence in the USA was unauthorized. This was especially striking, given that she had previously worked for a cleaning company that was contracted to clean ICE offices.

In spite of her legal status in the USA, Magdalena spoke of needing to be a better citizen in the USA. The kind of citizenship that Magdalena was talking about went beyond actual legal documents, to a sense of contributing to the larger community, to a greater public good. Ong (2003) makes a distinction between Citizenship (with a capital C), which is about the state's ability to confer documents on someone and citizenship (with a small c), which is about the practices that are part of people's everyday lives. Small c citizenship is characterized by behaviors that, "suggest, define, and direct adherence to democratic, racial, and market norms of belonging" (15). This small c citizenship is what Magdalena seems to be referring to. Magdalena longs to be a better citizen in the nation in which she lives, and she also wants to actively create meaning in her life. She cites formal education as central to achieving that goal. Her vision is profoundly democratic, and her desires and dreams are in sharp contrast to the decidedly neoliberal discourses that Angel, María, Raul, and Mirna have embraced. Rather than focusing on freedom and choice and the primacy of individual initiative, Magdalena is thinking about how she can participate in democratic citizenship and make her small contribution to society, even though her Big C citizenship is technically in Mexico, and not the USA.

Through her reference to cooking, Magdalena also addresses questions of gender. She suggests that the traditional role of women working in the home and raising children might not result in a meaningful life, or might not be the only contribution a woman can make to better the world. Beneath this statement is a search for meaning, for contributing to something bigger than oneself. Magdelena did not reject the traditional role of wife and mother, but she did call it into question as the only path to fulfillment.

Invoking God, she points out that, "God gave me a brain, and I can learn something more/Dios nos dió cerebro y lo, pudo aprender algo más." Here, Magdalena suggests that perhaps people are destined to develop their God-given abilities. And finally, Magdalena framed her own educational aspirations as her "grain of sand for society," her own small contribution to the nation in which she lives.

Magdalena's talk is an implicit critique of the neoliberal model. She questioned the neoliberal notion of self-actualization through acquiring skills and making choices. Instead, she suggests a model of self-actualization that can be achieved through contributing to the community good, and through finding meaning in life that goes beyond superficially prescribed roles.

By living in the USA without authorization and expressing a strong commitment to social citizenship within that nation, Magdalena is practicing a new kind of interstitial citizenship.

Concluding thoughts

Indeed, the discourses that circulate through these interviews make clear that national belonging for Mexican migrants in the USA involves producing themselves as neoliberal subjects. The learning of English along with the consumption of *Inglés Sin Barreras* are central to this struggle for personhood. It is a clever trick that some of these migrants, who are so closely surveilled and governed, come to think of themselves as free, in the neoliberal sense. At the same time, people like Magdalena are resisting this discourse, and refusing to be "made free" in the neoliberal mold, demonstrating the tension between resistance and regulation. And among the study participants, none is more clearly the object of surveillance than Magdelena. If neoliberal discourses depend for their success on the disciplining and disempowering of the working class, this tactic, while it is pervasive, is fortunately, not monolithic. People like Magdalena have refused to believe that the only way to authentic selfhood is through "the continual exercise of freedom" (Rose 1999, 87). Through her daily practices and discourses, Magdalena is conceptualizing citizenship and national belonging in ways that do not fit neatly into the neoliberal mold.

The participants in this study have made clear that the pressure to create oneself as a neoliberal subject, through becoming an "entrepreneur of the self" is powerfully present in their everyday lives. Learning English (preferably on one's own), consuming *Inglés Sin Barreras,* and responsibilizing themselves for the instability of the neoliberal world are activities that preoccupy them. At the same time, those who have embraced this neoliberal subjecthood see themselves as failing to achieve it. They cite their own lack of personal will and their commitment to other roles, such as that of parent, that impede their success as neoliberal subjects.

Perhaps we as individuals are no longer participating in a singular nation, but are experiencing citizenship as multiple and bound to the present. Rose (1999) suggests that the new vision of citizenship, what I term interstitial citizenship, "appears to inhere in and derive from active engagement with each of a number of specific zones of identity – lifestyle sectors, neighborhoods, ethnic groups, some private, some corporate, some quasi-public" (178). These data offer a grounding for what Rose suggests, making clear that interstitial citizenship exists in a kind of multiplicity. People like Magdalena ask us to question how one finds a sense of meaning through a neoliberal identity, and she urges us as scholars to think about citizenship in ways that are mobile and that emphasize the ways in which we engage with our local world through language and social connection, regardless of legal status.

Acknowledgements

The Spencer Foundation generously funded the larger ethnographic project, *Consuming English: How Latin American transmigrants produce/reproduce themselves as new Americans through ideologies of language and the nation,* from which the data analyzed for this article are derived.

Notes

1. I self-consciously use the term *migrant*, as per De Genova (2002), because it is a term migrants use for themselves, rather than *immigrant*, which represents them from an outsider's point of view.
2. I thank an anonymous reviewer for helping me to think about this idea.
3. All names of study participants are pseudonyms.

References

Appadurai, Arjun, ed. 1986. *The social life of things: Commodities in cultural perspective.* New York, NY: Cambridge University Press.
Bansel, P. 2007. Subjects of choice and lifelong learning. *International Journal of Qualitative Studies in Education* 20, no. 3: 283–300.
Brown, W. 2006. American nightmare: Neoliberalism, neoconservatism, and de-democratization. *Political Theory* 34, no. 6: 690–714.
Burchell, G., C. Gordon, and P. Miller, eds. 1991. *The Foucault effect: Studies in governmentality with two lectures by and an interview with Michel Foucault.* Chicago, IL: University of Chicago Press.
Butler, Judith. 1997. *The psychic life of power: Theories in subjection.* Stanford, CA: Stanford University Press.
Cammarota, J. 2009. The generational battle for curriculum: Figuring race and culture on the border. *Transforming Anthropology* 17, no. 2: 117–30.
Canclini, N.G. 2001. *Consumers and citizens: Globalization and multicultural conflicts.* Minneapolis, MN: University of Minnesota Press.
Chavez, Leo. 2008. *The Latino threat: Constructing immigrants, citizens, and the nation.* Palo Alto, CA: Stanford University Press.
Chiswick, B. 2000. Are immigrants positively self-selected? In *Migration theory: Talking across disciplines*, ed. James Hollinfield and Caroline Brettel, 61–76. New York, NY: Routledge.
Davies, B. 2005. The (im)possibility of intellectual work in neoliberal regimes. *Discourse: Studies in the Cultural Politics of Education* 26, no. 1: 1–14.
Davies, B., and C. Banks. 1992. The gender trap: A feminist post-structuralist analysis of primary school children's talk about gender. *Journal of Curriculum Studies* 24, no. 1: 1–25.
Davies, B., and P. Bansel. 2007. Neoliberalism and education. *International Journal of Qualitative Studies in Education* 20, no. 3: 247–59.
Davies, B., and P. Bansel. 2010. Governmentality and academic work: Shaping the hearts and minds of academic workers. *Journal of Curriculum Theorizing* 26, no. 3: 5–20.
De Genova, N. 2002. Migrant "illegality" and deportability in everyday life. *Annual Review of Anthropology* 31: 419–47.
Douglas, Mary, and Baron Isherwood. 1979. *The world of goods.* New York, NY: Basic Books.
Duncan, J. 2007. New Zealand free kindergartens: Free or freely forgotten? *International Journal of Qualitative Studies in Education* 20, no. 3: 319–33.
Foucault, M. 1977. *Discipline and punish: The birth of the prison.* New York, NY: Pantheon Books.
Foucault, M. 1988. Politics and reason. In *Michel Foucault: Politics, philosophy, culture: Interviews and other writings, 1977–84*, ed. L. Kritzman, 57–85. New York, NY: Routledge.
Foucault, M. 1994. The subject and power. In *Michel Foucault: Power*, ed. J. Faubion, 326–48. New York, NY: The New Press.
Gay, Geneva. 2000. *Culturally responsive teaching: Theory, research, and practice.* New York, NY: Teachers College Press.
Giddens, Anthony. 1991. *Modernity and self-identity: Self and society in the late modern age.* Oxford: Polity Press.
Harvey, David. 2005. *A brief history of neoliberalism.* Oxford: Oxford University Press.
Hondagneu-Sotelo, Pierette. 1994. *Gendered transitions: Mexican experiences of immigration.* Berkeley, CA: University of California Press.
Hornby, A.S. 1950. The situational approach in language teaching (I). *ELT Journal* 4, no. 4: 99–103.
Immigration Works. 2010. To copy or not to copy: State lawmaking on immigration after Arizona SB 1070. http://www.immigrationworks.org.
Keynes, John Maynard. 2009. *The general theory of employment, interest and money.* New York, NY: Classic Books.
Ladsen-Billings, G. 1995. But that's just good teaching! The case for culturally relevant pedagogy. *Theory Into Practice* 34, no. 3: 159–65.

Lemke, Thomas. 2000. Foucault, governmentality, and critique. Paper presented at the Rethinking Marxism conference, September 21–24, at the University of Amherst, Amherst, MA.

Martin, Luther H., Huck Gutman, and Patrick H. Hutton. 1988. *Technologies of the self: A seminar with Michel Foucault*. Amherst, MA: University of Massachusetts Press.

Nairn, K., and J. Higgins. 2007. New Zealand's neoliberal generation: Tracing discourses of economic (ir)rationality. *International Journal of Qualitative Studies in Education* 20, no. 3: 261–81.

Ong, Aiwa. 2003. *Buddha is hiding: Refugees, citizenship, and the new America*. Berkeley, CA: University of California Press.

Porter, Eduardo. 2002. Quirky English course evolves into a fixture of Latino pop culture – Poor immigrants flock to buy pricey home-study set. *Wall Street Journal*, February 13, Business, National section.

Rose, Nicolas. 1999. *Powers of freedom: Reframing political thought*. Cambridge: Cambridge University Press.

Terrill, Lynda. 2000. Civics education for adult English language learners. National Center for Literacy Education (NCLE). http://www.cal.org/adultesl/resources/digests/civics-education-for-adult-english-language-learners.php.

Ulllman, C. 2010a. Consuming English: How Latin American transmigrants form identities and construct symbolic citizenship through the English language program *Inglés Sin Barreras* [English without Barriers]. *Linguistics & Education* 21, no. 1: 1–13.

Ullman, C. 2010b. The ideological production of ESOL learner identities in their lives outside/inside the classroom: Language learning, consumption, and citizenship. *Adult Basic Education and Literacy Journal* 4, no. 3: 162–72.

US Census Bureau. 2010. State and country quick facts: Arizona. http://quickfacts.census.gov/qfd/index.html.

Warriner, D.S. 2004. "The days now is very hard for my family": The negotiation and construction of gendered work identities among newly arrived women refugees. *Journal of Language, Identity, and Education* 3, no. 4: 279–94.

Warriner, D.S. 2007a. "It's just the nature of the beast": Reimaging the literacies of schooling in adult ESL education. *Linguistics and Education* 18, nos. 3–4: 305–24.

Warriner, D.S. 2007b. Learning language and the politics of belonging: Sudanese women refugees *becoming* and *being* "American". *Anthropology & Education Quarterly* 38, no. 4: 343–59.

Warriner, D. 2008. Competent performances of situated identities: Adult learners of English accessing engaged participation. *Teaching and Teacher Education* 26, no. 1: 22–30.

Watkins, M. 2007. Thwarting desire: Discursive constraint and pedagogic practice. *International Journal of Qualitative Studies in Education* 20, no. 3: 301–18.

Appendix 1. Question protocol

1. How long have you had access to *Inglés Sin Barreras?*
2. Tell me how you use it.
3. How often do you use it?
4. How far have you gotten in the program?
5. If you haven't gotten very far in the program, why do you think that is?
6. Are there other people in your family or your circle of friends who use your copy?
7. Do you know other people who have used the program? If so, how far have they gotten?
8. Do you think *Inglés Sin Barreras* is good, bad, or neutral? Why?
9. Do you think the program has been useful for learning English? Why or why not?
10. Have you watched the volume on citizenship? Did you watch the movie at the end, *La Ultima Aventura*? What did you think of them?

Appendix 2. Transcription conventions

Lines in transcription are broken up into breath groups.

CAPITALS	higher pitch and volume
:	stretching sound represented by preceding letter
()	setting the scene
((cough))	description of non-verbal behavior
...	pause of fewer than three seconds

Floating migration, education, and globalization in the US Caribbean

Mirerza González and Nadjah Ríos-Villarini

This article follows a research project that collects oral histories of bilingual education teachers from Puerto Rico who migrated to the US Virgin Islands in the late twentieth century. The teachers' oral histories are used as a case study that provides in-depth analysis of competing discourses related to education and globalization in these two US Caribbean territories. The paper begins by examining intersections between migration and globalization in the Caribbean. Analysis of oral teachers' accounts of events experienced in both islands is provided, with a focus on how they dealt with tensions tied to floating migration, constructions of "otherness," language use, and racial formations in their articulation of transnational identities and cultural differences.

Introduction

As Jules (2008, 207) notes, "Caribbean people have always been a migrant people." From centuries of inter-colonial trade of slaves and products to recent efforts toward regional integration movements represented by the Caribbean Community and Common Market and the Organization of Eastern Caribbean States (OECS), the flows of human and material capital are foundational to the Caribbean experience.

Certainly, globalization has only increased and accelerated a human movement that is characteristic of the region. Jules (2008, 207) reports that the United Nations Population Division has revealed that the Caribbean has one of the highest net migration rates worldwide and that over the last 50 years, the region – with a current population of 37 million people – has lost about five million through migration.

This mobility has created blurry social and cultural geographies, where the boundaries and limits of the territories disappear, creating interconnected social exchanges and transcultural Caribbean contacts (Chinea 2005). Indeed, as Stephens (1998) and Basch (1994) argue, the Caribbean experience challenges conceptualizations of migration and the immigrant and teaches us something new about the very construction and use of hegemonic categories of race, nation, and ethnicity.

While research has provided insights into the experience of Caribbean migrants (Basch 1994; Chinea 2005; Duany 2002), few studies have addressed migration processes that take place between the US territories of Puerto Rico and the US Virgin Islands. This article is an analysis of oral histories collected among teachers from Puerto Rico who migrated to the US Virgin Islands in the late twentieth century. The teachers' oral histories are used as a case study that provides in-depth analysis of competing discourses related to education and globalization in these two US Caribbean territories.

We argue that the linguistic performance of teachers' fluid cultural identities reveals expressions of "otherness" forged through formal schooling. These expressions articulate social geographies that are tied to global forces. We also contend that these understandings can be explored with the help of the teachers' oral histories when reading them as a case study. In that sense, our aim is to describe issues related to cultural, linguistic, and racial differences where teachers and students are stakeholders as *floating migrants*.

Floating migration, education, and globalization in the US Caribbean

Floating migration is a concept used by scholars in Migration Research, Asian Studies, and related disciplines to describe labor migration in China. This phenomenon is produced by globalized forces and unbalanced economic developments in China that force rural workers to move back and forth to their place of origin (Li 1999; Liang and Ma 2004; Mrázek 2010; Roberts 2002; Zhang 2002). In China, floating migration brings difficulties to the state as it challenges the traditional registry of "hukou" (family household registration), while expanding inter-country movement and labor migrant networks (Chan and Zhang 1999; Qingle and Yu 1997; Zhang 2002).

In the 1980s, Durand (2004) and Massey (1987) addressed institutionalized Mexican migration processes through the Bracero Program in their foundational work with the Mexican Migration Project, while Chavez (1988) used the term "floating migration" to identify Mexicans' migratory patterns to the United States due to new globalized corporations' increasing need for cheap labor. The term "floating" also refers to the nature of the migratory experiences of workers, who come to the cities in search of work and return to their homes in search of a meaningful life (Zhang 2002, 314–5). As Durand suggests, in the case of Mexican migrants, the Immigration Reform and Control Act (IRCA) passed in 1986, "radically modified the traditional pattern of back-and-forth migration by men by legalizing 2.3 million Mexican immigrants and paving the way for even more to enter the US through a family reunification program" (2004, 3), resulting in the inadequacy of the term "floating migration" to identify its fluid nature.

However, as in the case of Chinese migratory processes, recent trends in the study of Mexican and Caribbean migration patterns (Basch 1994; Foulkes and Newbold 2000; Stephen 1998; Winders 2005) support the need to locate these in the global and transnational context of the new economy, triggered by what Giddens (1990) and Harvey (1989) identify as more flexible modes of capital accumulation by reconfigurations of spatial and temporal conditions of production due to information technologies (109). In that sense, migration provides a good frame of reference for understanding how globalization as a socio-political phenomenon, merges with technology's relaxation of space and time constraints (Held et al. 1999). This creates fluid scenarios – such as floating migration – that demand innovative approaches to understanding identity constructions. Globalization relates to the constant changes in the development of technologies that have influenced how space and time are experienced and conceived, exposing the interrelation of the local with the global (Harvey 1989; Heller 2011; Massey and Jess 1995). In fact, King (1995, 23) relates floating migration to uneven development produced by new experiences of place and space that get represented through language as people perform their cultural identities. He argues that migrants are not exceptional people; they play a crucial role in the complex movement of capital flow. Massey and Jess posit the idea that colonial migrations, particularly to the Caribbean, are early expressions of globalization as they facilitated uneven development by means of the control of capital flows (1995, 10).

As the global and the local reconfigure new geographies, the flows of capital, migrants, and cultural meanings transform group identities, particularly those related to cultural categories of gender, class, ethnicity, and race, that challenge what Gilroy calls the "logic of binary coding" (1994, 198). Paying attention to constructions of race in post-industrial Detroit, Hartigan (1999) calls this phenomenon the "localness of race," as "racial identities are produced and experienced distinctly in different locations" (14). Winders (2005) also provides a good example of how migration triggers changes in the formation of racial identities in his review of studies that trace the 2000s trends of Latino migration to the southern United States. He argues that these studies provide evidence of how changing trends in Latino migrations are restructuring racial formations in the South. Following Omi and Winant's work on race in the US (1994), Winders proposes that a reconfiguration in the geographies of Latino migration in the United States promotes new approaches to racial formations, as "racial formations are not only temporally but also spatially dynamic" (2005, 685).

Regardless of the fact that migratory processes have been in place for a long time, Heller (2011) argues it is not until recently that sociolinguists have started to explore people's movements across borders. She supports this engagement as such movements "have promoted language-related practices that need to be explored in theoretical and methodological ways" (51). In other words, assessing human experiences tied to flux means of capital:

> is not a form of expert knowledge, but rather an informed and situated social practice, one that can account for what we see, but which also knows why we see what we do, and what it means to tell the story. (2001, 6)

Floating migration and globalization: the case of Vieques and St. Croix

Small countries in general and the Caribbean region in particular are not exceptions to migratory movements. Cobas and Duany (1995), Chinea (2002), and Dookhan (1994) maintain that the Caribbean region has always received human flow since its colonial conception. Across the Caribbean region, migration processes mostly comprised involuntary and voluntary movements of African slaves, seasonal workers from British colonies in Asia, and mainly male European nationals who left behind their wives and children in Europe (2002, 143). But in the case of the colonial Hispanic Caribbean, more particularly Puerto Rico, a number of historical events contributed to contradictory conceptions of migrants. The local Spaniard colonial government allowed from 1700 to 1800 the entry of slaves who had escaped from nearby islands under British, Danish, and French control. Many of these people were enslaved again in Puerto Rico, and this prompted the growth of the non-white population, a phenomenon that jeopardized the control of the White Iberian population (Chinea 2002, 179–86). Worries of having very few families of proven Iberian "pure" blood resulted in the welcoming of the 1815 immigration decree *Cédula de Gracia*, "a major boost to White immigrants and slave owners" meant to promote the "whitening" of Puerto Rico (Chinea 2002, 196).

There is recorded history of floating migrations among Puerto Ricans, US Virgin Islanders, and other Caribbean islanders from the Lesser Antilles (Dookhan 1994; Rabin 2009) since early in the nineteenth century. At that time, Eastern Caribbean seasonal sugarcane workers came to the Puerto Rican islands of Vieques and Culebra (considered as municipalities of Puerto Rico), to work on sugarcane plantations. Using historical records, Rabin (2009) identifies these workers as: "thousands of free Black working men from the English colonies of the Windward Islands: Anguilla, Antigua, St. Kitts, Nevis, and Tortola [who] lived and worked in the sugarcane *haciendas* in Vieques" (21).

However, this first flow was inverted when the sugar industry in Vieques and Culebra declined as a result of the establishment of two US military bases. This movement from Puerto Rico to the US VI, and particularly to St. Croix, was first registered as starting in the 1920s, when the United States promoted the agricultural development of the new territory (Boyer 1983). At the same time, the military government abolished the free entry of seasonal contracted sugarcane workers from the Eastern Caribbean islands of St. Kitts, Nevis, Guadalupe, and Dominica, only allowing workers who were American citizens, "even though their labor was more expensive" (Dookhan 1994, 269).

This scenario was ideal for the thousands of *Viequenses* who became unemployed when the US military base was granted ownership of three-fourths of Vieques' land. Most of these migrants were working-class, light-skinned, monolingual Spanish speakers who moved to St. Croix in search of economic improvement. Additionally, these migrants were also American citizens, as the US Congress granted citizenship to Puerto Ricans by means of the 1917 Jones Act.

The US VI Department of Education was forced to offer bilingual education in response to the growing numbers of Spanish-speaking students who were now in need of schooling. As early as 1918, teachers from Puerto Rico were recruited to satisfy demands made by members from the Puerto Rican community who lived in St. Croix (Gill Murphy 1977). Since then, and in order to fulfill the needs of the Spanish-speaking community to comply with the right of free education, the Department of Education had recruited and trained bilingual teachers from Puerto Rico to the US Virgin Islands, and particularly to St. Croix.

Because of this educational setting, a second migratory wave came to St. Croix starting in 1960, when the Civil Rights Act created the Bilingual Education Program. Schoolteachers were recruited in Vieques, starting a new floating migration composed of educated and professional workers.

All of these developments structured tensions between Puerto Rican migrants and Virgin Islanders. In their classrooms, teachers had to deal with differences in language (Spanish vs. English/Creole) and cultural identity. Competing discourses about language ideologies that privileged English education over bilingual education and the linking of Spanish use to Puerto Rican migrants are two main elements that mediated the teachers' experiences. These competing discourses resonate with those previously reported by Zentella (1997) in her study about Puerto Rican children in

New York City. Similarly, Heller's study about bilingual education in Toronto (Canada) demonstrates that, regardless of the symbolic capital that bilingualism entails, teachers tend to enforce institutional policies that privilege one, culturally homogeneous space (2011, 109).

Skin color also constituted one of the main triggers of conflict between both groups. Lynn (2008) explains that multiple studies on the Caribbean register how skin color, in the sense of physiognomy, carries ideological weight in terms of race and social segmentation. He uses the term "pigmentocracy" to describe racial formations in the Caribbean, a term that refers to societies in which wealth and social status are determined by skin color (2008, 25). As Puerto Ricans' ideological constructions of race are strongly supported by the myth of *mestizaje*/hybridity (Duany 2002), Virgin Islanders' race constructions are deeply linked to Black slavery. As a consequence, differences in the discursive representations of skin color have promoted a highly contradictory articulation of racial formations among Puerto Rican migrants, particularly those who live and work in St. Croix (Krieger 1988).

The geographical configurations of education in two US territories: St. Croix, US VI and Vieques, Puerto Rico

Regardless of the fact that Puerto Rican migratory flows comprise an important area of research within Puerto Rican Studies, there is a gap in scholarship about the migratory movement that takes place between these two US territories. If it is true that, as a social experience, "Boricuas abroad"[1] embodies the complex and transnational cultural intersections that result from voluntary and forced migrations (Duany 2002), it is also true that recent scholarship still emphasizes the study of the Puerto Rican diaspora in cities such as New York (Dávila 1997; Flores 1993), Chicago (Cruz 2005), Philadelphia (Whalen and Vázquez 2005), and most recently, Orlando and Kissimmee, Florida (Duany 2010). Scholars barely remember a Puerto Rican migratory movement that began as early as the 1920s and that found in the US VI, particularly in St. Croix, an economic, climatic, and cultural refuge.

Puerto Rico and the US Virgin Islands are two different groups of islands in the Caribbean region that share a common political present, but have distinct colonial pasts. Although today both groups of islands are considered political territories that belong to the United States, they were part of two important colonial empires, Spain and Denmark, in the nineteenth century. Puerto Rico was acquired by the United States as a result of the Spanish-American War and the US Virgin Islands were sold by the Danish government to the United States in 1917. Both political transactions were part of a US military effort to control the Caribbean and protect the Panama Canal.

Another commonality of these islands relates to the establishment of the Department of Public Education as one of the most important institutional entities. Prior to the establishment of US military government in both Puerto Rico and the US Virgin Islands, educational efforts were led by the Catholic Church and the Moravian Church. This scenario was interpreted by the US as a chaotic and elitist system that required a centralized organization to enhance public access. As expressed by Evans in relation to the US Virgin Islands: "the single greatest weakness of the American education was the secularization of the schools" (1945, 33).

On the other hand, these educational efforts also promoted a political project to assimilate and acculturate the native citizens in the newly acquired territories (Hurwitz, Menacker, and Weldon 1987). This educational move created a new ideology of democracy aligned to the cultural values and economic needs of the United States. The effort of creating a public system of education in the new territories was a political and economic strategy used in other recently acquired territories like the Philippines and Guam. According to Evans (1945), the education system imposed on the new US territory was previously used in New Mexico and Arizona, where it was aimed at assimilating Native Americans. The educational model implemented in the new territories was most likely replicated in Puerto Rico and later in the US Virgin Islands following the US model.

These early educational efforts on both islands were characterized by extended experimentation in terms of the curriculum, instructional strategies, learning materials, and teacher training and development. In both cases, teachers from the United States were recruited to work as teachers and administrative personnel in order to make sure that the establishment of a new educational order was aligned with the educational, political, and economic project of Americanization. This idea is clearly stated in the House of Representatives Special Investigative Report on Minimum Wages and Education in Puerto Rico and the Virgin Islands (1949, 187):

> Of all public services in Puerto Rico, education is among the most important. Upon it, rests not only immediate values for the individual and his community but, even more profoundly, the long range good of society. The philosophy of the school system in Puerto Rico is firmly grounded on the American belief that education contributes to the perfectibility of man.

In both educational systems, the American project placed particular emphasis on vocational education including agriculture, home economics, and industrial arts. Such a move proved that the Americanization process through schooling was part of a broader economic and political project aimed at harmonizing the educational system of the territories. As suggested by Jules (2008), "harmonization is essential for several reasons: it will facilitate the realization of economies of scale in the provision of education; it will ensure some compatibility between the education systems that will further facilitate the free movement of persons" (210). Furthermore, this idea seems to align with the 1949 House of Representatives Report, which in the case of Puerto Rico stated that:

> [...] trade and industrial education in our island has the enthusiastic backing of the government and the people. We are now conscious that one of the best ways to promote industry is by creating and building through vocational training the skilled workmen who will operate the tools, instruments, and machinery in the new established factories and in those which are sure to come in the future. (193)

By promoting the development of competent subjects able to deal with both products and processes, the ideal of Americanization fostered the mobility of people, previewing also labor flux tied to globalization in the two territories. In that sense, education promoted the institutional development of skilled workers capable of adapting to flexibility on the basis of the American model of economic development.

Events as narratives: exploring language ideologies through oral accounts of events

Teachers' oral descriptions of events provide for what Polkinghorne (1998) calls "linguistic and hermeneutical understandings of ordinary experiences" (13). Accordingly, Polkinghorne proposes the concept of narrative as a "cognitive scheme" (1998, 15) that social agents use to organize events into schemas of meaning, while Luke (2002) suggests that narratives promote a balanced perception of the social agent as a creative, yet socially determined individual.

Teachers' oral histories, as qualitative accounts of academic research, have gained interpretative ground and reoriented how scholars think about the field of educational history (Dougherty 1999). Scholars such as Curry (1995) and Weiler (1998) provide good examples of how teachers' oral histories offer a more interdisciplinary reading of the lives of educators, the tensions they experience, and how they represent those tensions as memories. As Dougherty suggests, educational narratives usually contain more than one story about the past, and even more about the present (1999). Following this idea, we have approached the oral descriptions of teachers as maps that chart their complex, and at times highly contradictory experiences as floating migrants.

We want to focus on bilingual education teachers' oral histories to explore the discursive role of narratives and memory in the teachers' negotiation of ideological tensions related to identity formation. We frame this analysis within the critical-hermeneutical discourse analysis model. We recognize that our analysis is not that of traditional coding of linguistic data; however, we follow Gumperz (1993, 92) in that:

> new conditions of economic and cultural globalization have created theoretical and empirical challenges for a critical applied linguistics. It is argued that these will require that critical discourse analysis augment its strong focus on ideology critique with the study of texts that model the productive uses of power and discourse in new conditions.

The teachers' oral histories were collected from 2007 to 2010. With the help of members of the Puerto Rican community in St. Croix, we contacted and interviewed 15 teachers who had worked or were currently working with the Bilingual Education Program, and either lived or had lived in St. Croix. An open-ended questionnaire[2] was developed after completing the first interview to organize the discussion of themes emerging during the conversations. We respected the choice of language use during the interviews, but only a few preferred English. We translated all of the transcripts into English.

Following Polkinghorne's (2004), Dougherty's (1999), and Gumperz's (1993) recommendations, the interviews were transcribed and the described events were analyzed for themes and concepts that were recurrent in the teachers' narratives. This research is part of a more comprehensive project currently underway. Due to the fact that the project has not been completed, we will refer to the narrators using pseudonyms to maintain confidentiality, as the territories under study are small. Although we recognize the importance of their work as collaborators in this research, we also respect their anonymity.

Floating migrants, fluid identities, and signifiers of exclusion: a case study

George lives in Puerto Rico and when we spoke he worked as a teacher in Vieques. He moved to St. Croix in 1993 to work as a teacher for four years, and then moved back to Vieques, due to family issues related to their acculturation process in St. Croix. Kate was born in St. Croix to *Viequense* parents, and during her childhood moved back and forth between Vieques, St. Croix and the continental United States. She completed high school in St. Croix but moved back to Puerto Rico to finish a college degree. At the time this research was conducted, Kate worked as an English teacher in Vieques. Rachel is a retired teacher from Puerto Rico who married a *Viequense* and has lived in St. Croix since 1966, but has worked as a teacher in Puerto Rico for 14 years. She had also worked for the Bilingual Education Program until 1995. Finally, Monica was born and raised in St. Croix to *Viequense* parents. She moved to Connecticut to start a college degree in Bilingual Education. Currently, she works as a monolingual elementary school teacher in St. Croix.

As we developed the interviews with the teachers, they shared stories of various situations related to their experiences as migrant workers at different times during the study. It was clear to us that the teacher usually pointed to what Urciouli (1998) called "signifiers of exclusion," types of discursive practices that established distinctions and "otherness." One of those practices relates to ways of dealing with their racial identity when asked about how they would define themselves and others in their community. As the teachers struggled with their status as migrants in both Vieques and St. Croix, they pointed to their place of birth as one element that provided a point of reference when making sense of their racial identities by means of their lighter skin tone. For example, George stated that:

> I am Puerto Rican, but I'm White, and those are two different things. [...] But by being White and Puerto Rican, it causes friction. I had a *Viequense* friend, he was a teacher over there in St. Croix, in Central High, and he gave me a lot of advice. He told me [...] three things only. Number one: "Good morning;" number two: "Good afternoon;" and number three: "How are you?" ... Three things.

As for Kate, who was born in St. Croix, struggling with racial differences was something that she understood to define her childhood. During our conversation, Kate recalled:

> No, no, no. I never perceived it [racism] from a teacher to a student, but yes, it was from other students against us. So, we hung out together and we were all Puerto Rican. I mean, Puerto Rican as the daughter of a *Viequense* ... And we would hang out together and such, every afternoon we had to go out with our crew, like we say, because we would be threatened every day. [...] We were threatened due to the fact that, how he [George] says, we were lighter skinned; it was a lot. [...] They even have an expression. We were called "Puerto Rican hookworm," which is a worm that ... [It is] many times the insult that quickly comes out when they want to insult Puerto Ricans.

Both George and Kate shared with us that they experienced racism while they were adapting as migrants because of cultural differences between "us" and "them" due to skin-tone differences. When using the term "race," they referred to tensions and experiences of exclusion/inclusion because of skin tone as Puerto Ricans and Black Virgin Islanders engaged in social relations.

When asked to explain these cultural differences, George said that moving to St. Croix was a: "huge transition. When you go, it's a different culture. Students are different, and as others tell you, there are even students that, are 'difficult' to deal with. There is also racism against Puerto Ricans." As George completed this description, Kate nodded in approval and expressed that, "as a student I also perceived racism." Again, Kate's statement related to cultural ideologies of difference based on skin tone. Her lighter skin tone was a signifier of her "otherness."

Interestingly, after completing the recording of our interview, we engaged in an informal conversation that proved to be highly enlightening. George and Kate were arguing about their connections with St. Croix and their emotional ties with a possible hybrid identity that has been labeled as *Puerto Crucian*. Their awareness of this hybrid culture, regardless of their place of birth, was expressed through Kate's pointing out to George: "[…] you know, even though I was the one who was born in St. Croix, you are more Crucian than me."

As these perceptions reveal, the teachers' attributions of racial difference are deeply linked to both their experiences as migrants and the geographical locations where they were taking place. These perceptions provide evidence that today there are socio-cultural variations of certain local and regional communities within the broader Caribbean context, as Hoetink identified over 40 years ago (1971). These differences are evidenced by Rachel and Monica, who identified language, and not race, as a signifier of exclusion. In that sense, language use is another typology expressed by the narrators as a common issue in their experiences as migrant workers. As a signifier of exclusion, Rachel and Monica's experiences exemplify the working of language ideologies, practices in which language and language use operate as both markers of identity and crucial means of the structuring of inequality in social relations (Bauman and Briggs 2003; Irvine and Gal 2000; Silverstein 1979). In spite of the fact that all four narrators expressed their constant use of both Spanish and English as a tool to connect and communicate in both Vieques and St. Croix, Rachel and Monica expressed contradictory perceptions in terms of how language use is perceived as both teachers and parents.

As we engaged in the interview with Rachel, she openly expressed that she often taught Puerto Rican students in Spanish, even though it was against school policies. Rachel explained that regardless of the fact that in St. Croix the primary language of instruction is English, she clearly stated that she lacked full fluency in English at the time. Furthermore, students from Puerto Rican migrant families were usually assigned to their classrooms. At the time, Rachel worked for the Bilingual Education Program for students from Puerto Rico who attended school and were lacking English-language proficiency. Nonetheless, Rachel identified the struggles that these students experienced and decided to go against school policies by fostering a learning environment in Spanish. Rachel recounted for us the consequences of this decision:

> Well, let me tell you that I began by helping them in Spanish because the majority of them did not understand what was happening. One day, the principal came in and took the three first grade teachers to her office, and told us the headquarters received notice that the teachers were speaking Spanish during class. The only one that spoke Spanish was me, because one teacher was American and the other was a local. I told the principal that I noticed that the kids were lost and they needed to be spoken in Spanish in order to understand what was happening. And it appears this was the stepping stone for understanding the need to do something, and then they began, about three years after my being there, to deal with the situation.

This idea is also articulated in comments shared by Monica:

> There are just so many things. I also have to take them [students from Puerto Rico] aside to sometimes teach them certain things in Spanish because I just cannot speak Spanish all throughout the class, considering that the majority of it is in English. And, if I give a lesson, I take the student aside and explain the lesson. Therefore, I minimize the workload.

As we engaged in more informal conversations, the idea of Spanish as a marker of Puerto Rican identity emerged. This happened several times when talking about the narrators' family dynamics at home. The use of Spanish as a marker of Puerto Rican identity was identified by Gibson (1976) in her research about ethnicity and schooling in St. Croix. Gibson identified that Puerto Rican students usually failed in school due to language barriers. Gibson (1976), Zentella (1997) and Urciouli's (1998) research register how Spanish is tied to common understandings of Puerto Ricans as a culturally homogeneous speech community, and their work makes clear the problems that such constructions produce for Puerto Rican migrants who experience transcultural identities.

As the project progressed, we engaged in more detailed conversations with all of the narrators regarding their experiences as parents and how they managed both languages at home. Kate, Rachel, and Monica provided us with contradictory descriptions. In fact, when we shared some of the data collected in the broader project of oral histories, all expressed that in most of the cases, teachers' attitudes toward Spanish language maintenance and English language acquisition were anchored in their perceptions of identity as linked to their experiences as migrants in St. Croix.

Particularly interesting is Kate, Rachel, and Monica's recognition of language ideologies tied to language use; they identified Spanish as a language they spoke to articulate their cultural identities. For example, Kate proudly explained that, regardless of growing up in St. Croix, family interactions were usually conducted in both languages. Also, Kate mentioned to us that the church was an important factor in the way connections were fostered with the Spanish language:

> At home, thank God, we practiced both languages [English and Spanish]. That means that Spanish was always spoken. And so, in school, all learning was in English. So, from Head Start all education was in English and we grew up with the two languages. At my place we spoke Spanish, and in church, we learned the Bible in Spanish ... so we grew with the two languages.

As in Rachel's case, the connection between perceptions of cultural identity and language use was evidenced by the following assertion:

> My daughter had a bilingual education. She majored in Education, in English as a Second Language. [...] In San Germán. [...] She was born in Puerto Rico. I had her there so she would be Puerto Rican. [...] But she was raised here [St. Croix]. She attended private schools here. And she is completely bilingual. We speak Spanish in my house.

On the other hand, Monica shared a different perception:

> For me, it was more difficult during elementary school, you know? As a child, I had comprehension problems, reading comprehension, because we spoke Spanish at home, and English in school, and I had problems there. [...] I'm going to use myself as an example because I have three girls and my three girls don't speak Spanish at all. And I blame myself, because when I had my girls, I did [not] want them to learn Spanish

as a first language in fear of them reliving my experience. Their father does not speak Spanish. Then, I said: "Well, I want my girls to learn English first, to learn it well and to master it, to push ahead with it significantly." And then I figured I did things wrong, because I have one girl that likes Spanish and says things in Spanish; she reads well in Spanish [...]. [Then] the oldest one and the middle one become interested and talk to Mami. And it's because of Mami that they understand Spanish.

As a bilingual person who was "othered" in St. Croix, Monica used English to perform everyday interactions. Hence, her English dominance was problematic, because as a Puerto Rican, Monica was expected to use Spanish when communicating with other Puerto Ricans. Failing to fulfill the expected fluency in Spanish, Monica struggled with others' perceptions about qualifying as a member of the migrant community.

We might argue that these ideological constructions are in constant tension. Dialectically speaking, the development of English proficiency collides ideologically with the use of Spanish as an identity marker. Monica expressed these anxieties in terms of language use and how she struggled with the power of language ideologies. Spanish use provided Monica with a tool to articulate her cultural identity. Moving away from the use of Spanish was, she said, "like losing one's identity."

Conclusion

While migration promotes cultural exchanges among different cultural groups, it also frames challenges for local educators as they face institutional requests and pressures related to teaching and learning goals. Some of these pressures relate to performance because teaching practices are expected to meet national and supranational learning standards. In addition, teachers have to work with diverse learners, which may hinder their ability to deal with classroom management. In their classrooms, these teachers are confronted with their students' multicultural contexts, forcing them to generate more comprehensive understandings of their students' realities and diversity.

Although related to distinctive geographical locations, Puerto Rico and the US Virgin Islands were influenced by the political and economic development of the United States in the Caribbean region. In addition, both Puerto Rico and the US Virgin Islands have served as a bridge that connects the Eastern and Western Caribbean with the continental United States. These movements, or "floating migrations," are often bi- or tri-directional as the migrant workers move, and return, often to their places of origins.

That is not to say, however, that new identities have not emerged from these interactions. In fact, Highfield (2009) argues that there is an emergent *Puerto Crucian* ethnicity that distinguishes itself from that of Puerto Ricans, and that is represented by language use. He proposes that when they arrived almost a century ago, these migrating *Viequenses* were stigmatized racially and ethnically. With time, they were called Puerto Ricans. More recently, other names have been integrated, perhaps demonstrating a new conception of the migrant *Viequense*, regarding the Crucian perspective (19).

While the teachers who acted as narrators in this study acknowledged two primary signifiers of cultural difference (racial formations and language), they also expressed anxiety related to how these signifiers operate in everyday interactions. One of these is the use of two languages by a bilingual person during a communicative interaction: while it communicates anxiety regarding the idea of identity as a coherent, well-rounded construct, it also validates that Puerto Ricans in St. Croix expose themselves to everyday practices that encourage them to conform to not one, but multiple cultural identities that do coexist effectively with their Puerto Rican-ness as a perception tied to their migratory condition.

Following Mrázek (2010), this paper proposes to reassess the term "floating migration" in order to name migratory flows that provide for bridging and linking people, and the resulting multilayered issues. The concept proves useful to name temporary labor migrations in times of globalized, information-based, new economies (Massey and Jess 1995). These interactions produce cultural exchanges among different groups. As suggested, the oral histories explored in this paper make clear that there are interconnections related to race and language use that should be further analyzed in the Caribbean. Since language is one of the fundamental practices of culture (Hall 1995, 177), we propose that human communication and language use are key to understanding the ideological constructions that challenge floating migrants' social mobility (Heller 2011).

We argue that school spaces constitute uneven contexts where flows and networks become tools to challenge normalized experiences. Schools have to constantly deal with receiving and discharging students because of floating migration. In their classrooms, teachers and students are confronted with what Massey and Jess called a "sense of place" (1995, 88), a term that refers to the idea that places are experienced by people in ways that communicate feelings and meanings to them. Once people move from one place to another, interactions with places permeate their sense of identity and consciousness, forcing them to generate a more global understanding of their reality.

The oral histories of floating migrants, particularly those of our informants, George, Kate, Rachel, and Monica, support Heller's suggestion to approach the globalized new economy by rethinking the social interconnections resulting from capital flow, as "social categories and relations of power are constructed in interaction" (2011, 6). Following Hall (1995) and Heller (2011), the events described by George, Kate, Rachel, and Monica are examples of why more work is needed in order to assess the role played by linguistic forms and practices in the everyday experiences of floating migrants. There is a need for more scholarship to explore how floating migrants articulate social change, normalizing practices, and "citizenship" in the context of "a fluid, globalized world" (2011, 20).

Acknowledgements

The authors would like to thank the anonymous reviewers of the *International Journal of Qualitative Studies in Education* for their feedback and suggestions. They express their appreciation to Denni Blum and Char Ullman for their extraordinarily helpful feedback on an earlier draft. Thanks also to Aitza Maldonado-Martich. Portions of this research were funded by the University of Puerto Rico Institutional Fund for Academic Research (Fondo Institucional para la Investigación, Universidad de Puerto Rico).

Notes

1. "Boricuas Abroad" is a term used to identify Puerto Rican migrants in the US and their descendants.
2. See Appendix 1.

References

Basch, Linda. 1994. *Nations unbound: Transnational projects, postcolonial predicaments and deterritorialized nation-states*. London: Routledge.
Boyer, William. 1983. *America's Virgin Islands: A history of human rights and wrongs*. Durham, NC: Carolina Academic Press.
Chan, K.W., and L. Zhang. 1999. The Hukou system and rural-urban migration. *The China Quarterly* 160, February: 818–55.
Chavez, L.R. 1988. Settlers and sojourners: The case of Mexicans in the United States. *Human Organization* 47, no. 2: 95–108.
Chinea, José Luis. 2002. Fissures in El primer piso: Racial politics in Spanish colonial Puerto Rico during its pre-plantation era, c.1700–1800. *Caribbean Studies* 30, no. 1: 169–204.
Chinea, José Luis. 2005. *Race labor in the Hispanic Caribbean: The West Indian immigrant worker experience in Puerto Rico, 1800–1850*. Gainesville: University Press of Florida.
Cobas, José, and Jorge Duany. 1995. *Los cubanos en Puerto Rico, etnia e identidad cultural* [Cubans in Puerto Rico, ethnicity and cultural identity]. San Juan: Editorial de la Universidad de Puerto Rico.
Cruz, Wilfredo. 2005. *Puerto Rican Chicago*. Chicago, IL: Arcadia.
Curry, Constance. 1995. *Silver rights*. Chapel Hill, NC: Algonquin Books.
Dávila, Arlene. 1997. *Sponsored identities: Cultural politics in Puerto Rico*. Philadelphia, PA: Temple University Press.
Dookhan, Isaac. 1994. *A history of the Virgin Islands of the United States*. Kingston, Jamaica: Canoe Press.
Dougherty, Jack. 1999. From anecdote to analysis: Oral interviews and new scholarship in educational history. *The Journal of American History* 86, September: 712–23.
Duany, Jorge. 2002. *The Puerto Rican nation on the move: Identities on the Island and in the United States*. Chapel Hill, NC: University of North Carolina Press.
Duany, Jorge. 2010. Puerto Rican Florida (edited with Patricia Silver). Special issue, *CENTRO: Journal of the Center for Puerto Rican Studies* 22, no. 1.
Durand, Jorge. 2004. From traitors to heroes: 100 years of Mexican migration policies. Migration information source. Migration Policy Institute (Marzo). http://www.migrationinformation.org/Feature/print.cfm?ID=203.
Evans, Leslie H. 1945. *The Virgin Islands: From naval base to New Deal*. Westport, CT: Greenwood.
Flores, Juan. 1993. *Divided borders: Essays on Puerto Rican identity*. Houston, TX: University of Houston, Arte Público Press.
Foulkes, Matt, and K. Bruce Newbold. 2000. Migration propensities, patterns, and the role of human capital: Comparing Mexican, Cuban and Puerto Rican interstate migration, 1985–1990. *Professional Geographer* 52, no. 1: 144–5.
Gibson, Margaret. 1976. Ethnicity and schooling, a Caribbean case study. Doctoral diss., University of Michigan, Ann Arbor.
Giddens, Anthony. 1990. *The consequences of modernity*. Cambridge: Polity Press.

Gill Murphy, Patricia. 1977. The education of the New World blacks in the Danish West Indies/US Virgin Islands: A case study of social transition. Doctoral diss., University of Connecticut.

Gilroy, P. 1994. *The Black Atlantic*. London: Verso.

Gumperz, J.J., and N. Berenz. 1993. Transcribing conversational exchanges. In *Talking data: Transcription and coding in discourse research*, ed. J.A. Edwards and M.D. Lampert, 91–121. Hillsdale, NJ: Lawrence Erlbaum.

Hall, S. 1995. New cultures for old. In *A place in the world? Places, cultures and globalization*, ed. D. Massey and P. Jess, 175–213. Oxford: Oxford University Press.

Hartigan, John. 1999. *Racial situations: Class predicaments of whiteness in Detroit*. Princeton, NJ: Princeton University Press.

Harvey, D. 1989. *The condition of postmodernity. An enquiry into the origins of cultural change*. Oxford: Blackwell.

Held, David, Anthony McGrew, David Goldblatt, and Jonathan Perraton. 1999. *Global transformations: Politics, economics and culture*. Stanford, CA: Stanford University Press.

Heller, Monica. 2011. *Paths to post-nationalism: A critical ethnography of language and identity*. New York, NY: Oxford University Press.

Highfield, Arnold. 2009. Conferencia Magistral: Apuntes históricos sobre las migraciones de puertorriqueños a la isla de Santa Cruz, US VI [Keynote: Historical notes on migration of Puerto Ricans on the island of Santa Cruz]. In *Seminar for teachers: Memoirs*, ed. Mirerza Gonzalez and Nadjah Ríos Villarini, 11–20. San Juan, PR: Puerto Rican Endowment for the Humanities.

Hoetink, H. 1971. *Caribbean race relations: A study of two variants*. Trans. E.M. Hooykaas. New York: Oxford University Press.

House of Representatives Special Investigation Subcommittee No. 3 of the Committee on Education and Labor. 1949. Investigation of minimum wages and education in Puerto Rico and the Virgin Islands. 81st US Congress, 3rd session, October 26.

Hurwitz, Emanuel, Julius Menacker, and Ward Weldon. 1987. *Educational imperialism, American school policy and the US Virgin Islands*. London: University of America Press.

Irvine, Judith T., and Susan Gal. 2000. Language ideology and linguistic differentiation. In *Regimes of language: Ideologies, polities, and identities*, ed. Paul V. Kroskrity, 35–83. Santa Fe, NM: School of American Research.

Jules, Didacus. 2008. Rethinking education for the Caribbean: A radical approach. *Comparative Education* 44, no. 2: 203–14.

King, R. 1995. Migrations, globalization and place. In *A place in the world? Places, cultures and globalization*, ed. D. Massey and P. Jess, 5–43. Oxford: Oxford University Press.

Krieger, M. 1988. Race and ethnic relations in the US Virgin Islands, 1917–1987. In *Taking bearings: The United States Virgin Islands, 1912–1987*, ed. P. Leary, 86–7. St. Thomas: Bureau of Public Administration, University of the Virgin Islands.

Li, Cheng. 1999. 200 million mouths too many: China's surplus rural labor. In *The China reader: The reform era*, ed. O. Schell and D. Shambaugh, 362–73. New York, NY: Vintage Books.

Liang, Z., and Z. Ma. 2004. China's floating population: New evidence from the 2000 census. *Population and Development Review* 30, no. 3: 467–88.

Luke, A. 2002. Beyond science and ideology critique: Developments in critical discourse analysis. *Annual Review of Applied Linguistics* 22, no. 5: 96–110.

Lynn, Richard. 2008. Pigmentocracy: Racial hierarchies in the Caribbean and Latin America. *The Occidental Quarterly* 8, no. 2: 25–44.

Massey, Doreen, and P. Jess, eds. 1995. *A place in the world? Places, cultures and globalization*. Oxford: Oxford University Press.

Massey, Douglas S. 1987. *Return to Aztlán: The social process of international migration from Western Mexico*. Berkeley, CA: University of California Press.

Mrázek, Rudolf. 2010. Floating. No gears shifting. *The Journal of Asian Studies* 69, no. 4: 1021–5.

Omi, M., and H. Winant. 1994. *Racial formations in the United States: From the 1960's to the 1990's*. New York, NY: Routledge.

Polkinghorne, D. 1998. *Narrative knowing and the human sciences*. Albany, NY: State University of New York Press.
Polkinghorne, D. 2004. *Practice and the human sciences: The case for a judgement-based practice of care*. Albany: State University of New York Press.
Qingle, Jiao, and Housen Yu. 1997. *Workers' flood: Moving toward stability. Management of transient population achieves initial results*. Beijing: Fazhi Ribao.
Rabin, Robert. 2009. Los Tortoleños Obreros de Barlovento en Vieques: 1864–1874. In *Seminar for teachers: Memoirs*, ed. Mirerza Gonzalez and Nadjah Ríos Villarini, 21–34. San Juan, PR: Puerto Rican Endowment for the Humanities.
Richard, Bauman, and Charles L. Briggs. 2003. *Voices of modernity: Language ideologies and the politics of inequality*. Cambridge: Cambridge University Press.
Roberts, Kenneth. 2002. Female labor migrants to Shanghai: Temporary "floaters" or potential settlers? *International Migration Review* 36, no. 2: 492–519.
Silverstein, Michael. 1979. Language structure and linguistic ideology. In *The elements: A parasession on linguistic units and levels*, ed. R. Cline, W. Hanks, and C. Hofbauer, 193–247. Chicago, IL: Chicago Linguistic Society.
Stephens, M.A. 1998. Black transnationalism and the politics of national identity: West Indian intellectuals in Harlem in the age of war and revolution. *American Quarterly* 50, no. 3: 592–608.
Urciouli, Bonnie. 1998. *Exposing prejudice. Puerto Rican experiences of language, race, and class*. New York, NY: Westview Press.
Weiler, Kathleen. 1998. *Country schoolwomen: Teaching in rural California, 1850–1950*. Stanford, CA: Stanford University Press.
Whalen, Carmen Teresa, and Víctor Vázquez-Hernández, eds. 2005. *The Puerto Rican Diaspora: Historical perspectives*. Philadelphia, PA: Temple University Press.
Winders, Jamie. 2005. Changing politics of race and region: Latino migration to the U.S. south. *Progress in Human Geography* 29, no. 6: 683–99.
Zentella, Ana Celia. 1997. *Growing up bilingual: Puerto Rican children in New York*. Malden, MA: Blackwell.
Zhang, Li. 2002. Spatiality and urban citizenship in late socialist China. *Public Culture* 14, no. 2: 311–34.

Appendix 1. Preguntas Guías para Entrevistas Maestros

Información personal

¿Cómo usted llegó a Santa Cruz?
¿Cómo se hace maestra/o? Cuáles fueron sus primeros cursos?
¿Cómo llega a ser parte del Programa Bilingüe de Santa Cruz?
  Si nació en Santa Cruz, ¿Usted fue estudiante de educación bilingüe? De ser así, ¿Qué recuerda de sus experiencias?

Información profesional: Programa Bilingüe

¿Qué tipo de adiestramiento reciben los maestros del Programa de Educación Bilingüe?
¿Cómo se implanta el Programa de Educación Bilingüe en Santa Cruz?
¿Cómo se reclutan los maestros del Programa Bilingüe?
¿Cuántas escuelas bilingües hay en estos momentos?
¿El Programa Bilingüe impacta otros profesionales de la educación como principales, cosejeros escolares y trabajadores sociales?
¿Reciben los maestros del programa apoyo de instituciones educativas locales y puertorriqueñas?
¿Cómo maneja la educación bilingüe en su salón?
¿Qué beneficios tiene la educación bilingüe sobre aquella de corriente regular?
¿Qué destrezas usted como maestro entiende debe promover en el salón de clases?
¿Cuáles son los retos de enseñar en un programa bilingüe?
¿Cómo usted describiría la comunidad escolar que se beneficia de un programa bilingüe?
¿Cómo describe un salón ideal para la educación bilingüe?
¿Qué conoce/conoció sobre la comunidad(es) de sus estudiantes?

Guiding questions
Personal information

How/why did you come to Saint Croix?
How did you become a teacher? What were the first courses that you taught in Saint Croix?
How/when did you become a Bilingual Education teacher in Saint Croix?
If you were born in Saint Croix, were you a student of the bilingual education program? What do you remember about your experiences as a student?

Bilingual education program

Do you know when/how/why was the Bilingual Education Program introduced to Saint Croix's public education system?
How are/were the teachers recruited to the program?
At the present time, how many schools offer bilingual education in Saint Croix?
Do/did teachers from the Bilingual Education Program participate in professional development activities to gain relevant skills, knowledge and understanding of bilingual education?
Does/did the Bilingual Education Program have an impact on other educational services (i.e. school counselors, social workers, and/or school administrators)?
Do Puerto Rican teachers of bilingual education in Saint Croix receive support from local and/or Puerto Rican organizations?
What is your approach to bilingual education? What is your teaching style?
What are the benefits of teaching bilingual education when compared to monolingual education?
What skills do you consider should be fostered in a bilingual classroom?
What are the challenges of teaching in a bilingual education program?
How would you describe the school community that benefits from the Bilingual Education Program in Saint Croix?
Can you describe your ideal bilingual classroom?
What/How much do/did you know about your students' community?

Neoliberalism and the demise of public education: the corporatization of schools of education

Marta Baltodano

> Neoliberalism has brought fundamental changes to the way schools of education prepare professional educators; among them is the pressure for schools of education to produce fast-track teacher preparation programs that bypass traditional requirements. Due to the privatization of public education, a new market has emerged to train educators and administrators for charter schools. The No Child Left Behind Act has made the old multipurpose PhD in education obsolete and has led to fast-track EdDs to train school administrators to raise test scores. In this era of corporate schooling, colleges of education are competing with online and for-profit colleges to increase student enrollment. Academic capitalism has entered into the classroom and it has redefined the academic premises upon which the entire higher education system was instituted. This article asks, what are the implications of this new educational arrangement for the purpose of education and the development of a critically informed mass of democratic citizens? This article proposes a critical dialog among educators, parents, labor groups, and grassroots organizations and an action plan to stop the dismantling of public education.

Introduction

Neoliberalism in the US has transcended the realm of economic policies to become a political rationale that is undermining the major structures, processes, and institutions of American liberal democracy, particularly public education.

This study documents how the tenets of American liberal teacher education represented in a vision of rigorous content knowledge, democratic schooling, and social justice have been distorted and appropriated by the corporate goals of education. This article illustrates how schools of education have been affected by neoliberal reforms including a drastic transformation in the preparation of teachers, the intensification of the business of accreditation, the appropriation of multicultural education, and the formation of a new managerial and professional middle class to support the privatization of education.

This article particularly examines how professional organizations and accrediting institutions, such as NCATE and AACTE,[1] along with other powerful players of neoliberalism, like Teach For America, and a handful of foundations, have shaped the current state of teacher preparation and contributed to the destruction of public schooling.

I examine the political and economic policies that have altered the structures, pedagogical practices, and intended democratic goals of teacher education. I reflect on schools as "little democracies" that are supposed to prepare citizens for active civic participation (Dewey 2004).

Inspired by the work of Maxine Greene, John Dewey, Martha Nussbaum, and others, I propose a new imaginative engagement with the conception of the "public good" to counteract 30 years of neoliberal hegemonic attacks against public education.

This article is a much-needed reflection on the compromised state of teacher education and its gradual deterioration as a result of neoliberal policies. It offers a framework for starting a critical dialog among the many constituencies of public schooling to reclaim education as a public good.

Methodology

This research study is part of a larger inquiry that uses critical policy analysis to examine the discursive relations that have naturalized the corporate agenda of schools of education. While the larger study involves interviews and additional fieldwork, the research for this article is based on critical textual analysis of documents. They include: (1) review of legislation approved during the civil rights movement, among them the Elementary and Secondary Act, the Higher Education Act, the Immigration and Naturalization Act, the Civil Rights Act, the Voting Rights Act, and the Education for All Handicapped Children Act; (2) critical textual analysis of public policy documents, like the affirmative action executive order, the No Child Left Behind Act (NCLB) and Race to the Top; (3) analysis of university records that provide information about the financial restructuring of three universities that are part of this study; (4) examination of NCATE policy documents, reports, and accreditation criteria; (5) critical analysis of the Obama administration speeches, including the president's statements on education and particularly, some of his secretary of education's speeches and press reports; (6) textual analysis of newspaper and digital media describing events related to the reconstitution of public schools and the attacks against teachers and their unions; and (7) fieldnotes of institutional and community practices in my workplace and the city where I live that has the second highest concentration of charter schools in the nation. This research is also informed by the everyday performances in the university in which I work that have been shaped and exacerbated by the current climate of educational accountability.

Critical policy analysis has evolved from the field of critical discourse analysis (Luke 1995–1996) and it is centered on the application of discourse theories to policy studies (Taylor 1997). Discourse theories encompass a broad application of Foucault's theories of discourse, Gramsci's theory of hegemony, and Fairclough's focus on language as a social practice, to critically scrutinize public policy (Codd 1988; Taylor 1997).

The application of these theoretical frameworks to the analysis of policy has resulted in a methodology that offers a more sophisticated examination of the intent, meaning, and discourse of public policy (Taylor 1997). Critical policy analysis focuses on three fundamental aspects: "contexts, texts, and consequences" of policies (Taylor 1997, 33), but always attending to the issues of meaning and interpretation.

It is important to note that *critical policy analysis* widely differs from the narrow, linguistic approach to policy statements (McHoul 1984), because the fine-grained analyses have to be juxtaposed with the larger political and economic context in which these policies have emerged. As Codd (1988) argues, "policy documents ... are ideological texts that have been constructed within a particular context. The task of deconstruction begins with the recognition of that context" (Codd 1988, 243–4; Taylor 1997).

Therefore, critical policy analysis unmasks the "workings" of the discourses, defined by Foucault as "power-infused systems of knowledge" (Muetzenfeldt 1992, 4). These discourses are formed and sustained by the construction of "trusts" about the social and natural world, trusts that become the taken-for-granted definitions and categories by which governments rule and monitor their populations and by which members of communities define themselves and others (Luke 1995–1996, 9).

I sought to reveal the master narratives that have been constructed around the dismantling of public education and the preparation of teachers in the US. What follows is a review of the principles of the American tradition of liberal public education as articulated by founding and contemporary philosophers of education.

Public education and the *common good*

As Maxine Greene (1982) asserted a long time ago, "there is little talk today about the connection between public education and freedom" (4). More than in any other period of American history, teachers hava been stripped of their most precious role: the duty to educate a generation of fully informed democratic citizens. Neoliberalism has taken away the joy of learning, the creativity of teaching, and the formation of strong public intellectuals. Public education is gradually fading and is being replaced by new privatized forms of schooling. The results are the lack of an articulate public and the reduction of public spheres to contest the dominant neoliberal vision of society. The humanities and the arts are being eliminated from the curriculum of public schools (Nussbaum 1998, 2010). As a result, the newer generation of students is losing: "the ability to think critically; the ability to transcend local loyalties and to approach world problems as a 'citizen of the world;' and, finally, the ability to imagine sympathetically the predicament of another person" (Nussbaum 2010, 7).

The realization that something has gone awry in education has gradually begun to sink in. As Ravitch (2010) reflects:

> At the present time, public education is in peril. Efforts to reform public education are, ironically, diminishing its quality and endangering its very survival. (242)

> As a nation, we need a strong and vibrant public education system [... which] is a fundamental element of our democratic society. Our public schools have been the pathway to opportunity and a better life for generations of America ... To the extent that we strengthen them, we strengthen our democracy. (241–2)

The tradition of liberal public education, although not without failures and contradictions, was an ongoing project grounded in the philosophical tenets of John Dewey. His vision of schooling was based on the fundamental principle that schools were indispensable for the establishment of a civil society that could enact and sustain a democracy. Dewey (1916, 1956, 2004) believed that if schools were "little democracies" they could prepare citizens for active civic participation. He assigned teachers with the responsibility to play a leading role in preparing American citizens for active engagement in a democratic society. Dewey visualized education as the "wellspring of democracy itself" (Dewey 1916; Wirth 1966). He believed the values of American democracy, such as equal opportunity and social justice[2] were the backbone of the school curriculum.

Dewey strongly opposed the assumption that schools were places for drills, discipline, and dull exercises. He visualized "teachers as scholars and as students of the psychology of the learning process" (Wirth 1966, 53), and he could not accept the widespread belief that children could be taught by someone who did not problematize the psychological and philosophical implications of teaching. His major contributions were a theory of learning based on experiential teaching in a social-cultural context; the incorporation of students' experience into the curriculum; the vision of students as full citizens; and the retreat from the false dichotomy between theory and practice (Dewey 2004).

Vital to that tradition of American liberal education have been the incorporation of Socratic teaching to resolve real life problems, the practice of public debate and role playing in the classroom to develop critical voice, and a strong integration of the arts and literature to release the imagination and develop empathy for the Other (Greene 1991, 1995; Nussbaum 2010). These components are fundamental to forming, "a certain type of citizen: active, critical, curious, capable of resisting authority and peer pressure" (Nussbaum 2010, 72).

In contrast to this educational model is the rote learning and teaching to the test of neoliberal education that negates the possibility of even fantasizing about achieving the values of equal opportunity, justice, and social mobility. The banking concept of education (Freire 1970) sanctioned by neoliberalism is training students to become docile citizens.

The rise of neoliberalism in the US

The decline of the American economy in the 1970s and 1980s, caused by an international restructuring of labor and capital, was the backdrop to the economic policies carried out during the Reagan presidency (Torres and Schugurensky 2002). Reaganomics was the popular term given to the implementation of the first neoliberal policies in the US, which were grounded on the work of Friedrich von Hayek and Milton Friedman of the Chicago School of Economics[3] (Brown 2003; Symcox 2009). This economic school of thought fully opposed the previous Keynesian policies that advocated strong regulation of the economy and had created the welfare state of the previous decades.

"Capitalism with a human face" (Brittan 1995) developed in the US after the stock market crashed in 1929. President Franklin Delano Roosevelt, who took power at the depths of the Great Depression, retreated from the previous *laissez faire* capitalism of Adam Smith and instituted the New Deal, which sought protection for American workers through the establishment of minimum wages, collective bargaining, and social security.

In the following years, John F. Kennedy's and Lyndon Johnson's presidencies advanced this welfare economy through the New Frontier and Great Society programs. Additional social legislation was enacted to protect the poor, the elderly, those with special needs, and other marginalized groups. Medicaid and Medicare were instituted, and funds for low-income students, childhood education, and bilingual instruction were allocated through the Elementary & Secondary Act, the Higher Education Act, and the Bilingual Education Act (Baltodano 2009; Symcox 2009). This was a time when the welfare society was consolidated to protect the civil and economic rights of US citizens.

However, by the late 1970s, the postwar economic accumulation had been exhausted (Compton and Weiner 2008, 14) and capitalism appeared to be arriving at the "point of no return" (Balibar 1995, 64). A world recession emerged and American corporations began complaining about the plunging of their profits due to labor demands to increase wages for workers, and the international competition to keep prices down. They demanded special protection from the government, as the international economic crisis was threatening their survival. These corporations called for a return to the unregulated market of the pre-Great Depression as the only way to continue being viable (profitable).

This time, "as the economy slowed, state revenues failed to keep pace with social expenditures, and taxpayers began to express resentment towards those who benefited the most from state revenues" (Torres and Schugurensky 2002, 431): the largely disenfranchised social groups that had benefited from the social gains of the civil rights movement. This precipitated the end of the social contract that Americans had established with the government to become a mediator of the economy (Torres and Schugurensky 2002).

The end of the welfare state led to a radically free market where maximized competition, free trade, elimination of tariffs, and government protection for business replaced social assistance for the poor. Many of the regulations that the government had imposed on the financial and manufacturing industries to protect the American worker were abandoned (e.g. NAFTA, CAFTA, outsourcing of jobs through maquiladoras). Gradually the US, along with other leading world economies, intensified the implementation of post-Fordist production and trade and formally entered into a new global market.

Unlike Fordism, "that involves mass production based on moving assembly-line techniques operated with semi-skilled labour, that is, a mass worker" (Amin 1994, 9; Jessop 1995), post-Fordism operates a highly hierarchical and specialized division of labor where labor protections are diminished. Post-Fordism is characterized by: "new methods of production based on microelectronics, by flexible working practices, a much reduced role for trade unions in society, a new individualism, a reduction of state intervention, and a new relation between production and consumption" (Bonefeld and Holloway 1991, 1).

The post-Fordist model is also called "Toyotism," which was inspired by the management and production system implemented by the automobile maker Toyota in Japan in the late twentieth century. One of the most important features of Post-Fordism or "Toyotism" is that it has created a new kind of division of labor in which a small, highly skilled, highly paid management oversees a disposable mass of very poor, immigrant, part-time alienated workers with no job security, union protection, or vested relationship to the work site.

Vanished is the social protection of previous generations of workers, as neoliberalism powerfully encouraged the deregulation of labor laws and targeted labor unions and public schools as the greatest obstacles to the "freedom" of the market (Torres and Schugurensky 2002, 432).

The development of neoliberalism as political rationality

The welfare society that preceded the rise of neoliberalism in the US was not only characterized by comprehensive economic reforms to protect the American worker and the poor; it also included significant legislation that reinterpreted the dimension of civil liberties recognized in the Constitution and the Bill of Rights. Some of these laws were: (1) the Immigration and Naturalization Act of 1965, which prohibits the use of racial quotas; (2) the ratification of the Civil Rights Act (1964) and the Voting Rights Act (1965) prohibiting racial discrimination; (3) the executive orders 10925 (1961) and 11246 (1965) demanding affirmative action; and (4) the passage of the Education for All Handicapped Children Act (1975) creating inclusive education. These policies were the result of the civil rights movement and the cultural revolution of the 1960s that brought to the forefront of America's consciousness the early liberal values of equal opportunity and social justice. The multicultural education movement later advanced these social reforms by developing awareness of the difficult experiences of the marginalized groups that were protected by these regulations and advocated for more inclusive policies.

However, a group of neo-conservative scholars (Crozier, Huntington, and Watanuki 1975) perceived these democratic events as clear attacks on American democracy. They argued that the participation of marginal groups that were previously politically apathetic (Kaase and Newton 1995, 25) risked the: "danger of 'overloading' the political system with demands which extended its functions and undermined its authority" (Huntington 1976, 37). The essential goal of the Report on the Governability of Democracies (Crozier, Huntington, and Watanuki 1975) was to create awareness about the need to make democracies and their citizens "more able to service capital" (Davies and Bansel 2007, 250), rather than creating additional needs for a government already overwhelmed with meeting the needs of all its emergent and diverse citizens:

> At the present time, a significant challenge comes from the intellectuals and related groups who assert their disgust with the corruption, materialism, and inefficiency of democracy and with the subservience of democratic government to "monopoly capitalism." The development of an "adversary culture" among intellectuals has affected students, scholars, and the media [...] In an age of widespread secondary school and university education, the pervasiveness of the mass media, and the displacement of manual labor by clerical and professional employees, this development constitutes a challenge to democratic government. (Crozier, Huntington, and Watanuki 1975, 6–7)

This facet of neoliberalism – to make democracies and people more governable – has rarely been examined. However, back in the late 1970s Foucault (1978/1979) addressed neoliberalism as a form of governmentality[4] when he was lecturing at the College de France. He discussed the implementation of Ordo-liberalism[5] in Europe and the Chicago School of Economics arising in the mid-twentieth century in the US (Brown 2003, 5).

Foucault's discussion did not focus on the economic policies of neoliberalism but on the ways that it becomes a "mode of governance." He contended that neoliberalism as political rationale morphs into a large ideological apparatus that transforms the nature of the state, the notion of citizenship, and produces new subjectivities, moralities, behaviors, and desires. The shifting of what was considered common sense becomes "a new organization of the social" (Brown 2003, 2).

What follows is a description of the characteristics of neoliberalism as a political rationale and as a form of governmentality, grounded in the work of Foucault (1978/1979), Brown (2003), and Davies and Bansel (2007):

- Neoliberalism takes control of the political sphere and subsumes it entirely to the needs of the market. The individual citizen becomes a *homo oeconomicus* and every single area of social, cultural, and political life is reduced to the simple economic principles of cost-benefit, production, and efficiency (Brown 2003, 9).
- Neoliberalism develops new discourses, institutional practices, rewards, norms, and new common-sense values to engulf every single aspect of human life into this form of governmentality. "Neo-liberalism involves a normative rather than ontological claim about the pervasiveness of economic rationality and advocates the institution building, policies, and discourse development appropriate to such a claim. Neo-liberalism is a constructivist project" (Brown 2003, 9).
- Neoliberalism as a political rationale does not mean *laissez faire* capitalism. In this form of governmentality, there is always active political intervention and manipulation of all the social institutions, from the media, the law, the arts, schools, and universities, to the most important protagonist of all, the state (Brown 2003, 9).
- Under neoliberalism the state acquires a new identity. It becomes the protector of capital and its role is reduced to the enactment of monetary, fiscal, social, and educational policies to nourish and protect the market. The legitimacy of the state is based on its ability to be true to this function (Brown 2003, 10).
- Under neoliberalism, government practices are reduced to the same calculating equations of profitability and cost-efficiency benefits. Gone are the commitments to equality and social justice grounded on the traditional liberalism of the founding fathers (Brown 2003, 10).
- Under neoliberalism the individual citizen becomes one of the most important targets. This is not related to the individualism of Adam Smith but it is a redefinition of the role of citizens as "entrepreneurial actors in every sphere of life" (Brown 2003, 15). In this form of governmentality, individuals become rational subjects whose goal in life is to be self-sufficient. They blame themselves for their own failures regardless of the structural constraints they may face. "A 'mismanaged life' becomes a new mode of depoliticizing social and economic powers and at the same time reduces political citizenship to an unprecedented degree of passivity and political complacency" (Brown 2003, 15). Nevertheless, the neo-liberal citizen defines herself as having the power of freedom, represented in the many choices that the free market offers.

As Davies and Bansel (2007) claim:

> Neoliberalism functions at the level of the subject, producing *docile subjects* who are tightly governed, and who, at the same time define themselves as free. Individuals, we suggest, have been seduced by their own perceived powers of freedom and have, at the same time, let go significant collective power, through, for example, allowing the erosion of union power. (249)

- Under liberalism the public-minded individual is replaced by the *homo oeconomicus* and the body politics is replaced by a group of entrepreneurs and consumers. "Civil society is reduced to a domain for exercising this entrepreneurship" (Brown 2003, 38). It is important to remember how Margaret Thatcher, the leader of neoliberalism in Europe summarized this concept: "There is no such thing as a society" (cited in Hursh 2005, 12).
- As a form of governmentality, neoliberalism corrodes the institutions, values, and processes of liberal democracies (Brown 2003). It seeks to eliminate the notion of education as "a common and public good in the public interest" (Luke 2005, 161).

The privatization of state institutions, particularly the defunding of public education, appears to have serious implications for the future of American democracy.

Neoliberalism and the demise of education as a public good

The assaults against public education during the 1980s responded to the allegations of neoliberalism that schools were not responding to the needs of the economy or supporting US efforts to consolidate its leadership in the emergent global market. The publication of several state and commission reports[6] convinced American society that something was wrong with public education. The alarming cries for educational reform centered on teacher education. Schools were accused of failing students and universities were blamed for the lack of preparation of teachers. Accreditation institutions assumed a greater role by assuring that the curriculum and pedagogical practices of teacher preparation were aligned to the goals of neoliberalism. Gradually the goal of public education was changed from forming critical citizens for a healthy democracy to focusing on their development of functional skills to be economically productive (Hursh 2005, 5).

The rhetoric of neoliberalism – the shifting of common sense – was displayed in the campaign to discredit public education.[7] Americans lost confidence in the revered institution of public schooling. Neoliberalism blamed schools for the inequalities created by the unregulated market while increasing stratification and exclusion through a militant standardization movement that relied on testing, publication of test scores, and ranking of public schools.

Simultaneously, neoliberalism instilled fear in the public that the decline of American economic power was imminent if schools were not fixed. Neoliberalism became associated with democracy, economic stability, accountability, and more importantly, school choice. Schools, teachers, and their unions were portrayed as institutions that were compromising the success of the American economy. This was the case in Wisconsin when in 2010 Governor Walker proposed a controversial bill to substantially diminish the collective-bargaining rights of thousands of public school teachers while increasing their contributions to their pensions and health benefits under the excuse that those cuts were essential to reduce the state deficit. The bill, which also included a provision limiting the percentage of property taxes that the state could raise to offset its debt, and would end enrollment caps for charter schools, was approved in the midst of one of the most powerful protests at the national level. This was a very symbolic piece of legislation as it signaled the path that other states might follow to continue undermining public school teachers and their unions.

The NCLB represents the culmination of 20 years of rampant attacks against public education and one of the most important achievements of neoliberalism. Through NCLB the federal government was able to enact legislation that erased the tradition of local control of schools, with the only exception being Indian reservations (McCarty 2008). Schools became at once standardized in the name of accountability. Under NCLB, schools are required to publish disaggregated data on students' test scores and use specific scientific curricula to make improvements on students' achievement. Teachers continue receiving permanent training on how to teach to the test and they are penalized if their students' test scores are not raised. Because test scores reflect a myriad of influences, including the students' family income (Hursh 2004), schools in these working class communities are being shut down, reconstituted, or offered "for sale" because they could not meet the intended academic improvements. As a result, they become charter schools managed by non-profit charter management organizations or for-profit businesses.

This is part of the reconstitution of public services under the new neoliberal state. Education is no longer a public good offered and protected by the government; it has become a commodity that can be traded in the market. "Neoliberalism, unlike liberalism, withdraws value from the social good. Economic productivity is seen to come not from government investments in education, but from transforming education into a product that can be bought and sold like anything else" (Davies and Bansel 2007, 254). Forgotten are the intended democratic goals of public education.

The appropriation of universities as cultural spaces

Universities, where the institution of tenure protects academic freedom, have been one of the few remaining public spheres where face-to-face communities have articulated the connection between education and freedom (Greene 1982). However, as educational institutions, they have also fallen prey to the expansion of neoliberal policies. Since the late 1970s, neoliberalism began introducing fundamental changes to the way universities operate, using the strategy of "piecemeal functionalism."[8]

University restructuring began in, "1978 when the US Business-Higher Education Forum was established to create partnership between corporations and universities to support science, math, and technology" (Torres and Schugurensky 2002, 436). However, it soon became clear later that the intention of this group was to align higher education institutions to the goals of neoliberalism. According to Torres and Schugurensky (2002, 436), since its inception the Forum was, "interested in influencing policy formation and creating ideological hegemony, aligning higher education with the business and corporate sector." Similar interest groups proliferated later, including a Canadian version, the Canadian Corporate-Higher Education Forum, launched in 1983 (Torres and Schugurensky 2002), and the Business Roundtable consisting of the top 300 CEOs in the nation, which focused on education from 1989 on (Kumashiro 2010).

Michael Useem (1984) argues that these changes in higher education respond to the implementation of what he describes as "institutional capitalism"[9] that seeks to intensify the alliances between corporations and cultural institutions (Torres and Schugurensky 2002, 435). The increasing presence of corporate executives in boards of regents and boards of trustees of universities aims to influence the direction of their academic and non-academic work to support the expansion of globalization (Torres and Schugurensky 2002, 435). As such, these reconstituted governing boards have diligently embraced the discourse of accountability and standardization initiated in the 1980s and supported the demands, "for a permanent assessment of the outcomes of the higher education system" (Torres and Schugurensky 2002, 443).

The power brokers of neoliberalism

The Business Roundtable, formed in 1972 and dedicated to influencing education since 1989, was responsible for organizing a powerful group of billionaires, philanthropists, and foundations with the purpose of implementing neoliberal reforms in public education. Part of this original group were the: "Annenberg Center, the Broad Foundation [from Los Angeles real estate magnate Eli Broad], Education Trust, Harvard Graduate School, and the editorial boards of major newspapers" (Kumashiro 2010, 59).

Later on, other powerful players joined this effort, among them: the Bill and Melinda Gates Foundation, the Walton Family Foundation, the Michael and Susan Dell Foundation, the Lilly Endowment, the David and Lucile Packard Foundation, the W.K. Kellogg Foundation, and the Doris and Donald Fisher Fund (Kumashiro 2010; Ravitch 2010). However, the three most powerful donors controlling the direction of public education are Eli Broad, the Walton Family Foundation from the founder of Wal-Mart, and Bill and Melinda Gates (Ravitch 2010).

The city of Chicago is one example of the changes that these powerful business groups are able to make by pouring millions of dollars into initiatives and groups that are dismantling liberal public education. Renaissance 2010 was the program initiated by Mayor Richard Daley and envisioned intellectually by the Commercial Club of Chicago to restructure Chicago Public Schools (Kumashiro 2010, 58). Arne Duncan, a non-educator and the CEO of Chicago Public Schools, was chosen as Obama's secretary of education because he pioneered the reconstitution of public schools under Renaissance 2010, and was responsible for implementing the goal of closing 60 low-performing public schools and opening 100 new ones as small schools, charter, or contract schools by 2010.

To date, 75 inner city schools have opened with mixed results and Chicago is one of the cities with the highest numbers of alternative certification programs and reconstituted schools because of the strong monetary support of philanthrocapitalists (Ravitch 2010) for educational initiatives that promote the privatization of public schooling (Kumashiro 2010; Lipman 2003).

Not coincidentally, another powerful player in the campaign to restructure teacher preparation is Teach for America, which has emerged as one of the most overlooked groups that has coalesced with neoliberalism to dismiss the notion that teachers need formal teacher education before stepping in a classroom.

Teach for America has an authoritative presence in Washington, DC,[10] Chicago, and other major metropolises across the nation. According to Miner (2010):

> TFA spends significant organizational time, energy, and money on its alumni, who are arguably the source of the organization's true political power. The most famous alumni are Michelle Rhee, former chancellor of the Washington, DC public schools, and Mike Feinberg and David Levin, founders of the KIPP Schools. (28)

It was in Chicago where Teach for America started and where Michelle Rhee ran the New Teachers Project, which created the Chicago Teaching Fellows Program, another replica of the Teach For America (TFA) alternative certification program.

TFA's permanent lobbying of major school districts has made their members authoritative participants in all the reform efforts to dismantle public education. For example, in the districts that are undergoing severe budget cuts, senior teachers are laid off and replaced by TFA corps. "More recently, in Washington, DC, former TFA corps member and current Schools Chancellor Michelle Rhee laid off 229 teachers in October, but only six of the 170 TFA teachers in the system, according to the *Washington Post*" (Miner 2010, 29). Miner, citing Peter Downs, president of the St Louis elected school board, says, "that the district pays $2000 a year to TFA for each of its recruits" (Miner 2010, 27–8).

TFA's major donors are the: "Broad Foundation, the Michael and Susan Dell Fundation, the Doris and Donald Fisher Fund, the Rainwater Charitable Funds, and the federal government via AmeriCorps and the US Department of Education" (Kumashiro 2010, 58). In 2008, TFA listed: "Wachovia as one of five corporations donating more than $1 million at the national level. The others are Goldman Sachs, Visa, the biotechnology firm Amgen, and the golfing tournament Quail Hollow Championship" (Miner 2010, 30). Included in this list are some of the corporations responsible for the financial debacle of the past few years. In addition the Walton Family Foundation, created by Sam Walton, founder of Wal-Mart, contributed $9 million to TFA, which is the single largest contribution to the organization (Miner 2010, 32).

In 2008, TFA spent more than 500,000 dollars[11] lobbying state and federal legislatures to pass legislation to approve alternative teacher certification and other pro-business educational initiatives (Miner 2010, 32).

These are certainly major concerns about an organization that plays such a powerful and authoritative role in the demise of public education and actively benefits from the restructuring of teacher preparation.

The commodification of schools of education

Schools of education are the most affected by these whirlwinds of neoliberal reforms.[12] Among the major changes are drastic transformations in the preparation of teachers, the intensification of the business of accreditation, the appropriation of multicultural education, and the formation of a new managerial and professional middle class to support the privatization of education.

Teacher education has been systematically degraded since the 1980s with the publication of dozens of reports attacking public schools, teachers, and the universities that prepare them. One of the most intense targets has been to dismantle traditional teacher preparation programs that have an extended residency component and a coaching model to prepare and induct pre-service teachers. For example, Teach for America, and Secretary of Education, Arne Duncan, have strongly criticized long-term teacher preparation because they deem it lengthy, expensive, and unnecessary.

The commanding forces of neoliberalism, among them the federal government, local states, business groups, and accrediting institutions, are urging the creation of fast-track teacher preparation programs. This happens in spite of the fact that abundant research links student achievement to traditional teacher credentialing (Cochran

Smith 2001; Darling-Hammond 2000, 2001; Darling-Hammond, Berry, and Thoreson 2001; Darling-Hammond and Young 2002; Weiner 2007, 275; Wilson, Floden, and Ferrini-Mundy 2002; Zeichner 2006).

As Kumashiro (2010) argues, the excuse that alternative routes to teacher certification challenge the monopoly of the universities has resulted in a proliferation of alternative teacher certification outside higher education institutions. These short-lived teacher preparation programs are reproducing at a fast pace while universities are also creating alternative teacher credentialing programs to remain competitive in that market.

Arne Duncan, Obama's secretary of education and one of the most recognized czars of neoliberalism, has spent most of his tenure encouraging the creation of alternative certification models and attacking schools of education, evinced by the speeches at Columbia Teachers College and at the AACTE conference. What follows is an excerpt from Duncan's (2009) speech at Teachers College:

> Now I am all in favor of expanding high-quality alternative certificate routes, like High Tech High, the New Teacher Project, Teach for America, and teacher residency programs. But these promising alternative programs produce fewer than 10,000 teachers per year. The predominance of education schools in preparing teachers is not the only reason this is a national priority and a critical concern for higher education ... America's taxpayers already generously support teacher preparation programs. And it is only right that this investment should be well spent.[13] (http://www.ed.gov/news/speeches/teacher-preparation-reforming-uncertain-profession)

This is an excerpt from Duncan's talk at AACTE (2010):

> In my talk last fall at the Teachers College at Columbia I called for a sea-change in our schools of education. I challenged schools of education for failing to teach aspiring teachers how to use data to differentiate and improve instruction, and boost student learning. Great teacher after great teacher I've talked with around the country told me that they learned those skills on the job, not in school. I criticized some ed schools for a lack of rigorous and relevant research, and for failing to provide sufficient high-quality, hands-on practical training about managing the classroom, especially for high-needs students. And I said that colleges of education had to do a much better job of gathering data on the effectiveness of their graduates in the classroom and their impact on student achievement. At present, most colleges of education know little to nothing about the impact of their graduates on student learning.[14] (http://www.ed.gov/news/speeches/preparing-teachers-and-school-leaders-tomorrow-secretary-arne-duncans-remarks-american)

These remarks are part of a campaign to prepare the public for new incoming changes to teacher certification. Duncan proposed a new national exam for all teacher candidates that would measure their teaching competence and the quality of their teacher preparation programs. Those schools of education that rank highest will be rewarded with money from the Race to the Top initiative (Berlak 2010).

In California, there are already several entrance and exit exams, among them the CBEST (California Basic Educational Skill Test), CSET (California Subject Examination for Teaching), RICA (Reading Instruction Competence Assessment), CalTPA (California Teacher Performance Assessment), and the additional evaluations of the NCATE and other credentialing commissions. Thus, Duncan's proposal to require PACT (Performance Assessment for California Teachers) as a national exit exam (which is being used as an alternative to CalTPA) would add another layer of federal control of what teachers need to learn in order to teach.

According to a teacher educator (Berlak 2010) whose department uses PACT to assess credential candidates: "teaching patterns valued by PACT are primarily aspects of explicit, systematic, direct instruction that will instill in students knowledge specified by the state-mandated standards and measured by standardized tests" (43–4). The creation of signature assignments in Live-Text and other commercial software paid for by the students is already interfering with the academic freedom of faculty to determine their own assessment methods.

The tactics of neoliberalism are multiple and concurrent. Alternative certification creates competition and deprofessionalizes teaching, while NCLB, Race to the Top, and accrediting institutions force schools of education to align their curriculum and pedagogical practices to the formation of the *homo oeconomicus*.

Marketing, accreditation, and diversity

As the "cash cows" of most universities, schools of education are also pressured to increase student enrollment and to compete with all the purveyors of public and private education, which in this era of corporate schooling includes online universities, for-profit higher education institutions, and private educational corporations. Therefore, schools of education are seeking accreditation at higher rates to become more marketable because what sells well is the promise of accountability and excellence.[15] Institutions like NCATE currently accredit 657 colleges of education and 100 more are in the process of being accredited nationwide. Arne Duncan highlighted the significance of national accreditation as part of his mission to align education to the needs of the market:

> As you know, the accreditation of schools of education is a voluntary process, and historically coursework had been given greater priority than clinical training for students in accreditation. But there also are encouraging signs that colleges of education want to make self-policing more meaningful, with clinical experience driving coursework. Both NCATE, the National Council for Accreditation of Teacher Education, and AACTE, the American Association of Colleges for Teacher Education, are firmly behind the new drive to link teacher preparation programs to better student outcomes. (Duncan 2009)

It is expected that the imminent establishment of a national exam for credentialing teacher candidates that will convey quantitative data on students' competence and quality of their program, will be used by national accrediting institutions to grant or refuse accreditation of teacher preparation programs.

National accreditation has also contributed to the reification of diversity. Schools of education in their quest to seek NCATE accreditation have developed mission statements and conceptual frameworks that articulate NCATE's commercial notion of diversity and social justice that attracts aspiring teachers. Nonetheless, the tendency of schools of education to link NCATE with the concept of social justice triggered an alarming response from conservative groups that support neoliberal policies. As a result, in 2007, NCATE withdrew the term social justice from its accreditation training documents in response to concerns that the council was emphasizing too much diversity:

NCATE has never required a "social justice" disposition; NCATE expects institutions to select professional dispositions they would like to see in the teachers they prepare. The term "social justice," though well understood by NCATE's institutions, was widely and wildly misinterpreted by commentators not familiar with the workings of NCATE. NCATE has never had a "social justice" standard and thus did not enforce such a standard. (NCATE 2007)

If there was any hope that NCATE would reaffirm its original role of advocating for the inclusion of social justice, diversity, and equity as it did in 1977 when it required the inclusion of multicultural education in teacher education, this statement leaves no doubts about its political orientation. Accrediting institutions, particularly NCATE, play an essential role as regulators of the educational market.

New degrees for the neoliberal society

Another change in schools of education has arisen as a result of the rapidly emerging and powerful managerial middle class that provides support to the policies of neoliberalism. According to Apple (2001), these are people with backgrounds in management and efficiency techniques who provide the technical and: "professional support for accountability, measurement, product control, and assessment that is required by the proponents of neoliberal policies [...] and tighter central control in education" (57).

Thus, neoliberalism has generated a new market to train teachers and administrators for charter schools, and leaders with expertise in management techniques. Schools of education are creating new academic programs and degrees with specialization in charter schools and leadership in urban education. In addition, because NCLB made the old multipurpose PhD in education obsolete (Guthrie 2009), schools of education are creating fast-track doctorates (EdD) in educational leadership[16] to train school administrators, with the ultimate goal of improving academic achievement as measured by student test scores.

This new market has proven so popular and profitable that schools of education have entirely reorganized their academic units to accommodate the large number of students who seek to obtain a doctorate in three years without the intensity of its research-oriented counterpart (Goldring and Schuermann 2009; Guthrie 2009; Levine 2005a, 2005b).

Public relations, national rankings, and managerialism

Another important development is related to the reconfiguration of schools of education as powerful players in the educational marketplace. Traditionally, the US News & World Report rankings have driven the academic and administrative decisions of schools of education, however, at present neoliberalism has exacerbated those demands. Deans of schools of education are forced to increase their standing as a basic marketing strategy to increase student enrollment. As a result, more often they devote an unprecedented amount of time to networking with the constituencies that provide feedback on the rankings,[17] in addition to their expanding fundraising activities.

Public relations have become so fundamental for schools of education that new positions have been created for communication managers, public relations officials, directors of development offices, and media coordinators within these academic units. The work of these new staff members has become crucial to make schools of education and their leaders significant players in the educational market.

Lastly, one of the most visible changes in schools of education can be observed in how these academic units are being financially administered. *Managerialism* has taken over the administration of universities (Apple 2001) and particularly schools of education. The corporate practices of performance-based assessments, recruiting, marketing, bottom lines, business reports, standardization, work norms, and tuition-based revenues have gradually penetrated the daily life of these academic institutions.

Academic capitalism has entered American universities and it is redefining the academic premises upon which the entire higher education system was instituted. Universities, which are the last public space protected by academic freedom to promote the development of public intellectuals, are losing ground to the globalization of higher education.

Reclaiming public education as a common good

Nussbaum (2010) proposes a *human development paradigm* to counteract the *education for profit* that is replacing American liberal education. This model emphasizes the dignity of all citizens and focuses on broadening the basic spectrum of human and political rights to include social and economic rights (e.g. education and health), which have not yet been ratified by the US government. This *human development* model seeks to inspire in its citizens:

- The ability to think well about political issues affecting the nation, to examine, reflect, argue, and debate, deferring to neither tradition nor authority.
- The ability to recognize fellow citizens as people with equal rights [...] to look at them with respect, as ends, not just as tools to be manipulated for one's own profit.
- The ability to have concern for the lives of others, to grasp what policies of many types mean for the opportunities and experiences of one's fellow citizens, of many types, and for people outside one's own nation.
- The ability to see one's own nation, in turn, as a part of a complicated world order in which issues of many kinds require intelligent transnational deliberation for their resolution. (Nussbaum 2010, 26)

These concepts should be taught through the integration of literature, arts, math, and science; the discussion of economic history, political geography, and global citizenship; and the examination of theories of social and global justice from a political theory perspective (Dewey 2004; Greene 1995; Nussbaum 2010, 91–2).

Fundamental to the teaching of this human development approach are the pedagogical model of Socratic teaching (or problem-posing pedagogy as Freire calls it), the teaching of debate, the integration of role-playing, the use of experiential teaching, and the practice of the arts. Among the important goals of this kind of education is the capacity to inculcate in students empathy for their fellow citizens. This has been one of the most significant components of traditional liberal education and a key concept for the preservation of the common good.

In addition, Andrzejewski, Baltodano, and Symcox (2009) propose a collective vision for social justice that includes transformative principles for protecting teachers and their work, transforming the curriculum of public schools and universities, and transforming the preparation of teachers beyond NCATE (281–5). Among some of these guidelines and declarations of rights for teachers and students are the following:

- Teachers must have the protection to form and join labor unions of their choice, and initiate grievance processes against those (union leaders as well as school leaders) who are not protecting the rights of teachers or are involved in corruption.
- Teachers must have protection to exercise academic freedom for research, creative activity, and dissemination of knowledge.
- Teachers must be able to teach human rights, social and environmental justice and peace.
- Teachers must be able to create their own curriculum as long as it meets the benchmarks for grade level. No teacher should be forced to follow teacher-proof curricula, or be threatened, harassed, or demoted for not implementing pre-package curriculum. (282)

- Teacher candidates must have the freedom to learn pedagogical skills and global political knowledge that will make them competent teachers and transformative intellectuals in the classroom.
- Teacher candidates must have the freedom to experience modeling of pedagogical models such as problem posing pedagogy, Socratic dialogues, questioning, feedback, authentic pre- and post-assessment, experiential learning, heterogeneous grouping, peer grouping, and so forth.
- Teacher candidates must have the freedom to experience student-teaching before being formally inducted into the classroom. (284)

These two frameworks (Andrzejewski, Baltodano, and Symcox 2009; Nussbaum 2010) are not driven by a utopian vision of education. They closely resemble the constitution of many industrial countries, including the US, are inspired by the work of recognized educators worldwide, and are based on human rights conventions ratified by the majority of the world's nations. These visions may be used as an initial platform to initiate a conversation and launch a movement to reclaim education as a public good.

Michael Apple (2001) remembered Paulo Freire saying that "education must begin in critical dialogue," (218) and this is the conversation that this article seeks to inspire. It proposes the immediate task of organizing a grassroots movement comprised of teachers, students, community activists, union leaders, and faculty at colleges of education and liberal arts who are concerned with the demise of education as a *public good*.

This organic process is essential to create historical blocs (Gramsci 1971) and counter hegemonic alliances to reclaim the public spheres that have been offered for sale (Apple 2001). This organizing effort may take the forms of teachers' study groups, student councils, neighborhood councils, faculty support groups, community meetings, teacher union convocations, and so forth. The most important thing is that Americans begin to have a conversation about what kind of education and what kind of democracy they seek to sustain.

Among some of the most pressing issues to consider for these constituencies may be the following:

- Reexamine, evaluate, and support the reconfigured role of unions in public schools.
- Reclaim local control of public schools and reconfigure local school boards where parents and teachers are the majority.

- Create strong and authentic partnerships between local schools, local unions, and universities' teacher education programs.
- Conceptualize and implement teacher preparation models that reflect the best practices and the best interest of students.
- Encourage greater involvement of educators and members of this movement in public office to enact legislation to protect education as a public good.
- Seek judicial protection to stop the federal government from interfering in the local control of schools.
- Create new teacher accreditation organizations that truly respond to a professional and civic vision of public schooling.
- Organize faculty groups to create awareness in departments and colleges about the advancement of neoliberalism in higher education.
- Reimagine teacher education in terms of professional identity, democratic goals, and structural arrangements with the larger society (Wilkinson 2007).

The issues to consider are far broader and deeper than what is suggested here, but a critical dialog about the state of education in the US would be a starting point in the quest to protect the most important of the social institutions of American liberal democracy, public education.

Notes

1. NCATE is the National Council for Accreditation of Teacher Education; AACTE is the American Association of Colleges for Teacher Education.
2. Dewey's beliefs in the intrinsic relationship between theory and practice were fundamental for his conception of teachers as transformative intellectuals who were morally attentive to larger social reforms. Dewey believed that schools were public spaces to critically assess the excesses of the industrial movement and to advocate for those who were being silenced.
3. Friedrich von Hayek and Milton Friedman were recipients of the Nobel Memorial Prize in Economics in 1974 and 1976, respectively.
4. Foucault's 1978 and 1979 College of France lectures had been recorded in audiocassettes and were unpublished and untranscribed until 2004, when the first edition of this work was published in French. In 2008, these lectures were translated and published in English.
5. Ordoliberalism is the term given to the neoliberal governmentality conceptualized by members of the Freiburg School after WWI in Germany and implemented in West Germany after WWII. In spite of the fact that this school had existed in parallel to the Frankfurt School of Critical Theory, it had opposite views on many of the key issues. Ordoliberalism impacted the development of the Chicago School of Economics in the US; however, the latter became more radical (Lemke 2001). Unlike Adam Smith's assumptions about the natural forces of the market, Ordoliberalism proposed that the market is not innate, and therefore, the government has to intervene in order to protect it. The state has to create competition, and encourage demand to keep the market alive. In this view, capitalism is a social construct, created and maintained by the government (Brown 2003; Lemke 2001). There is no such thing as the "logic of the market." It is the state that defines the life and direction of the economy.
6. Among these reports were: *A Nation at Risk: The Imperative for Educational Reform* (National Commission on Excellence in Education 1983); *A Nation Prepared: Teachers for the 21st Century: The Report of the Task Force on Teaching as a Profession* (Carnegie Forum on Education and the Economy 1986); *Tomorrow's Teachers* (Holmes Group 1986); *Time for Results: The Governors' 1991 Report on Education* (National Governors' Association 1991), and *Goals 2000* (United States Department of Education 1985).

7. See for example popular films like "Waiting for Superman" (2010).
8. This technique is defined as the way norms and changes are introduced gradually, "lessening the chance people will grasp the overall scheme and organize resistance" (Sklar 1980, 21, cited in Davies and Bansel 2007, 251). "Piecemeal functionalism" has been one of the most successful methods that neoliberalism has used to render itself invisible and gradually consolidate its platform of governmentality (Davies and Bansel 2007). The invisibility of neoliberalism makes it difficult to challenge the depth of the social reorganization carried out by this ideology.
9. Useem uses the term "institutional capitalism" to differentiate it from the *family* and *managerial* capitalism of previous eras (Torres and Schugurensky 2002, 435).
10. TFA is so influential in the White House that it successfully orchestrated a campaign against Linda Darling-Hammond, one of its most vociferous critics, when she was considered for a key position in the Obama administration (Miner 2010).
11. This is the maximum amount allowed for political lobbying for a 501(c)3 organization.
12. For example, during spring 2010, a graduate school of education in a public Tier-1, research university in the Southwest was "de-established" and collapsed into a teachers college because the university board of regents and the state legislature considered it more profitable to focus on teacher preparation than subsidizing an entire academic unit devoted to research. Tenure and non-tenure faculty were told they were "free agents" and were instructed to search for jobs somewhere else.
13. Arne Duncan's 2009 address at Columbia Teachers College, "Teacher Preparation: Reforming the Uncertain Profession."
14. Arne Duncan's 2010 address at the American Association of Colleges for Teacher Education Conference, "Preparing the Teachers and School Leaders of Tomorrow."
15. According to the NCATE's mission (2010), "Applicants to an NCATE accredited institution will have the assurance that the institution's educator program has met national standards and received the profession's 'seal of approval'" (3).
16. See for example the EdD programs in educational leadership at Vanderbilt University, University of Southern California, Pepperdine University, Arizona State University, and St Louis University among many others.
17. Some of the people who provide feedback on the quality of schools of education are alumni, superintendents, principals, and other deans of schools of education. The names of participants cannot be revealed because their participation was confidential according to the protection offered by the Institutional Review Board (IRB) that approved this research.

References

Amin, A. 1994. *Post-Fordism: A reader*. Oxford: Blackwell.
Andrzejewski, J., M. Baltodano, and L. Symcox, eds. 2009. *Social justice, peace and environmental education. Transformative standards*. New York, NY: Routledge.
Apple, M.W. 2001. *Educating the right way. Market, standards, God, and inequality*. New York, NY: Routledge.
Balibar, E. 1995. *The philosophy of Marx*. London: Verso.
Baltodano, M. 2009. The pursuit of social justice in the United States. In *Social justice, peace and environmental education. Transformative standards*, ed. J. Andrzejewski, M. Baltodano, and L. Symcox, 273–87. New York, NY: Routledge.

Berlak, A. 2010. Coming soon to your favorite credential program: National exit exams. *Rethinking Schools* 24, no. 4: 41–5.
Bonefeld, W., and J. Holloway. 1991. *Post-Fordism and social form*. London: Macmillan.
Brittan, S. 1995. *Capitalism with a human face*. Cambridge, MA: Harvard University Press.
Brown, W. 2003. Neoliberalism and the end of democracy. *Theory & Event* 7, no. 1. DOI: 10.1353/tae.2003.0020.
Carnegie Forum on Education and the Economy. 1986. *A nation prepared: Teachers for the 21st century. The report of the task force on teaching as a profession*. New York: Carnegie Forum on Education and the Economy.
Cochran Smith, M. 2001. Reforming teacher education. *Journal of Teacher Education* 52, no. 4: 263–5.
Codd, J. 1988. The construction and deconstruction of educational policy documents. *Journal of Education Policy* 3, no. 3: 235–47.
Compton, M., and L. Weiner, eds. 2008. *The global assault on teaching, teachers, and their unions*. New York, NY: Palgrave Macmillan.
Crozier, M., S.P. Huntington, and J. Watanuki. 1975. *The crisis of democracy: Report on the governability of democracies to the trilateral commission*. New York, NY: New York University Press.
Darling-Hammond, L. 2000. Teacher quality and student achievement: A review of state policy evidence. *Education Policy Analysis Archives* 8, no. 1. http://epaa.asu.edu/ojs/article/view/392.
Darling-Hammond, L. 2001. *The research and rhetoric on teacher certification: A response to "teacher certification reconsidered"*. National Commission on Teaching and America's Future. Palo Alto, CA: Stanford University.
Darling-Hammond, L., B. Berry, and A. Thoreson. 2001. Does teacher certification matter? Evaluating the evidence. *Educational Evaluation and Policy Analysis* 23, no. 1: 57–77.
Darling-Hammond, L., and P. Young. 2002. Defining "highly qualified teachers": What does "scientifically-based research" actually tell us? *Educational Researcher* 31, no. 9: 13–25.
Davies, B., and P. Bansel. 2007. Neoliberalism and education. *International Journal of Qualitative Studies in Education* 20, no. 3: 247–59.
Dewey, J. 1916. *Democracy and education*. New York, NY: Macmillan.
Dewey, J. 1956. *The child and the curriculum; and the school and society*. Chicago, IL: University of Chicago Press.
Dewey, J. 2004. *Democracy and education. An introduction to the philosophy of education*. Mineola, NY: Dover.
Duncan, A. 2009. *Teacher preparation: Reforming the uncertain profession*. New York, NY: Columbia University Teachers College. http://www.ed.gov/news/speeches/teacher-preparation-reforming-uncertain-profession.
Duncan, A. 2010. Preparing the teachers and school leaders of tomorrow. Speech given at the American Association of Colleges for Teacher Education Conference, February 19, in Atlanta, GA. http://www.ed.gov/news/speeches/preparing-teachers-and-school-leaders-tomorrow-secretary-arne-duncans-remarks-american.
Foucault, M. 1978/1979. *The birth of biopolitics. Lectures at the College de France*. Trans. G. Burcher and ed. A. Davidson. New York, NY: Palgrave Macmillan. (Original work published in 2004 in French by Editions du Seuil/Gallimard).
Freire, P. 1970. *Pedagogy of the oppressed*. New York, NY: Seabury Press.
Goldring, E., and P. Schuermann. 2009. The changing context of K-12 education administration: Consequences for Ed.D. program design and delivery. *Peabody Journal of Education* 84, no. 1: 9–43.
Gramsci, A. 1971. *Selections from the prison notebooks*. Trans. and ed. Q. Hoare and G. Smith. New York, NY: International Publishers.
Greene, M. 1982. Public education and the public space. *Educational Researcher* 11, no. 4: 4–9.
Greene, M. 1991. Values education in the contemporary moment. *Clearing House* 64, no. 5: 301–4.
Greene, M. 1995. *Releasing the imagination: Essays on education, the arts, and social change*. San Francisco, CA: Jossey-Bass.

Guthrie, J.W. 2009. The case for a modern doctor of education degree (Ed.D.): Multipurpose education doctorates no longer appropriate. *Peabody Journal of Education* 84, no. 1: 3–8.

Holmes Group. 1986. *Tomorrow's teachers*. East Lansing, MI: The Holmes Group.

Huntington, S.P. 1976. The democratic distemper. In *The American Commonwealth*, ed. N. Gazer and I. Kristol, 9–38. New York, NY: Basic Books.

Hursh, D. 2004. Undermining democratic education in the USA: The consequences of global capitalism and neo-liberal policies for education policies at the local, state, and federal levels. *Policy Futures in Education* 2, nos. 3–4: 607–20.

Hursh, D. 2005. Neoliberalism, markets and accountability: Transforming education and undermining democracy in the United States and England. *Policy Futures in Education* 3, no. 1: 3–15.

Jessop, B. 1995. The regulation approach, governance and post-Fordism: Alternative perspectives on economic and political change? *Economy and Society* 24, no. 3: 307–33.

Kaase, M., and K. Newton. 1995. *Beliefs in government*. Vol. 5. Oxford: Oxford University Press.

Kumashiro, K.K. 2010. Seeing the bigger picture: Troubling movements to end teacher education. *Journal of Teacher Education* 6, nos. 1–2: 56–65.

Lemke, T. 2001. The birth of biopolitics: Michel Foucault's lecture at the College de France on neo-liberal governmentality. *Economy and Society* 30, no. 2: 190–207.

Levine, A. 2005a. *Educating researchers: The education schools project*. Washington, DC: The Education Schools Project. http://www.edschools.org/EducatingResearchers/educating_researchers.pdf.

Levine, A. 2005b. *Educating school leaders: The education schools project*. Washington, DC: The Education Schools Project. http://www.edschools.org/pdf/Final313.pdf.

Lipman, P. 2003. Beyond accountability: Toward schools that create new people for a new way of life. In *High stakes education: Inequality, globalization, and urban school reform*, ed. P. Lipman, 169–92. New York, NY: Routledge.

Luke, A. 1995–1996. Text and discourse in education: An introduction to critical discourse analysis. *Review of Research in Education* 21, no. 1: 3–48.

Luke, C. 2005. Capital and knowledge flows: Global higher education markets. *Asia Pacific Journal of Education* 25, no. 2: 159–74.

McCarty, T. 2008. The impact of high-stakes accountability policies on Native American learners: Evidence from research. Queensland Study Authority. http://www.qsa.qld.edu.au/6322.html.

McHoul, A.W. 1984. Writing, sexism and schooling: A discourse analytic investigation of some recent documents on sexism and education in Queensland. *Discourse* 4, no. 2: 1–17.

Miner, B. 2010. Looking past the spin. *Rethinking Schools* 24, no. 3: 24–33.

Muetzenfeldt, M., ed. 1992. *Society, state and politics in Australia*. Sydney: Pluto Press.

National Commission on Excellence in Education. 1983. *A nation at risk: The imperative for educational reform*. Washington, DC: US Department of Education.

National Council for Accreditation of Teacher Education (NCATE). 2007. NCATE issues call for action; defines professional dispositions as used in teacher education. http://www.ncate.org/public/102407.asp?ch=148.

National Council for Accreditation of Teacher Education (NCATE). 2010. NCATE's mission. http://ncate.org/Public/AboutNCATE/tabid/179/Default.aspx.

National Governors' Association. 1991. *Time for results: The governors' 1991 report on education*. Washington, DC: National Governors' Association.

Nussbaum, M. 1998. *Cultivating humanity: A classical defense of reform in liberal education*. Cambridge, MA: Harvard University Press.

Nussbaum, M. 2010. *Not for profit: Why democracy needs the humanities*. Princeton, NJ: Princeton University Press.

Ravitch, D. 2010. *The death and life of the great American school system: How testing and choice are undermining education*. Philadelphia, PA: Basic Books.

Sklar, H. 1980. *Trilateralism: The trilateral commission and elite planning for world management*. Montreal: Black Rose Books.

Symcox, L. 2009. From a Nation at Risk to No Child Left Behind: 25 years of neoliberal reform in education. In *Social justice, peace and environmental education. Transformative standards*, ed. J. Andrzejewski, M. Baltodano, and L. Symcox, 53–65. New York, NY: Routledge.

Taylor, S. 1997. Critical policy analysis: Exploring contexts, texts, and consequences. *Discourse: Studies in the Cultural Politics of Education* 18, no. 1: 23–35.

Torres, C.A., and D. Schugurensky. 2002. The political economy of higher education in the era of neoliberal globalization: Latin America in comparative perspective. *Higher Education* 43, no. 4: 429–55.

United States Department of Education. 1985. *Goals 2000*. Washington, DC: Author.

Useem, M. 1984. *The inner circle: Large corporations and the rise of business political activity in the US and UK*. Oxford: Oxford University Press.

Waiting for Superman. Directed by Davis Guggenheim. Hollywood, CA: Paramount Vintage, 2010.

Weiner, L. 2007. A lethal threat to US teacher education. *Journal of Teacher Education* 58, no. 4: 274–86.

Wilkinson, G. 2007. Civic professionalism: Teacher education and professional ideals and values in a commercialized education world. *Journal of Education for Teaching* 33, no. 3: 379–95.

Wilson, S., R. Floden, and J. Ferrini-Mundy. 2002. Teacher preparation research: An insider's view from the outside. *Journal of Teacher Education* 53, no. 3: 190–204.

Wirth, A.G. 1966. *John Dewey as educator: His design for work in education (1894–1904)*. New York, NY: Wiley.

Zeichner, K. 2006. Reflections of a university-based teacher educator on the future of college- and university-based teacher education. *Journal of Teacher Education* 7, no. 3: 326–40.

Index

Note: Page numbers in **bold** type indicate tables.
Page numbers followed by an 'n' indicate notes.

AACTE (American Association of Colleges for Teacher Education) 121, 132, 133
academic capitalism 4 *see also* corporatization of US schools
accreditation of schools of education 122, 133; accreditation institutions 128, 131, 137
affect from personal investments 54–6 *see also* fourth-grade classroom study of risk and affect
Alteños, the, of El Alto, Bolivia 33, 35, 45, 46 *see also* hip hop music
Arizona state laws 89, 92–3 *see also* ethnographic project on migrant status in Arizona

Bloomberg, Michael 10–12, 26n4
Bojórquez, Abraham 31, 36, 41, 44
Bolivia 34, 43; education 44; El Alto 31–49; neoliberal policies in 31, 32–3; privatization 32–3 *see also* hip hop music
Business Roundtable, the 129, 130

capitalism 6, 125; economic change and the new capitalist discourse 51, 52–6; migration of human capital 105, 106–7, 116; philanthrocapitalism 11–12, 13–14, 23, 24; racial philanthrocapitalism 15, 20, 25 *see also* neoliberalism
capitalist mindsets 63–4 *see also* fourth-grade classroom study of risk and affect
capital movement restrictions 4
Carnegie, Andrew 13
citizen, the, and citizenship 4, 65; neoliberal idea of 72–3, 88, 89–90, 91, 92, 100–1; preparation for 123–4, 135
civil liberties legislation 126
civil rights movement in US 122, 126
College Prep (College Preparatory Academy) 12–15; and professionalism 9–10, 15–18, 19–24; use of students for image management 18–19, 25
colorblindness and racial disparity 14, 17, 22, 25

consumption as mark of identity 53, 88, 89, 91, 100, 128
corporate links to higher education 129–30
corporatization of teacher education research study 122, 123–4, 131–5
corporatization of US schools 3–4, 10, 11–12, 23, 133–5
critical policy analysis 122–3
Critical Race Theory 14
Critical White Studies 14–15, 19
cultural capital of Whites 25

deregulation of the labor market 125
Dewey, John 123–4, 137n2
discourse theories, meanings of 51, 122
dress code and student professionalism 9, 18–19, 22, 24
Duncan, Arne 130, 131, 132, 133

economic change and the new capitalism 51, 52–6
education: neoliberalism in 1, 2–4, 6, 121–2, 128–35, 138n8 *see also* corporatization of teacher education research study
EIL (English as an international language) 73–4, 75–82
emotional intelligence 55–6 *see also* fourth-grade classroom study of risk and affect
employees in the new capitalism 53, 55
English-language voluntourism 69–70, 71–4, 76–7, 78–83
English-language voluntourism research study in Costa Rica 74–6, 78, 79, 80, 81–2
enterprise culture of the new capitalism 52–4
entrepreneur of the self 21; as neo-liberal subject 4, 6, 89–90, 98, 100–1, 127; and risk-taking 52–3, 55, 60–3, 65–8
ethnographic project on migrant status in Arizona 92–101, **93**; transcript excerpts and conventions **94, 95, 96, 97, 99,** 104
European colonization of Latin America 41–2

INDEX

faith-based organizations and mission work 70–1
fear, overcoming of 63–5
floating migration 106–8, 111–12, 115, 116
Fordism and post-Fordism 53, 125
Foundation, the, at College Prep 10, 12, 17–19
fourth-grade classroom study of risk and affect 56–60, 63–5; and individualistic risk-taking 60–3, 65–8
Friedman, Milton 124, 137n3
funding of public schools 15, 19, 21, 24, 128, 134; of ethnic studies in Arizona 92, 95; by philanthropic donors 130, 131

Gates Foundation, the 11, 130
globalization 1, 31, 52, 82–3, 106–7, 129–30 see also English-language voluntourism; neoliberalism
Global South, the 69, 75, 76–7, 80, 83n1
Goldsmith, Steve 11–12
governmentality, notion of 88–90
government and the welfare state 52, 124–6
graduation rate of New York public school students 11, 18

Hayek, Friedrich von 124, 137n3
healthcare 2
hip hop music 34–6; as protest movement for equity in El Alto, Bolivia 5, 31–2, 33, 34–41, 43–4, 46–7
human development paradigm for education 135–7
humanizing pedagogy 24
hyperglobalism 5, 72

image management through college matriculation 17, 18–19, 24–5
indigenous people of Bolivia 31–3, 34, 36–7, 39–40, 41–3, 45–6
individualism: as entrepreneurial neoliberal subject 6, 88–90, 94, 98, 100–1, 127; risk-taking and entrepreneur of the self 60–3, 65–8
individualization and economic activity 52–3, 72, 88, 127–8
Inglés Sin Barreras (English without Barriers) 5, 87–8, 89, 91–2, 93, 94–100
institutionalization of schooling practices 3–4

Johnson, Lyndon 124

Kennedy, John F. 124
Keynesianism 1–2, 88, 124
Klein, Joel 11, 12

labor migration 4–5 see also ethnographic project of migrant status in Arizona; oral histories of migrant Puerto Rican teachers to US Virgin Islands
labor protections in the global market 125
language and identity in educational practice 4–5, 108–9, 113–16
language use and globalization see EIL (English as an international language)
Latin America, vision of a united 41–2
Latino migration to the U.S. 106, 107 see also ethnographic project of migrant status in Arizona; migrant status in Arizona
legislation and social reforms in US 122, 126
Lima, Alto, Bolivian hip hopper 43
Living Books, fourth-grade student journal 60, 61
Llajuas, Bolivian hip hopper 38, 39, 40, 43–4, 46–7
Lozada, Gonzalo Sánchez de 33

market, role of the 2–3, 6, 89 see also globalization; neoliberalism
mattering zones and personal affect 54–5
migrant status in Arizona 87, 89, 92–3 see also ethnographic project of migrant status in Arizona
migration in the Caribbean 105–6, 107–8, 109; oral histories of Puerto Rican teachers in Virgin Islands 106, 111–16, 120
mindsets and motivation 63–4
mission work and faith-based organizations 71
Morales, Evo 34, 45, 46

nationalization of Bolivian industry 34
nation-state, the 5, 53, 72, 76, 83n1
NCATE (National Council for Accreditation of Teacher Education) 121, 133–4, 138n15
NCLB (No Child Left Behind) policy 122, 129, 133, 134
neo-conservative perceptions of civil liberties legislation 126
neoliberal discourses 4–5; and the individual 87, 88, 89–90, 94, 97–8
neoliberalism 4, 6, 72, 89, 126–7; in education 1, 2–4, 6, 121–2, 128–35, 138n8; the individual as entrepreneurial subject 6, 88–90, 94, 98, 100–1, 127; and individual freedom 87, 88, 127–8 see also English-language voluntourism; globalization
neoliberalism in the US 124–5
neoliberal policies in Bolivia 31, 32–3
neoliberal subject, formation of 4, 5, 89–90
new capitalism, the 51, 52–3
New Visions for Public Schools 11

INDEX

oppressed and oppressor, relationship between the 43–4, 45, 46, 47
oral histories of migrant Puerto Rican teachers to US Virgin Islands 106, 111–16, 120
Ordo-liberalism 126, 137n5

PACT (Performance Assessment for California Teachers) 132–3
parasitic interdependence between races 19
pedagogy in hip hop 34, 35
pedagogy of professionalism 24, 25
personal investments and their affect 54–6
philanthrocapitalism 11–12, 13–14, 23, 24, 130, 131; racial philanthrocapitalism 10, 15, 25
philanthropy for public schools 11–12, 14, 130
post-Fordism 125
professionalism curriculum at College Prep, New York 9–10, 15–18, 19–24
public education in the US 3–4, 109–10, 128–9, 130–1, 135–7; graduation rates in New York 11, 18; philanthropy for 11–12, 14, 130
public relations in schools of education 134–5
public school closures 11
public school reform in New York 10–11, 12
Puerto Rico 105–6, 107–8, 109; education in 108, 109–10

race and philanthropy 13–14
Race to the Top initiative 132, 133
racial formation and social privilege 13, 24, 26n8
racial identities and migration 107–8, 109, 112–13
racial philanthrocapitalism 10, 15, 25
racism and capitalism 10
"reindianization processes" 45
restructuring of closed schools 10–11
risk taking and individualism 52–3, 55, 60–3, 65–8
Roosevelt, Franklin Delano 124

schools and teaching as preparation for citizenship 123–4, 135
social programs in liberal democracies 1–2, 52, 124–5
Spanish-speaking migrants in the US 90, 91 *see also Inglés Sin Barreras* (English without Barriers)

SSCs (small themed schools of choice) 10, 11, 12
state, role of 88–9, 124–5
state support of education 1–2, 6, 129
student attitudes to professionalism curricula 9–10, 15, 16, 21–4, 25, 26n5
student test scores 11, 128, 129, 134
surplus value and personal investments 54–5

teacher education and accreditation 121, 130–3
teachers, declaration of rights of 135–6
teachers and professionalism 20–3
teachers and student test scores 129
TFA (Teach for America) 130–1, 138n10
Thatcher, Margaret 128
TIPNIS highway in Bolivia 45, 46

Ukamau y Ke, Bolivian hip hop group 38, 42, 43
Uma, Nina, Bolivian hip hopper 5, 33, 35–6, 37, 40–1
universities, governance of 3
universities and corporate links 129–30
US corporations and 1970s economic recession 124–5
US Virgin Islands 109 *see also* oral histories of migrant Puerto Rican teachers to US Virgin Islands

voluntourism (volunteer tourism) 5, 69–72, 82–3; English-language voluntourism 69–70, 71–4, 76–7, 78–83

Wayna Rap, hip hop group 34, 35, 37, 39–40, 41, 42, 43, 44, 47
Wayna Tambo cultural center 36–7, 38
welfare state, the 1–2, 52, 124–5; under neoliberalism 65, 72, 88, 91, 125–6
Whitestream, as cultural capital 25
White supremacy upheld through social policy 25
White teachers as neoliberal saviors 22

www.routledge.com/9780415672276

Related titles from Routledge

The Internationalisation of Higher Education
Towards a new research agenda in critical higher education studies
Edited by Eva Hartmann

We are in the middle of a fundamental transformation of the global architecture which is challenging the supremacy of the US, and to a certain extent of Europe, in economic and also in normative terms. The essays in this volume shed light on the role of higher education (HE) and its internationalisation in this transformation, focusing on the different regions of the world. These empirical studies are part of a new research agenda in HE studies, going beyond a 'higher educationism' limiting itself to a simple description of institutional changes in HE in the light of internationalisation. They advance an interdisciplinary perspective drawing on accounts from critical theory, international relations and international political economy. This perspective analyses the strategic selectivity, transformation and struggles related to this major transformation of HE and its contribution to a new global architecture.

This book was originally published as a special issue of *Globalisation, Societies and Education*.

June 2011: 246 x 174: 160pp
Hb: 978-0-415-67227-6
£85 / $145

For more information and to order a copy visit
www.routledge.com/9780415672276

Available from all good bookshops

www.routledge.com/9780415693240

Related titles from Routledge

Internationalization of Teacher Education

Creating Globally Competent Teachers and Teacher Educators for the 21st Century

Edited by Reyes L. Quezada

This book proposes to excite readers to engage in conversations on how Schools and Colleges of Education can internationalize teacher education programs so that graduates have global teaching experiences, that teacher education curricula include global perspectives, and that there are opportunities to have faculty think and teach from a global perspective. The contributors in this book have the knowledge and expertise in international teacher education to answer many questions regarding the development of a 21st century competent global teaching force. They describe their experiences, programs, and support for the goal of continuing to internationalize Schools and Colleges of Education. The book is designed to be interactive - readers are encouraged to engage themselves in the conversation as the editor invites them to e-mail any of the authors to discuss questions posed.

This book was originally published as a special issue of *Teaching Education*.

November 2011: 246 x 174: 128pp
Hb: 978-0-415-69324-0
£85 / $145

For more information and to order a copy visit
www.routledge.com/9780415693240

Available from all good bookshops